LIFE IN THE VICTORIAN VILLAGE

The Daily News Survey Of 1891: Volume 1

In the autumn of 1891, at the height of the agricultural depression, the Liberal newspaper, the *Daily News*, published a series of articles on rural life by their 'Special Commissioner', George Millin. The reports covered the agricultural economy in great detail, but the main focus of the series was the state of the rural poor. Millin travelled through southern England, recording the living conditions and the opinions of the agricultural labourers, seeking solutions to the associated problems of rural poverty and migration from the countryside. His reports generated immense interest and a large volume of correspondence, as readers of the *Daily News* contributed their ideas to the debate. Farmers, landowners, labourers, artisans, trade unionists and clerics all wrote in response to the survey, recounting their experiences and suggesting ways in which rural life could be improved.

This material has been brought together for the first time into two volumes and provides a fascinating insight into the circumstances of life in the late Victorian village, with accounts of wages, working hours and practices, housing, sanitation, the cost of living, social life and class relations. Millin attempts to convey the experiences of the working people he meets, as well as their ideas, attitudes and fundamental beliefs. From his reports and from the letters of his correspondents, we get a vivid picture of what life was like for the farm worker and artisan, representing a key source for economic and social historians.

LIFE IN THE VICTORIAN VILLAGE

The Daily News Survey Of 1891

Volume 1

Caliban Books

EDITOR'S NOTES

The material contained in these volumes consists of verbatim copies of letters, extracts, and editorials which appeared in the original daily editions of *The Daily News*. They appear in date order as shown in the contents pages listed at the beginning of each volume, thus making them easy to find. Where reference is made by correspondents to earlier letters, page numbers are shown in brackets denoting the first page of the letters in question. This method, it is hoped, will enable readers to follow the threads of discussion on any topic. Where no Volume number is shown, the pages refer to the current Volume.

Caliban Books would like to acknowledge the contributions of Liz Bellamy, Edward Razzell and Jeremy Ward in compiling these publications.

LIFE IN THE VICTORIAN VILLAGE

List of Articles and Letters Printed in the Daily News August – September
1891

DATE		NAME	PLACE
Sent	**Printed**		
	14/08/91	Editorial	-
	"	Special Commissioner	Chelmsford
14/08/91	15/08/91	P.	London
	"	Special Commissioner	-
	18/08/91	" "	-
	"	A.W.Marks	Sheerness on Sea
	"	'One of That Stamp'	-
17/08/91	19/08/91	Arnold D.Taylor	Honiton
	20/08/91	Special Commissioner	-
19/08/91	21/08/91	Geo. Loosley	Gt.Berkhampstead
"	"	'South Lincoln'	-
"	"	'Wanderer'	-
	"	'Churchwoman'	-
	22/08/91	Special Commissioner	Stisted
20/08/91	"	W.Pearson	Stapleford, Cambs.
21/08/91	"	W.H.Hall	Newmarket
22/08/91	25/08/91	Arnold D.Taylor	Honiton
	"	Alfred R.Wallace	-
22/08/91	"	'A Country Vicar's Wife'	-
	27/08/91	Special Commissioner	-
	"	An Oxfordshire Landlord	-
25/08/91	"	F L.Soper	Highgate
"	"	'A Countryman'	-
"	28/08/91	A.W.	-
26/08/91	"	Chas.Wills	Bristol
	29/08/91	Editorial	

DATE		NAME	PLACE
Sent	Printed		
	29/08/91	Special Commissioner	Ixworth
	"	Henry Taylor	Stockport
26/08/91	"	'Western Counties'	-
	"	A.H.J.	-
28/08/91	"	A.W.	-
	"	John Higgins	Pylle, Somerset
	"	The Speaker, The Graphic	-
	"	Dr.Morris	-
29/08/91	31/08/91	Alfred Thomas Brett	Watford Hse, Brks.
	"	'A Leicestershire Farmer'	-
28/08/91	"	E.B.	-
	"	'An Oxfordshire Landlord'	-
	"	'Reporter'	Langport, Somerset
	"	C.G.C.	Downside, Surrey
	"	Richard	Taunton Dean
	"	Sunday Sun	-
	"	The Spectator	-
	01/09/91	Special Commissioner	Barnham
	"	William Jameson	Manor Park, Essex
	"	'A Farmer's Son'	-
	"	A.B.	-
30/08/91	"	B.W.	-
	02/09/91	Arthur Clayden	-
	"	W.S.Swayne	-
01/09/91	"	W.G.	-
"	"	G.Nicholls	-
	"	'A Devonshire Squire'	-
	"	Thomas Pickworth	Loughborough
	"	L.	-
	"	J.F.S.	-

ii

DATE		NAME	PLACE
Sent	Printed		
	02/09/91	James Rayner	Aldington, Hythe
	"	John Higgins	Pylle, Somerset
	03/09/91	Special Commissioner	Norfolk
31/08/91	"	Arnold D.Taylor	Honiton
	"	'An Out & Out Radical'	East Kent
	"	Frederic C. Rivers	Oxford
	"	"farmed in it over 30 years"	Berkshire
	"	John Chandler	W.Kensington
	"	R.W.Perkins	King Stanley,Glos.
	"	Andrew Reid	Leyton
	"	Leeds Mercury	-
02/09/91	04/09/91	'A Farmer's Son	Banbury
"	"	Sydney Hallifax	-
"	"	'A Town Dweller In The ...'	-
	"	'A Lover of Suffolk'	-
	"	B.W.	-
	"	'A Villager'	Yorkshire
	"	'A Cornish Farmer's Son'	Cornwall
	"	Daniel Rogers	Wimbledon
	"	'A Lover of the Old Country'	Wales
	"	A.W.	-
	"	'One from the Plough'	-
	"	'Bedfordshire'	-
04/09/91	05/09/91	'A Wiltshire Landlord'	-
	"	M.B.Rhys	-
03/09/91	"	W.H.P.	-
	"	W.J.M	-
	"	Mr.G.Gunnell	Lynn
	"	J.F.S.	-
	"	'A Kentish Man'	Weald
	"	T.W.C.	Leicester
	"	Rev.Walker Legerton	Brentwood

DATE		NAME	PLACE
Sent	**Printed**		
	05/09/91	Rev.E.J.Dukes	Bridgwater
	"	'A Wiltshire Minister'	-
	"	Rev.R.D.Morgan	Stroud
	"	Rev.Thos.G.Crippen	Milverton, Som.
04/09/91	07/09/91	Frederick Impey	Longbridge, Worcs
	"	T.H.Phelps	Tibberton, Gloucs.
	"	The Spectator	-
	"	Sunday Sun	-
	08/09/91	Special Commissioner	Woodstock
	"	T.M.	-
	"	Arthur Clayden	-
	"	John Higgins	Pylle, Somerset
	"	'Cantab'	-
	"	George Webb	Plumstead
	"	'Oxfordshire Tenant Farmer.	-
	"	'Western Counties'	-
	"	Charles Fox	Gloucester
	"	'West Somerset'	-
	"	Henry Norton Palmer	-
	"	W.M.Hawkins	Hundon, Suffolk
	"	E.C.H.	-
	"	A.Martin	-
	"	Stuart Erskine	Buck.Palace Mans.
	"	'Dorset'	-
	"	'North Herefordshire'	-
	09/09/91	William Saunders	E.L.R.L., London
08/09/91	"	W.W.	London
	"	B.K.	-
	"	'South Beds.'	-
	"	J.Standring	Epworth,Doncaster
	"	W.H.Cooper	Cheltenham
	"	W.H.Pearson	Stapleford, Cambs.

iv

DATE		NAME	PLACE
Sent	**Printed**		
	09/09/91	R.C.R.	Hampstead
	"	Rev.J. Denny Gedge	Methwold, Norfolk
	"	'Devonshire Squire'	-
08/09/91	10/09/91	F.C.Rivers	Oxford
	"	'Hodge'	-
09/09/91	"	E.Heys-Jones	Kensington
	"	Rev.Jos.Ferguson	(British Weekly)
	"	Rev.M.T.Myers	" "
	11/09/91	Special Commissioner	-
08/09/91	"	'A Constant Reader'	Oxford
	"	'A Lincolnshire Landlord'	-
10/09/91	"	Joseph Hyder	London
	"	H	-
10/09/91	"	H.H.Watson	London
	"	Philip Lewis	Chipping Camden
	"	Rev.Henry Brandreth	Norfolk
	"	'A Woman'	Shrewsbury
	"	Henry B. Soden	Upper Clapton
	"	T.G.M	-
	"	'A Constant Reader'	-
	"	J.P.Sheldon	Sheen, Ashbourne
	"	'A Bucks.Farmer'	-
	"	O.C.	-
	"	'An Out & Out Radical'	-
	"	'A Daily Reader'	N.Northumberland
	"	William Jameson	-
	12/09/91	'Agricola'	-
	"	W.M.Reynolds	-
	"	'A Country Vicar's Wife'	-
	"	'A Village Parson'	-
	"	Het Varke	Norwich
	"	'Blankney Heath'	-

v

DATE		NAME	PLACE
Sent	Printed		
	12/09/91	J.Crawford	Sherburn, Durham
	"	F.W.H.	-
	"	'A Farmer's Daughter of S.B.'	-
	"	'A Bucks. Radical'	-
	"	'East Sussex'	-
	"	H.	Ealing
	":	Herbert G. Moberly	-
	"	J.D.	Loughborough
	14/09/91	Special Commissioner	Woodstock
	"	'Rusticus'	-
	"	'Rayat'	-
	"	'Countryside'	-
	"	H.A.	-
	"	Wm. H. Paine	Willesborough
	"	Maltus Q. Holyoake	-
11/09/91	"	'A Country Vicar'	-
	"	J.W.D. Kingsley	Kilburn
	"	'An Oxfordshire Landlord'	Kingham
	15/09/91	Rev. Denny Gedge	Methwell, Norfolk

.

vi

INTRODUCTION

In 1891 the *Daily News* appointed a 'Special Commisioner', George Millin, who was charged with the task of investigating 'the present conditions and future prospects of social life in the country villages of England'.[i] For two months, from August to October 1891, Millin walked and rode through the countryside of Essex, Suffolk, Norfolk, Oxfordshire, Berkshire and Buckinghamshire. He observed the state of agriculture and rural life, not as an informed expert, but as an interested urban visitor, and above all, he talked to the people he met - carters, publicans, vicars, cobblers, agricultural workers and their wives. He wrote up his findings in a series of lengthy and polemical reports to his paper, combining factual observations on the state of the land, housing, wages, grain prices etc. with 'the ideas and speculations ... occupying the minds and stirring the hearts of many of the most thoughtful and farseeing of those [he] ... met'.[ii]

These reports were subsequently published in a single volume entitled *Life in Our Villages* (1891) but this gives only half the picture. For Millin's reports generated huge interest amongst readers of the *Daily News* and also in other papers and periodicals. Alongside the Special Commissioner's reports appeared a mass of letters from correspondents from a range of backgrounds and political persuasions, offering comments and advice on what Millin in a later work was to term 'The Village Problem'.[iii] The letters from farmers, parsons and labourers published in the *Daily News* soon outweighed the offerings of the commissioner, while in other papers the debate itself became an item of news. For the first time this material has been reproduced in its totality within a single volume, and it provides a fascinating insight into how rural life was perceived in the late Victorian period.

While little known today, the *Daily News* was the third most popular newspaper in the mid nineteenth century. Established in January 1846, its first editor, Charles Dickens, set out its ideological stance claiming that 'the Principles of the *Daily News* will be Principles of Progress and Improvement, of Education, Civil and Religious Liberty and Equal Legislation'.[iv] For the rest of the nineteenth century the *Daily News* was the main instrument for the articulation of liberal views, leading the campaign to repeal the Stamp Tax on newspapers, supporting Italian unification and the abolitionists in the

American Civil War, and challenging conservative social and economic policies through the advocacy of Free Trade and social justice. It attracted contributions from prominent writers of liberal persuasion (including around 1600 pieces from Harriet Martineau) and after the abolition of the Stamp Tax made possible a reduction in price to a penny, it sold 150,000 copies a day.[v] By the end of the nineteenth century circulation had begun to decline, prior to a revival with the recovery of liberal fortunes in the early twentieth century, but the *News* was still the established and recognised voice of progressive liberalism at the time when Millin was filing his reports. The interest generated by Millin indicates the importance of rural issues within the liberal agenda of the late Victorian period, despite the increasingly urban nature of society at this time. A healthy agricultural system and a happy agricultural workforce were seen as essential for the general well-being of the nation. Yet as both Millin and many of his correspondents noted, the rural economy seemed to be in a parlous condition.

For much of the nineteenth century English agriculture had boomed. The Napoleonic Wars had brought spiralling prices and profits, and although depression had immediately followed the peace of 1815, by the 1830s farmers were flourishing. The 1850s and '60s were an agricultural golden age, in which 'high farming' was widely adopted in the lowlands. This was a high-input/high-output system, based on heavy investment, in which ever-greater quantities of grain and livestock were produced through the use of artificial fertilisers and manufactured animal feeds. Farm buildings and field drainage were improved and machinery was increasingly introduced. But the high levels of investment required for this kind of farming could only be maintained while the market for agricultural produce remained buoyant. When prices began to fall from the late 1870s, farming started to slide into depression.

The decline was largely due to the expansion of the American rail network into the prairies of the mid west, which meant that British markets were flooded with large quantities of cheap imported grain. This coincided with a string of poor harvests which initially served to obscure the true causes of the farmers' problems. Prices, rents and land values fell rapidly in the early 1880s, and, after a brief period of stabilisation, a further intense depression occurred in the early 1890s. This time livestock producers were affected as well as arable farmers, as cheap meat and dairy products came into the country from Australia and the New World.[vi]

The impact of these changes was patchy, not all regions being affected in the same way or to the same degree. The Commissioner focussed his attention on eastern England, particularly Essex, Suffolk and Norfolk, because it was here that the effects of the depression were most keely felt. These were districts in which the principles of 'high farming' had been most enthusiastically adopted in the middle decades of the century and intensive stock-corn production had been taken up not only on the better soils but also on more infertile land, such as the heavy clays of south Essex, and the sands of the Breckland. The Commissioner makes little reference to soil or topography, but it was in these areas that he found the worst examples of rural decline. The clays were particularly badly affected, for these were used for growing wheat, the price of which fell disastrously through the 1880s and 1890s. The Commissioner's descriptions of abandoned and weed-choked fields, and of Essex as a 'civilised waste', are not exaggerations. Hunter Pringle, in the Royal Commission report for 1894, described parts of the county where 'whole farms and tracts of country have been abandoned and given up to nature', and he produced maps which showed an abundance of derelict land.[vii]

Elsewhere, however, the effects of the depression were less drastic, as was made clear by some of the correspondents to the *Daily News*. While many writers concurred with the bleak picture of rural depopulation and decay presented by Millin, others, particularly in the West of England, saw the situation in a more sanguine light.[viii] In *Our Villages: Another View. A Reply to the Special Commissioner of the 'Daily News'*, reproduced as an appendix to this volume, A.N.Cooper celebrated the improvements that had taken place in the rural life of the East Riding in recent years, although his divergence from Millin may have been motivated by ideological as much as geographical differences. Even within Essex, however, there were variations in the extent of rural degeneration, and only a few miles from the clayland wastes, Pringle was able to observe areas of more fertile soils where the land was well farmed and no fields were left uncultivated.

The main response to depression was a marked shift in patterns of land use and over large areas of lowland Britain, the area under arable contracted. In the period 1866-75, 45% of land in Britain had been under crops. In the period 1896-1905, this fell to 32%. There was an even more striking decline in the acreage under wheat: in 1866-75 more than three million acres had been under the crop, but after 1893 this dropped to less than two million, occasionally falling below one and a half million.[ix]

Livestock prices held up rather better than those for arable products, and dairying in particular remained a profitable enterprise, with large urban conurbations providing an expanding market for fresh milk and other dairy produce. In addition, a range of alternative forms of agricultural production flourished where land was suitable and good markets available. There was a massive expansion of fruit-growing and horticulture in areas like the Isle of Axholme and the East Anglian Fens. Between 1873 and 1904 the area of land devoted to orchards in Britain went up by some 60%[x] and poultry production also increased. Many of the correspondents to the *Daily News* saw the development of these forms of diversification as an important means of improving the wages and standards of living of the rural poor. Nevertheless, although the picture was not one of unrelieved gloom, available statistics confirm the views expressed by most of the voices within this volume - that English farming at the turn of the century was, overall, in a poor way.

All classes involved in agriculture claimed to be suffering from the effects of the depression, and economic hardship accentuated the tensions inherent in the structures of rural production. Rents went unpaid, or fell into arrears and some landowners were forced to take farms in hand, rather than leave them uncultivated. Average rents had reached a peak of 29s 9d per acre in 1877, but by 1885 they had fallen to 24s 1d.[xi] It is true that many of the landed rich possessed alternative forms of non-agricultural income, but the scale of economic decline was striking nevertheless. Farmers, however, suffered more than their landlords and throughout the 1880s and 1890s bankruptcies were widespread. Here, again, there was much variation from area to area, depending on soils, location, and the type of farming practised. In general, the small pastoral farms and horticultural enterprises, and the large arable farms, were better able to weather the depression than medium-sized holdings. In the case of the former the farmer could rely on his own hard work and frugality. The latter benefitted because the rents of large farms were relatively low per acre (because of the difficulty of attracting tenants) and extensive arable enterprises enjoyed considerable economies of scale. There were examples of individual success, as in the case of the farmers who left Scotland and other parts of highland Britain for lowland regions such as Essex and East Anglia, exchanging relatively small and high rented pastoral farms for larger arable holdings with lower rents. But few farmers really flourished in the period and most responded to falling prices by curtailing investment and economising on labour. They not only shifted into less labour-intensive forms of agricultural production, such as livestock grazing, but also reduced the thoroughness with which the land was worked and farmland maintained. Weeding was carried out less efficiently, hedges grew tall and wide. The neat countryside of the high farming years was replaced by a more untidy, unkempt scene.

While Millin noted with regret the poor state of the land and the hedges, and the lack of cultivation of the fields, his main focus of interest was in the plight of the agricultural workers, the rural labourers and artisans. Like the liberal readers of the *Daily News*, he had little sympathy for the Tory landowners and capitalist farmers, and for him the most striking consequences of the depression in agriculture were the poverty of the people within the countryside and the steady migration from the land. In *The Village Problem* Millin quoted figures for the decline in the number of agricultural workers in England and Wales. Whereas in 1871 there had been 434 agricultural workers for every 10,000 of the population, by 1891 this figure had dropped to 255. For the United Kingdom as a whole the decline was from 531 to 318.[xii] In an article in *Longman's Magazine* in July 1883 entitled 'The Dorsetshire Labourer', Thomas Hardy had observed that 'A depopulation is going on which in some quarters is truly alarming'.[xiii] The Commissioner and his correspondents frequently lament that it is 'the bold peasantry', 'the young, the strong, and the enterprising' who quit the land, leaving behind only 'the old people and fools'.[xiv]

Many explanations for this flight from the countryside were proposed, but two in particular found favour with the readers of the *Daily News*. The first was the low level of agricultural wages. The second was the poor quality of life in the countryside and the superior attractions offered by towns. But in spite of what many correspondents appear to have believed, agricultural wages were not in fact falling in the 1890s.[xv] The improvements achieved in the 1870s, largely as a result of the success of the short-lived agricultural workers' union established by Joseph Arch, had been maintained throughout the period of falling prices in the 1880s: the rural depopulation which many saw as a *consequence* of poor wages was, in fact, one of the main reasons why wages remained relatively high, in spite of the depression. Indeed, they shrank much less than prices. At the same time, the exodus of workers ensured that long-term unemployment in the countryside was comparatively rare. Nevertheless, this line of argument should not be taken too far. The condition of farm workers may have improved to some extent compared to the situation in the middle decades of the century, but wages remained low in comparison with those of urban workers. There were no old-age pensions and long periods of winter unemployment (exacerbated by the general economies in hedging and ditching) meant that many workers could expect repeated spells in the workhouse. The letters included here, and the comments to the Commissioner, expose the resentment that was felt at this enforced dependence, and at the lack of regular and reliable work. It was often claimed that low wages were offset by other benefits enjoyed by agricultural workers, and in particular by the provision of housing at little or no rent. But as the Commissioner makes clear, this accommodation was often inadequate and insanitary, poorly maintained and without proper sewerage systems and water supplies. To urban eyes, imbued with a late Victorian consciousness of public health issues, the conditions in which rural workers had to live were simply appalling and the sensations of shock and horror come through in Millin's reports, despite his attempts to maintain a temperate tone. It is clear from the material in this volume that although agricultural wages may not have been falling at this time, the life of the rural poor was extremely hard. The picture painted by Millin supports the words of Canon Girdlestone, the North Devon radical, that farm workers 'did not live in the proper sense of the word, they merely didn't die'.[xvi]

In such a situation, accelerating migration to the towns was a matter of little surprise to the Commissioner, his interviewees, or his correspondents. Most of the contributors to the debate agreed, however, that there were also more intangible factors which ensured that rural life was less attractive to the poor, and particularly to the younger generation, than life in the towns and cities. There was simply more to do in the town - more amusements, more educational facilities - and in the urban environment men and women were less subject to the patronage, dominance and interference of their social superiors.

The reports of the Commissioner reveal the extent of the desire for independence amongst the rural poor, and their resentment at both the patronising attitudes of squires, parsons and their wives, and the 'tyrannical, domineering, nigger-driving sort of treatment' to which they were submitted.[xvii]

The increasingly urban nature of the population therefore formed the subject of the Commissioner's scrutiny, but it was also part of the social and ideological background to his reports. Late Victorian England was divided into great estates and farmed by tenant farms of various sizes, but it was no longer a primarily agrarian economy. At both a local and national level, the established political power of the landed elite was being challenged. Adult male suffrage was achieved in 1884, and in 1888 elected county councils replaced the oligarchic quarter sessions which had formerly administered the shires. An urban and industrial agenda dominated the concerns of national government. Through the 1850s and 1860s British military power permitted an unprecedented dependence on imported food to feed the urban masses, and the problems of the countryside tended to be forgotten. Parliamentary debates and newspaper editorials were primarily concerned with the great questions of India, the military power of foreign competitors, and Irish Home Rule, rather than with the social and economic problems of the countryside. In the words of the historian P.J.Perry, 'Rural Britain was ... in most respects *terra incognita* to the masses ... It could be safely ignored by the urban middle class, and sacrificed by the political elite'.[xviii]

This neglect of rural Britain was largely a result of the ignorance of conditions in the countryside on the part of the urban majority. Yet from the 1880s the isolation of agricultural communities began to break down. With the completion of the last stages of the rail network and the spread of the bicycle, the increasingly affluent urbanites were able to gain access to the world beyond the city and the suburbs. At the same time, a deep seated anxiety about progress and industrial change sparked off what has been described as a 'pastoral impulse', a nostalgia for rural life which swept through the culture of late Victorian Britain.[xix] Whereas the spirit of the mid nineteenth century had been characterised by the industrial novels of Charles Dickens, Elizabeth Gaskell and Benjamin Disraeli, the end of the century saw an efflorescence of prose and verse exploring and eulogising rural life. In the year when Millin produced his *Daily News* reports, Thomas Hardy published *Tess of the D'Urbervilles* and in 1893 Robert Blatchford brought out his socialist *Merrie England*.

The end of the nineteenth century has been identified as the period which saw the construction of a concept of Englishness which was based on the celebration of a romanticised vision of village life in the Home Counties.[xx] Yet while Millin's reports clearly stem from this urban interest in things rural, and focus on the southern counties of England, they cannot really be characterised as simple manifestations of the 'pastoral impulse' or the 'Southern Metaphor' which have been outlined in accounts of writing on the countryside of the late nineteenth and early twentieth century. Indeed, the *Daily News* material highlights the extent to which the loose use of this kind of conceptual framework tends to suppress the diversity of writings on, and analyses of, rural life, assimilating the nostalgic, romanticised visions of the Georgian poets with the informed and precise accounts of writers such as Mary Mann into a single homogenous tradition. The Commissioner's reports are clearly infused with a belief in the value of country life and the agricultural economy, but they draw on a tradition of observation, investigation and critique rather than a literature of pastoral celebration, and while the two discourses share an emphasis on the importance of her countryside, their differences are as significant as their similarities.

The obvious antecedent for the *Daily News* reports was William Cobbett's *Rural Rides* which initially appeared in his *Political Register* from 1821. Cobbett, like Millin, travelled through the countryside of southern England, seeking to record the experience of agricultural workers and making observations on the condition of the rural economy to support his radical but idiosyncratic political agenda. This tradition of using newspapers to investigate social problems was continued through the nineteenth century with the surveys by the *Morning Chronicle* of the lives of workers in cities, towns and the countryside.[xxi] There was also a precedent in the work of the various parliamentary commissions into social and economic problems, with their 'blue book' reports. In 1880-2, for instance, The Royal Commission on the Depressed Condition of the Agricultural Interest (the Richmond Committee) reported on the issues of rural decline and depopulation that were of interest to Millin.

The *Daily News* reports therefore need to be seen in the context of the growing urban interest in rural life that marked the end of the nineteenth century, but, in the tradition of William Cobbett, Richard Jefferies, Mary Mann and to some extent Thomas Hardy, they manifest a questioning and analytical rather than a complacent and nostalgic attitude towards the countryside. The focus is on the difficulties, particularly of poverty and depopulation, and as such these works can be seen to represent a Liberal interpretation that can be contrasted to the mythology of Merrie England that was to become incorporated as a central strand of conservative ideology in the twentieth century.[xxii] Millin aimed to describe and explore the problems of the rural community, but both he and his correspondents also sought explanations for, and solutions to, those problems.

The solutions to the rural crisis proposed by the Commissioner and his readers were certainly varied. They ranged from the cranky and bizarre - such as the encouragement of country dancing and the drying of apple slices - through the eminently practical, to the out-and-out radical. Improvements in housing and wages were high on the agenda of the Commissioner and most of the correspondents, but more far-reaching changes in the structure of rural society and in patterns of landholding were also advanced. There was much debate about the relative merits of small as opposed to large farms in terms both of what they could produce, and of the numbers of men which they would employ. Many believed that the provision of allotments would help to make rural life more attractive, while others considered that they would instead serve to depress wages, and that the large-scale creation of small-holdings was the answer. Only these could provide a rung on the farming ladder for the labourer, and thus give the ambitious some hope for future improvement. Many wrote of the benefits to be gained from the expansion in horticulture, fruit-growing, and poultry-keeping, which rendered such smallholdings more viable than ever before.

Some believed that wholesale expropriation of the landed rich, and nationalisation or 'municipalisation' of land were the answer. Parish councils were also the focus of considerable interest, with many correspondents advocating an extension of their powers. It was suggested that they should be able to acquire land for smallholdings, and construct a range of facilities to improve the conditions of the rural poor, such as reading rooms, baths and schools. It was felt by many whom Millin met that only this kind of far-reaching change could effectively challenge the stranglehold of the wealthy landowners and their allies in the clergy over the life of rural England. Indeed, the radicalism of the solutions considered by Liberal opinion in late nineteenth-century Britain tends to expose the ideological timidity of society a century later.

The reports published here contain fascinating if anecdotal evidence about the character of rural life in England in the last decade of the nineteenth century. Equally interesting, however, is the light that they and the responding letters shed on contemporary understanding of the problems of the countryside. With hindsight we can see that their understanding was frequently flawed, and that cause and effect were not always effectively linked. Dereliction and weed-choked fields were not, for example, principally caused by a labour shortage resulting from the flight of workers to the towns - as many seemed to believe - but rather by a depression resulting from factors of international trade. What is revealed here is not so much a collection of facts about the condition of the countryside, as an account of how these conditions were perceived and the terms in which they were analysed in late Victorian Britain. As evidence of liberal views on society and the economy, and of the nature of the debate over rural issues, the material presented here is invaluable.

Liz Bellamy and Tom Williamson

---

[i] See below p. 1.

[ii] See below p. 424.

[iii] George F. Millin, *The Village Problem* (London: Swan Sonnenschein and Co., 1903).

[iv] Quoted in Stephen Koss. *Fleet Street Radical: A.C.Gardiner and the Daily News* (London: Allen Lane, 1973) p. 34.

[v] *ibid.*

[vi] P.J.Perry, *British Farming in the Great Depression 1870-1914* (Newton Abbot: David and Charles 1974), pp. 21-33.

[vii] Royal Commission on the Agricultural Depression, First General Report, 1894, XVI, Pt 1, pp.704, 801.

[viii] See, e.g. 'Dorset' p. 145 below.

[ix] Perry, *British Farming,*, p.107.

[x] Board of Agriculture Report on the Fruit Industry, 1905, XX, p.546.

[xi] R.J. Thompson, 'An Inquiry into the Rent of Agricultural Land', *Journal of the Royal Statistical* Society 70 (1907), 587-616.

[xii] Millin, *The Village Problem*, p. 15.

[xiii] Thomas Hardy, 'The Dorsetshire Labourer', *Longman's Magazine* (July, 1883), reprinted in *Hardy:The Tragic Novels* ed. R.P.Draper (Basingstoke: Macmillan, 1975, 1989) pp. 42-51.

[xiv] p. 1 below.

[xv] Perry, *British Farming*, p.127.

[xvi] Quoted in J.Burnett, *Plenty and Want: A Social History of Diet in England from 1815 to the Present Day* (London: Nelson, 1966).

[xvii] p. 44 below.

[xviii] Perry, *British Farming*, p.16.

[xix] Jan Marsh, *Back to the Land: The Pastoral Impulse in England, from 1880 to 1914* (London: Quartet, 1982) p. 4 and passim.

[xx] Donald Horne, *God is an Englishman* (Harmondsworth: Penguin, 1969); Martin Wiener, *English Culture and the Decline of the Industrial Spirit, 1850-1980* (Cambridge: Cambridge University Press, 1981) pp. 41-3; Marsh, *Back to the Land*, p. 4.

[xxi] P.E.Razzell and R.W.Wainwright (eds.), *The Victorian Working Class: Selections from Letters to the Morning Chronicle* (London: Frank Cass, 1973).

[xxii] Simon Miller, 'Urban Dreams and Rural Reality: Land and Landscape in English Culture, 1920-45', *Rural History: Economy, Society, Culture*, 6:1 (April, 1995), 89-102.

EDITORIAL

The Countryside. We publish this morning the first in a series of letters from the Special Commissioner who is investigating for the benefit of our readers the present conditions and future prospects of social life in the country villages of England. Our Commissioner begins with a gloomy picture of the state of the agricultural labourer. It is a picture with which we are all more or less familiar in its main features, but it is one that will always admit of new rendering illustrative of the conditions of the hour. The rural districts are still emptying to fill the towns. Our Commissioner has walked and driven through Essex, and Essex, as he sees it, is fast becoming a civilized waste. The bold peasantry are forsaking it in ever-increasing numbers. It is eminently the bold ones who play this truant part – the young, the strong, and the enterprising. Only "the old people and fools" remain behind to take the statement, as our Commissioner received it, on local authority. The young men go into the police, into the army, or into the railway service. Where the soldiers and the policemen are, there the young women are apt to be, and the village maiden enters her Paradise through the area gate of town. The old people and fools are an eternal object-lesson to those who feel tempted to remain. Wages are low, work is hard, field employment is at a stand-still during a large part of the year. Many of the labourers go into the workhouse, as a matter of course, during the winter season.

The wages are not altogether to blame for it. Those who are best able to judge say that the dulness of the country must also be taken into account. The work is most fatiguing, the relaxations are few, especially those of a stimulating kind. There are the fields in the day time, the walk home in the twilight, the village life without events, and the chimney corner without news. It is not gay, yet, while earnings remain at their present level, there is no way of making it brighter. Amusement follows the money, and a sense of the daily quickening of life is the luxury of opulent, or at any rate, of populous communities. In our huge town districts, the mere numbers make their own news, and supply their own excitement. The village must always be content to import those from without, and the one form in which alone it is able to import

12

them is the very one for which circumstances make it the least inclined. The village library is more or less of a failure as it must be in the very nature of the case. There are a·thousand reasons of fact, as distinguished from benevolent fancy, why MACAULAY's Essays or the poems of LORD TENNYSON cannot give much imaginative exhilaration to the rustic mind.

What is to be done? To take this world as we find it, the prosperity of the agricultural labourer must still depend on the prosperity of the farmer. The final question for the practical man, therefore, is how can the English farmer hope to do well? There is one ray of light in our Commissioner's picture. The large farmer still holds his own.; only the small one has to pay wretched wages proportional to his profits, and has practically to turn his holding into a waste. What is this but a confession that agriculture may still hope to thrive in this country when it is conducted, like any other large industry, with all that science can bring to its aid. If we spun or made machinery upon the principles in which many of us till the ground, our cottons and our steam-engines would soon lose the markets of the world. British farming has to be freed from its feudal fetters of custom quite as much as those of law. Its present state demands nothing less than an economic revolution, in which the landowners, for their own sake, must learn to lead the way. Such a revolution would no doubt largely destroy the present beauty of the rural scene. It would give us large areas of cultivation, and a remorseless method in the manner of cultivating them that would be fatal to all the minor amenities of country life. The land would have to be made to do its best, and all the idle people – gentle as well as simple – would have to be cleared out of the way. Landlords will probably accept the authority of the late LORD BEACONSFIELD as unimpeachable. If they know how to read one of his memorable utterances between the lines it will tell them that the land will no longer keep three persons – the landlord, the farmer, and the labourer. It is for them to consider in their own interest which of them should offer to make some equitable arrangement for giving way. In his next stage of development the agricultural labourer must become the agricultural artisan, with only one master between him and the buyer.

It is idle to look to mere legislation for a remedy, or at any rate to Protection. It is a matter of history that British agriculture was never more prosperous than in the two or three and twenty years ending in 1874, and following the repeal of the Corn Laws. The Royal Agricultural Society had been formed before the passing of that measure, but with a knowledge of what was coming. LORD ALTHORP, who may be regarded as its founder, had warned the farmer against putting his trust in legislative nostrums, and had urged him to study the facts of the hour, and confide in himself. The result was seen in a wonderful development of scientific farming, which, combined with a Providence of a run of good seasons, gave us nearly a quarter of a century of fat years. Then, to be quite fair in the retrospect, America which had been partially distanced, began to overtake us once more. New railways and improved steamers brought the corn to our doors at nominal rates, and British agriculture again fell out of the race. This is the situation as it exists today. But as new methods saved us in the past, newer methods may save us now if we have the wisdom and energy to adopt them. The new ideas of the olden time were ideas of cultivation; perhaps nothing but new ideas of tenure will serve our turn today.

We want a social Rothamstead and a social Woburn to teach us how the land should be held, as well as how it should be farmed. American competition may not threaten us forever; at least such is the opinion beginning to be widely prevalent in the United States. Mr. WOOD DAVIS's striking papers in *The Forum*, based on the figures supplied by the Department of Agriculture show that, in four or five years, the American people may themselves require all the produce that can be grown on American soil; the entire product, at any rate, of cereals, potatoes, and hay. In ten years, Mr. DAVIS thinks, some of them will have to be fed on imported wheat. He is not in the least distressed at the prospect. He regards it as a good time coming for the American farmer, when all his produce will be taken at profitable rates at home. It is no part of his business to show that it may be a good time for the farmers of both worlds. In so far as his prophecy is also a warning, it carries a recommendation of more thorough methods of culture. This, and happily for America this alone, is the lesson for our kinsfolk beyond the sea. We in this country have to deal with a more complex problem. Until we solve it, agricultural England must continue to wear the melancholy aspect described by our Commissioner today.

(FROM OUR SPECIAL COMMISSIONER)

CHELMSFORD, THURSDAY

Beyond all dispute the agricultural labourer is abandoning the land he was born on and is making his way into the towns. I have to-day driven and walked a good many miles through parts of this country of Essex which have from time to time impressed me with a conviction that Hodge must not merely be going into the towns but has actually gone. "Whom have you left then?" asked one Nonconformist minister of another who had for many years been the pastor of a village congregation that had dwindled and dwindled in the district I have been jogging through to-day. "Whom have you left then?" "Old people and fools," was the bitter reply. "You see very few young men about these parts now-a-days," said the landlady of a little inn into which I turned for some bread and cheese to-day. "It's only the old folks as be left. As soon as the young 'uns be able to do for theirselves, they be off to better theirselves as they think. They go into the towns and get into the police or the army or on the line. A good many go on the line." "You can't get men of any sort," said an Essex farmer. "I've done all I can to keep mine, and except the old men that I have had twenty or thirty years - and one of 'em I've had five and thirty years - I've got none. I began farming in forty-one, and I've brought up over forty lads to the farming, and they no sooner get to be eighteen, or from that to five and twenty, than they're off. You can't keep them." "And your land no doubt is suffering for want of labour?" "Of course it is. It isn't producing half what it might. How can it? Why, things are choked up with squitch and thistles, and I can't clear them."

Yes, there is no doubt that Hodge is giving up farming in these parts, but if you think you are going to get Hodge himself to tell you why, you will very like be greatly mistaken. While to-day sitting over my bread and cheese at the cross-legged table within the settee of the bricked-floored little public-house, a little old patriarch came in for his mid-day glass of beer to drink with his bread and bacon. He peeped, I thought bashfully, round the screen, and seeing a stranger within, squatted down upon the seat outside close to the door. "You needn't be afraid to come in, my lad," I said, wishing to have a little chat with the old man. Perhaps there was just a touch of the patronising in my tone. If there was, my priggishness was promptly rebuked. "Oh, I ain't afeared of o' you mate," said the old man. "No, no, of course not." "It ain't the first time I ha' set 'ere." "No, I expect not." "Nor you ain't the first man I ha' seen with a good coat on his back." Clearly the old man was troubled with no bashfulness at the presence of a stranger, and I went on trying as cunningly as I could to inveigle him into some little self-revelation, but it was a total failure. He parried all my questions, assumed an air of the blankest ignorance on matters with which he must have been perfectly familiar, and steadfastly refused to be pumped. But when presently the landlady joined in with the observations I have just recorded, he put in, I thought very acutely. "You see, sir," said the landlady, "if they settle on the land they just make a living, and I think as on the whole they be more happy and contented than a good many'd think for; but you see there's nothing afore 'em. They never get on. They don't get no higher wages. They get just enough to keep 'em; but since prices ha' gone down so the farmers can't afford to give 'em more." "What prices ha' gone down?" demanded the old man. "Why, corn." "Well," was the retort, "and ain't the price o' stock gone up? Don't a bullock fetch twice as much as it used to since I can remember? And don't a calf fetch twice as much, and ain't the price o' 'osses double what they used to be? They talk about their wheat and their barley, but they never say nothing about the price o' bullocks."

Clearly the old man wasn't so utterly incapable of observation as he would have had me think. But the landlord, who now came to the front, said he was of a contented mind, and had always been satisfied with his lot, though to look at the old fellow, and by the tone of his remarks, I should hardly have judged so. "That's what they get," he growled at one point, as he sliced off a lump of fat bacon on his bunch of bread. "What they earn is another thing." The old fellow was between 70 and 80 years of age - 77, I think they said; and his day's work was 11 hours of hoeing or nine hours with allowances for meals. And every winter the old man spends in the workhouse. "And does he find any fault with the workhouse?" I asked of the landlord as we presently jogged along in his light cart. "No; he don't find no fault. He takes it all quiet enough." At threescore years and fifteen or thereabout, I suppose nine hours of hoeing leaves a man little spirit even for grumbling, but here is an object lesson for all the sturdy young fellows from 18 to 25 - 11s. a week - on piecework - and nine hours' of hoeing and the much-dreaded workhouse, and a pauper's grave at the end of it all. What wonder if, as the landlady says, they go into the town to "better themselves."

And it is the same with the young women. "We get no women to work now," said the farmer I have already quoted. "Some of the old ones 'll do a day now and again, but we get no young women in the field now. They all go into the town to service. While ladies'll give thirty or five-and-thirty pounds for a cook, and sixteen and eighteen pounds for a housemaid, of course we can't keep 'em here." "And no doubt when the lasses go, the lads soon begin to follow?" "Of course they do." A Baptist minister of this county gave me a striking illustration of the influence of the young women in assisting the draining of the country of its labourers. Before he came into his present ministry, he was in charge of a church in a village, where pillow lace-making was a staple industry of the people, and while it lasted they were thriving, and the church was prosperous. But foreign competition, or something else, ruined the lace-making. Things grew worse and worse till twelve hours of close working wouldn't pay twopence. Every girl in the place who was good for anything at all - eighty or ninety per cent - flitted into the towns, and all the young men followed.

"I don't think it's altogether wages," said a very able observer, another Congregational minister of eight years' standing in an Essex village. "The country you see is very dull, and it is difficult to see how it can be made otherwise. The people have to be up at five in the morning, and they require to be in bed by seven or eight o'clock." This gentleman's opinion was that their long day's work was too exhausting to permit of any kind of social life in the evening, and indeed he said it was evidently with the utmost difficulty that the people kept awake in church or chapel on Sundays. He had tried to get up evening entertainments, and had tried to start a library, indeed he did start one with two or three hundred volumes, and for a short time it seemed to be appreciated. But he couldn't keep up an interest in it, and it had to be dropped. "The hours of labour are so long, and the work so heavy, that it leaves the people fit for nothing in the way of mental improvement at the end of the day?" "It leaves them fit for nothing but bed." "Then, apparently, if social life in the village is to be made brighter and more attractive some shortening of the hours

17

of work seems to be indispensable?" "Yes; but then I confess I see a great difficulty. There has been some talk of the union here, and I suppose it is coming." "Yes; they say in London that the great difficulty in the way of effective union there is the disorganized agricultural labourer, who is always ready to pour in ·from the country to defeat gas-workers and others in their efforts to improve their condition. And Tillett and the rest of them say that the labourers must be organized, and they are preparing to do it." "Well, when the movement reaches here I shall find myself in a great difficulty.

There are one or two large farmers - men farming on a large scale and with ample capital - who are doing well. But the great majority of them round here have hardly a pound in their pockets, and to give shorter hours and better pay at their expense means just knocking them over. Even as it is their land is not half cultivated, and they simply cannot stand any further drain upon them. What is to be done it is very difficult to say." "Your observation convinces you that the large farmers have an advantage over the small ones?" "A very decided advantage. They can keep horses and men regularly employed by shifting them about from place to place, and they can buy to greater advantage and sell too. I'll give you an instance. I know two men at this moment who buy oilcakes of precisely the same kind. One buys in large quantities for cash and gets it £3 a ton cheaper than the other, who cannot afford to do so. I know two other men who had hay to sell when the price was low. One was obliged to sell, and got £2 a load for it. The other kept it for a time, and got £4. I know one farmer who buys oats, when he wants them, first hand. He goes down to the docks, buys direct from the importer in considerable quantities, and entirely saves the profit of the middleman." "The small farmer, then, seems likely to go to the wall?" "He is bound to go to the wall," and it seems, moreover, that the large farmer can do, in proportion, with fewer men, can afford better machinery, and more of it, than the small man. According to all the testimony I have met with down here, thus far things are moving in something of a circle. The want of money and the scarcity of labour are evolving the system of large farms, and the system of large farming is tending to dispense more and more with the need to labour. "Well, what is to be done?" "I cannot undertake to suggest. What we seem to want is a great statesman to come forward and take the matter in hand."

Saturday, August 15, 1891.

LETTER TO THE EDITOR

(OUR VILLAGES)

SIR,- Your Special Commissioner's letters on "Village Life" should prove of value to all who are interested in labour questions. Undoubtedly one of the most difficult problems to be solved is how to keep the labourer on the land. But surely, judging from a recent visit to the district, your Correspondent is drawing too dark a picture of village life; *e.g.*, he refers to the very long hours of labour. True, the hours are long, but still they are precisely the same as those of the labourers and artisans in the towns. The normal working day is nine hours, and overtime is paid during haymaking and harvesting. Another point greatly in favour of the country labourer is the comparative lowness of rent. In London, for example, a man has to pay five or six shillings for two or three rooms in an overcrowded locality. In the country for less than one-half of the above amounts he can get a fairly good cottage, in most districts, though unfortunately not in all, and garden large enough to supply the family with vegetables. Under these circumstances I think a steady, industrious man is better off in the country than in the town. Unfortunately, owing perhaps to the dullness of the village life, many men spend far too much of their time in the village alehouse, with deplorable results. Probably the introduction of parish councils and the spread of technical education will check this evil. I notice the reverend gentlemen quoted by your Corespondent do not speak well of the labourers. Probably the labourers would be as disrespectful to the parsons. It is perhaps not altogether the fault of the people or their work that they find it difficult to keep awake on Sundays. The preacher to stir the somewhat stolid breast of the labourers has yet to be discovered.- I remain, yours obediently,

P., London,   August 14

Saturday, August 15, 1891

(FROM OUR SPECIAL COMMISSIONER)

Starting from Chelmsford this morning, I have driven some fifteen or twenty miles through the country of Essex. If I had done merely this I should have brought back with me the pleasantest possible impression of prosperous villages and charming little homes, embowered in orchards and flower gardens, and tenanted by a comfortable and contented peasantry, healthy, thriving, happy, and beyond all comparison better off that the corresponding class in our great towns. Knowing what I know of life in lower London, I might well have regarded the constant draining away of this population thither as due to the infatuation of mere ignorance, doomed to a speedy enlightenment by a bitter experience, and certain to be followed by repentance. Life here as we drive along looks so placid, so pleasant, so easy that, by comparison, the life of those who are crowding our dock gates, or are pent up in gas factories, or slaving at our great railway stations, conducting omnibuses, tramping the dull streets by night as policemen, or going through the drudgery of a city warehouse - such life seems by comparison a sort of nightmare.

Here is a little place, just a few yards back from the highway, a semi-detached cottage. The windows full of flowers look out across fields of waving corn, and pleasant meadows, and dark green woods. Its doorway is sheltered by a porch that has been a mass of sweet-smelling honeysuckle. Its forecourt garden is full of cloves and fuchsias, geraniums, and sweet peas, and under a canopy of old trees and shrubs is a rustic seat where, when the labourer's work is done, he may sit and smoke his pipe and watch the sunset, and see the evening primroses unfold, and enjoy

The gleam - the shadow - and the peace supreme.

It is a house that would have inspired Cowper or Wordsworth to break out in song, or George Leslie to sit down before it and paint. Here is another. A pebbled pathway edged by mossy stones leads up to it through beds of roses and petunias, nasturtiums and phloxes, interspersed with currant bushes and raspberry canes. Its red-tiled roof and crumbling chimney stack stand picturesquely out against a background of plum and walnut, apple and pear trees, and its latticed windows peep cosily out of a cluster of vines. "Delightful little houses!" you exclaim as you rattle past them. Photograph one of these places with the weather-beaten old rustic smoking his pipe in the arbour, and the old dame with her knitting at the door, and perhaps a buxom lass feeding a coop of chickens, and you will have the picture of a lowly home that it seems madness for the young people to run away from for life in Brick-lane, Spitalfields, or Dockhead, or Shadwell. Show such a picture as this, and say that Ben Tillett and Tom Mann are coming down here to commence an agitation among such people, and Ben Tillett and Tom Mann will strike you at once as demons of discord who richly deserve to be flung into the nearest horsepond. Reform in the villages, indeed! Let the people alone. God made the country, and man made the town. These Essex villagers have fresh air, and flowers and fruit in their season. They have all the delights of the open country - green fields and shady woods, waving cornfields and laden orchards, and peace and quiet and Sunday rest. If their wages are low, so are their expenses, and though they get none of the excitements and stir of town life, they know nothing of its struggle and strain either. Let them alone. That is how it would naturally strike the stranger who should spin along behind a good horse, as I have been spinning to-day, through Writtle, Cooksmill Green, Highwood, and the neighbourhood.

I have been doing a little more than this however. The Chelmsford guardians, to their infinite credit, and unlike many other Boards in Essex, have taken an enlightened and thoroughly progressive view of their duties as the sanitary authorities of their district. Instead of appointing at a salary of fifteen or twenty pounds a year a medical officer who is in practice for himself, and who is expected to attend merely to such matters of health, or rather of sickness, as the sanitary officer may call his attention to, they have taken the far more sensible and public spirited course of engaging the whole time and strength of a thoroughly competent man. Dr. Thresh, a D.Sc., an M.B., I suppose one of the youngest and certainly one of the ablest medical officers in the kingdom, devotes himself entirely to travelling about the district, looking after matters of water supply, drainage, the general sanitary condition of house property, and all other matters bearing on the public health. It was in company with Dr. Thresh that I made my round to-day, and I was able thus to

21

see not only the outsides of these attractive little houses, but the insides also and the people who live in them.

The first thing which struck me was the fact that "absenteeism" and its evils are by no means peculiar to Ireland. "In that row of houses," I was informed, "some of the people have lived twenty or thirty years, and they have none of them ever seen their landlords." We step down and look at one or two cottages. I cannot pretend to any that I was greatly shocked at what I saw. But I certainly ought to have been, and if I had peeped into the same rooms up a court in Lambeth or Poplar I should have been. But it was a delightful summer morning. The cottage doors opened into thriving little garden plots, and it was all so breezy and pleasant without that it really seemed to matter very little what was within. But the cottages were in a scandalous condition, and evidently the agent could not have spent a penny piece upon them for many years. Tumble-down ramshackle, damp and draughty, any landlord ought to have been heartily ashamed of drawing rent for them. "This is how I manage to keep out the damp, sir," said one woman cheerily from the interior of her little low-raftered den, the floor of which was sunk below the level of the yard. And as she spoke she turned up two or three thicknesses of old rugs and carpets from the brick floor beneath them. "The place is wretchedly damp," observes the doctor as he makes a note or two, and we move on. "The people suffer a good deal from rheumatism and pleurisy, and that sort of thing, what with their brick floors and their broken plaster walls and clay soil." We rattle on past a village school with a score or two of youngsters out in the playground in front. "Some of those children," says my cicerone, "have to come three miles to school, and in the winter time the cross roads are swamps of mud. This road here," he continued, as he pulled up at the end of a lane and dismounted," was last winter a foot or a foot and a half of liquid slush, and the children had to get along here to school.

No wonder they got bronchitis and influenza. I want to go and see whether the landlord has finished a well at one of these cottages down here." No, the well was not finished, and the landlord would have to be touched up again; but progress had been made, and soon these cottages would have a fair supply of wholesome water. "Come and see where they used to get their water for drinking and cooking," said the doctor, leading the way down an unusually large garden plot. I stepped down a bank, pulled the boughs aside, and found a little stinking pond, into which the surface water drained from the land around. It was all the water they had had for drinking till the authorities insisted on a well being sunk - a mere stagnant ditch. Another cottage - indeed a whole row of cottages - were still drawing supplies from a similar source - just a stagnant puddle under some trees at the bottom of the garden. The woman in whose garden was this water supply for herself and her neighbours, complained bitterly of what they had to put up with at times. The continuous rains of late had freshened up the ditch and rendered the water comparatively wholesome, but at times it was almost black and the stench was dreadful. It made her sick. An attempt had been made to get water by sinking a well, but it had failed. The land round that part seems unusually capricious in this respect. Within a few yards of the front garden gate Dr. Thresh had found reason to believe that water could be got at, and an experimental sinking had proved that he was correct. The boring or digging, or whatever it was, had been undertaken on a bit of waste ground by the roadside. The land, however, belonged to Wadham College, Oxford, and the agent had refused permission to make a well there. So the poor people had been compelled again to resort to their wretched ditch, and when another attempt had been made to sink for water only a few yards away, it had entirely failed.

"What on earth could have been the reason for that agent's refusal?" I inquired afterwards. "I don't know at all," was Dr. Thresh's reply. No doubt this gentleman has a reason, and it ought to be an exceptionally strong one, and the authorities of Wadham would do well to ask for it and scrutinise it closely. The want of good water is one of the great troubles of these villagers, but in the case of some of them it is only one of many evils that make life a misery and a burden. I mentioned just now a cottage, whose latticed windows peered out from a luxuriant grape vine, beneath a roof of picturesque red tiles. "I could get along for water," said the tenant. "I can fetch that from the well over yonder," he said, indicating a supply at some distance across the fields," and I wouldn't mind if he'd jest put the windows in. I like th' ole place, and I don't want to leave it." Outside and from the road the place looked the picture of cosy comfort, but go up to it and peep inside, and go round the back, and you will find it is a filthy, dilapidated pig-stye sort of place, in a condition utterly unfit for habitation. The latticed windows are actually tumbling out, and some of them at the back have really gone, and the whole are stopped up with sacking or pieces of board, while the reeking walls are all mouldy and crumbling. But a place worse than this by far stood a little way off on the same road. It was not one of the most attractive of the cottages about there, but it stood in an open and sunny position; the luxuriant garden plot at the back showed prettily through the open passage leading from the front door, and the children playing about it gave a homely, cheerful aspect to it. But such a house inside I never saw in my life, though I think I have seen a good many of the worst rooms in London. The poor woman begged we would go upstairs and look at the front bedroom. She had had to move out of it, she said, for she was afraid her bedstead would have tumbled through in to the room below. This was not in the least an exaggeration. I really felt it unsafe to stand upon the floor. The walls were cracked and broken. Throughout the house they were patched with tarred sacking or bits of sheet iron, the roof was leaky, and rain was free to come in from above, and all the winds of heaven had free course through broken floors and ramshackle windows. And that unfortunate family had had to shiver in that miserable ruin - condemned twelve months ago - all through the last dreadful winter. "I was nearly perished to death, sir," said the poor woman, "and they've been threatenin' to put the brokers in for the rates. Can they do it, sir, for a place like this?" Why did they stay there? it will be asked. Well, the simple answer is that they couldn't help it. Why they couldn't help it is a question which I must leave to a future letter. "In a locality where you can find somebody who will sell suitable plots of ground for erecting cottages, and at a reasonable price," says Dr. Thresh, as we drive along, "guardians can erect cottages; but where you have to put compulsory powers into operation, the legal expenses become so heavy that you can't do it." "That is to say in the only cases where the Act is required you find it is of no use?" "Precisely so. It breaks down just where it is most needed." Some further comments on our house to house visitation I must leave for another letter.

(FROM OUR SPECIAL COMMISSIONER)

"Cherchez la femme," said the Oriental philosopher whenever mischief arose. Inquiry into the causes of the influx of agricultural labourers into the towns strongly supports the wisdom of that eastern potentate. I am fast arriving at a conviction that the main source of the trouble is to be found in the influence of the young women. In one of the cottages we went into in the course of the round of visits I partly described in my last letter, there were three bonny lasses who seemed to ‘have completely outgrown the parental wigwam which, notwithstanding its flowery, picturesque exterior, was a low-raftered, pokey little place with a general air of sordid poverty. They had all three been out to service, but were temporarily at "home." "You wouldn't like to come back and settle down here?" they were asked. "No," was the emphatic reply. "You wouldn't catch us settling down here." They flit out of the old nest into the towns, these pretty cherry birds, and very likely with at least three young swains looking wistfully after them. They become familiar with quite a different world, get new ideas of home life, acquire quite a different standard for men and their wages. Presently they come home for a holiday, full of tales of this higher life and the wonderful earnings of smart young men of their acquaintance. There is the milkman - who sees all the life of the busy streets, and spends his pleasant days in serving pretty girls with milk and eggs, and gets a pound a week for it.

The groom was a villager once, and not a bit smarter than young Hodge, and when he came to town knew no more about horses. He now gets what is equivalent to five and twenty or thirty shillings a week, and has to drive out his master and see all the sights. Dull work turnip-hoeing in the middle of a ten-acre field at a maximum of eleven shillings a week after this. "One of my servants is going to marry a labourer," said a gentleman. "They have been waiting till he got his eleven shillings - full man's wages that is. He has got that now, and he is thinking of getting married. But the girl wants him to come into the town, and it is certainly only natural. She sees that my groom and gardener is getting twice a labourer's wage, though he is no sharper or smarter than the other. She doesn't care to go and settle down for life on eleven shillings a week and no prospect of any rise. She doesn't see why he shouldn't come into the town and get on a bit."

That, no doubt, is a very common case. "When they begin to think about getting married," said this gentleman, "is the time when they begin to be restless and begin to think about getting away from the land" - from about eighteen to five and twenty, that is, just the period of life mentioned by the experienced farmer whose pessimistic view of things I gave in my first letter. "It's the young 'uns as can go," said an old labourer in the rather doleful tone of a man who had missed his opportunity. "It's the young 'uns as can go; it's o' no use for the old 'uns to think about it." Many and many a long year's work had the old man done.

> Oft did the harvest to his sickle yield,
> His furrow oft the stubborn glebe had broke:
> How jocund did he drive his team afield!
> How bowed the woods beneath his sturdy stroke!

But it was all over; he could work no more, and now had, I suppose, to depend upon the parish. He sat there quite alone in the world. His sons had gone from him, and his wife had died two years ago. His breezy little room, with the sunbeams pouring in upon its red brick floor, looked decidedly pleasant, and I couldn't help thinking how different it might have been with the old fellow if one or two of his sons could have been working on the land around, much of which was so manifestly in need of their labour. It is evidently a great grief to many of the old people that their boys will run off to the towns. "I grieved more over my boy as went away to London, than I did over the four I'd lost," said a pleasant-faced woman; "I didn't eat a ha'porth o' food for a fortnight." "But I dare say he likes to come back and see the old home sometimes?" "Ah, that he do, sir," replied the woman, looking delighted at the thought. "He comes down for a day or two whenever he can, and he says 'there's no place like home after all, mother.' Bless you, when he was at home he'd ha' thought it shame to kiss his mother, but" - "Ah, and now when he comes back he'll do it, eh." "I should just think he would," laughed the rosy little woman. "But it do improve 'em to go to London," said another comely little matron, as she stood at her cottage door and told us how her boys had got on, evidently divided between her sentiment of pride in the lads and her grief at parting with them. "Somehow they seem quite different when they come home," she said. "And have all your boys gone to London?" "No, I got two at 'ome, now." "And why haven't they gone too?" "One of 'em had a bad attack of rheumatic fever and can't go out, and the other has fits." "That" it was remarked as we moved down the garden, "gives you some idea of the sort of people who are being left in many of these villages - just those who can't get away."

To a great extent this exodus from the fields to the towns is an exodus of the spirited and ambitious young man in quest of a more promising sphere. But it is by no means entirely so. In a great many cottages we looked into, the question was put as to why the sons had migrated, and the answers elicited seemed to show unmistakably that it was a case of Hobson's choice. "Your son has left the neighbourhood?" was put again and again, and in a great many instances the answer was in effect, "Yes, sir; he had to go." "How was that?" "Well, where was he to find work?" "But ar'nt the farmers employing so many hands as they used to do?" "No, that they aint, nothing like." "How is it?" "Because they ain't got the money, sir." Among the people I have met, there seems very little disposition to blame the farmers. It's everywhere put down to their want of means. With the exception of a few large farmers, everybody who is cultivating land at all seems to be doing it in the most economical style possible, and it seems to be the rule now with the greater number to turn their men adrift as soon as they have got in their harvest. "We had at least a dozen men out of work in my parish last winter," said a clergyman whom we met on the road to-day. I have not been sufficiently long in the neighbourhood to be very familiar with affairs, but with half an eye I could see as soon as I came here that all the usual winter work of the farms was entirely untouched - such as the clearing out of ditches and the trimming of hedges. The men are discharged and the work is not done.

So far as I have seen the county of Essex, I should say that with the average farmer this is the invariable rule. Men are being turned off after harvest. and are compelled to drift into the towns or the workhouse. They go away in the winter, and when autumn comes round again it is not surprising that farmers don't find them at their beck and call. A large farmer whom I have talked with to-day apparently regarded this as the secret of the whole difficulty. He himself kept his staff of men on steadily through the winter, and had lost none of his hands. He is, I should say, a man of ample means, and can afford to farm well, and though, like most other people about here, he did a little grumble at the low price of corn, he evidently considered himself fairly thriving. There were, he frankly admitted, considerable advantages in farming on a large scale, and some of these advantages seemed to accrue to the village adjacent, which was one of the few places I have been through from which the labourers are not migrating, and which seems to be in a fairly thriving state. Here, however, as in so many other parts of the county of Essex, the water supply is a source of difficulty. The villagers have wells, but unfortunately they have also cesspools which often drain into them, and typhoid fever is a frequent scourge here as a consequence. They had formerly one good well to which they could resort if they would, and be safe. The new railway line, however, came along and cut off their supply and appropriated the water, which the railway company now pump up for their own purposes, and sell it to the villagers through a public pump at a shilling a thousand gallons. They have of course to pay this in the form of a rate, and then they have to pay for its being brought to them or fetch it themselves, often from a long distance. In their difficulty the people, or their representatives, approached the owner of a neighbouring estate for permission to make use of a spring of good water bubbling up and running to waste. Nobody ever heard of the spring being of a ha'porth of use to anybody till it was wanted for villagers who were dying with typhoid. I saw to-day a man who had just lost his wife from typhoid - for want of it, and who proposed to bring it down to their homes in a pipe, and then the prohibitive charge of fifty pounds a year was made. I have this on the common knowledge of the village.

I hear that a communication has been received from Wadham College about the well that I said their agent would not allow to be sunk on a bit of roadside ground. The facts are precisely as I stated them; but it now appears that no formal application was made either to the agent or to the College authorities. The experimental well was made without permission, and when the agent objected to it there seemed to be no reason to doubt that the well might just as well be sunk a few yards off on the ground belonging to the cottages. Here, however, no water could be found; moreover the ground had long been polluted by pig-styes. In justice to the agent, whoever he may be, I am glad to make this explanation, though I am equally glad to have directed

28

attention to a matter in which I have no doubt the Wadham authorities and their agent will do whatever is right. Dr. Thresh had no knowledge of the matter beyond his knowledge of the sinking of the experimental well, and in answer to my inquiry he merely stated that he didn't know, as my letter represented.

TO THE EDITOR OF THE DAILY NEWS

Tuesday, August 18, 1891

OUR VILLAGES.

SIR,- The article by your correspondent who recently explored part of Essex clearly shows that life in our villages is not particularly worth living. His view as to the profitableness of large farms will not apply to some other home counties, but his description of the average labourer, and his dismal social surroundings and prospects, is true of nearly all rural districts. He says; (page 18) "What we seem to want is a great statesman to come forward and take the matter in hand." That may be true, but the coming statesman, whatever his measures may be, cannot bring relief to the labourer until public opinion is thoroughly made up on the questions involved. We hear now, from time to time, views advanced which may appear to be sound, but so far they are little more than speculative theories. Instead of being brought to the front, most of these theories are pushed back into a very secondary position in all the speeches of our leading statesmen. What statesman of first-class position has so far put land law reform in the fore-front of his programme? What may be the next great question when Home Rule for Ireland is settled, as it will very shortly be, as yet it is difficult to forecast; but I fear it will not be land law reform. There are too many class ties and influences existing to hope for this reform at the hands either of land owners, great capitalists, or their relatives and social friends. It is much more probable that the cry for land law reforms, tending perhaps toward the nationalisation or the municipalisation of the land, will in the first instance come from below - that is, from the people themselves. As yet the labourer knows very imperfectly what his real voting power is. The potency of this is being revealed to him little by little by passing events. Even

29

the hysterical efforts of the Primrose League in our darkest villages are confirming the shrewd labourer in the suspicion that so much fuss would not be made over him and his vote were it not that his political power is known and seriously feared by the whole Tory party. The power of great statesmen may be very potent in swaying the opinions of a nation, but it must have the ground prepared first. It may be that the ever-increasing intelligence and better information of the once despised "Hodge the labourer " will presently force the hands of those in high places. We are steadily moving on in the right direction to afford the necessary conditions for a popular land law reform movement. Free village schools will secure better education for the next generation. The answers now given by the village clergyman to his subservient deputy, the village schoolmaster, will ere long fail to satisfy Hodge junior that contentment under injustice is a virtue, and that it is a good and proper way of spending his life to drudge on day by day, till old age comes on him, with the union-house and a pauper's grave as the finale. That being so, he will, it is most likely, "Come forward and take the matter in hand" himself, without wearily waiting the event of a "great statesman."- Yours truly,

A.W. MARKS, Sheerness-on-Sea.

SIR, - We have read with interest both your Commissioner's letters and your own article upon the above subject. Most of the impressions conveyed by your Commissioner are correct, but he has certainly been misled by his informant regarding the advantages of large holdings and the likelihood of their being the farms of the future. Doubtless there is considerable advantage attendant on the application of labour-saving machinery which can only be attained on the larger holdings, but any gain in this line is more than counter-balanced by numerous drawbacks. I have myself had some experience as a small farmer, first in Aberdeenshire and now in Kent, and my observation fully corroborates the truth of the old adage - "He that by the plough would thrive, himself must either hold or drive." Small holders are certainly handicapped in the matter of rent, for all over Britain I should say 300 acres and upwards can be hired for at least 25 per cent. less than 100 acres and under. But as to the advantages of large purchases of cake or manure in these times of keen commercial competition they are gradually disappearing, and the example furnished by your correspondent is certainly a very exceptional one. A small holder whose credit is good can purchase the ton of cake at twelve months' credit for 7½ or 10 per cent. above the price payable for twenty tons purchased for cash, which would mean 12s. or 15s. per ton of difference, and as a rule in consumption more than this difference would be found in the greater waste where the larger quantities are used. On the other hand, according to present indications, our agriculture of the future must be more on the model of our Continental neighbours, where the farmer and his family own and occupy only as much land as they can labour themselves, and their industry is devoted to dairying and poultry and stock-rearing. In such pursuits the large holder is at once excluded from the race, or virtually so; and in any case if the large holder be dependent upon the profits of his farming for a living - the majority of them are not - it is, and has been rather a rugged one lately, and in many cases has vanished entirely.

Whereas, although in many cases rack-rents and confiscation of improvements have crippled the small holder, he is undoubtedly the man who has survived the depression. There are not many very large holdings in this neighbourhood, but there is one whose operations come under my notice. In this case the time lost by men and horses going long distances to work and carrying produce from outlying portions of his farm, certainly implies an additional expenditure of 20 per cent. for team labour, compared with farmers holding under 200 acres. To this must be added the difficulty of management and the certain deficiency of labour where a large number of hands are employed, whose only interest is to put in the time and receive the pay. The finding of economic labour is certainly the question of questions for the farmer of to-day, but it will not be solved by occupying such a holding as will require fifty men to labour it with two or three bailiffs over them at 70*l.* a year, a steward over the bailiffs receiving 200*l.* a year. No, the successful farmer of the future is undoubtedly the man who wears the sleeved waistcoat.- I am, yours, &c.,

"ONE OF THAT STAMP."

LETTERS TO THE EDITOR.

OUR VILLAGES.

SIR,- I am very glad to see that you are calling attention to English Village Life. So much has been said lately concerning the lives of the workers in London that the problems which face us in the country have to a large extent escaped notice. Yet it is evident that here, if anywhere, is to be found the key to the solution of the difficulties which arise from unrestricted competition for employment in our great towns. If you begin with the towns you are putting the cart before the horse. Stop the immigration of young and strong labouring men to your already overcrowded centres, and then you will have made some good progress towards a substantial improvement of the lot of the town workers. Otherwise you are in the position of a man who should try to pump his well dry while a spring is flowing in at the bottom. You must improve the lot and brighten the prospects of our agricultural labourers. You must give them a permanent interest in the land of their native village.

I have known them intimately for 15 years as a parish priest, and I knew them well as a layman before that; and I say emphatically that it is no wonder that they rush to the towns. They have no prospects in their native place, except the workhouse or a paltry outdoor relief of 2s. or 2s. 6d. a week. They feel there is at least a chance for them in London, or Bristol, or Cardiff - to name the towns they chiefly go to from these parts. But you must not think that the movement has been altogether a voluntary one. "I don't like cottages on my estate," says a landlord, "they are only harbourage for poachers;" so down go the cottages. Moreover, large farms have for some time past paid the landlord better than smaller holdings. So the small farms are thrown into one, and away go the men. And those who are left - what is their fate? Well, Sir, I could tell you a great deal about this which even your Commissioner does not seem to have discovered yet. How should he have done so? It takes a very long time to gain the confidence and understand the lives of these people. You must live among them to do it. They are very brave, very patient, and very reticent. They are noble fellows in short, and woe to the country that allows some of its

finest manhood to be treated as English agricultural labourers are treated now!
Yours obediently,

ARNOLD D. TAYLOR, (G. S. M.) Churchstanton Rectory, Honiton,   August 17.

Thursday, August·20, 1891.

(FROM OUR SPECIAL COMMISSIONER.)

It ought not to be, though apparently it is, necessary to point out to the readers and correspondents of *The Daily News* that when I quote a man's words I do not necessarily endorse his opinions or vouch for his statement. I am, I see, supposed to have been misled with regard to the advantages of large farming. I have certainly expressed no opinion in favour of large farms. I have merely recorded the opinions of intelligent local observers who take that view. Without for the moment expressing an opinion one way or the other I may say as a mere matter of fact that I have met with several people more or less competent to speak on the point who have unhesitatingly asserted the advantages of large farming. The last man I questioned on the point was himself a large farmer and he seemed to be in no doubt about it. "It is worth your while to get the best machinery," he said. "You can always find work for your horses and a regular staff of men." That is the opinion of a practical farmer of long experience. It is for the readers of *The Daily News* to say what the opinion may be worth. I have heard none to the contrary of this except in the case of those who have insisted on the necessity for getting back to the good old times, when the farmer turned up his shirtsleeves and worked with his men in the fields, while his daughters milked the cows and his wife made the butter and cheese. If I thought that any word of mine could assist in bringing about this, I can only declare that I should be delighted to say it. A prosperous farmer among his men, pitchfork in hand, leading, directing, stimulating those who will share his prosperity with him, is a king among men. His lot is among the brightest and the happiest on earth. By all means let his daughter milk the cows - in a shed constructed on sanitary principles, of course. The lasses will have the wholesome, dignifying sense of a useful life, and when they have done

33

their daily work, I hope they will dress themselves as prettily as they know how, and have an evening at the piano, or help in the village choral society, or manage the village library, or attend a lecture. Hoorah for the good old times plus the culture and education that we are nowadays coming to regard as quite consistent with solid work in the world, and which we may rest assured must somehow work in with any general scheme of things if that scheme is to be expected to fall in with the march of human progress, and is permanent. The old style of farmer - sordid, ignorant, opinionated, contemptuous of science and new-fangled notions did for the old times. But let it be laid down as an axiom that the future has no place for him. He has to go the way of blunderbusses and sedan chairs, and·anything tending to reproduce him is a tendency against all the forces of the times.

I repeat that I have again and again heard opinions to the effect that at all events in this part of the world the small farmers are going down, and unquestionably the appearance of the country I travelled through yesterday, say from Wickford to Althorne and Southminster and thence back by road to Chelmsford bears out this view. A more dreary and depressing stretch of badly-farmed crops and land out of cultivation, dilapidated cottages, and deserted fields, it would be difficult to find. "That field," said a worthy rector - a downright good old Tory, who had nothing but scathing denunciation for technical education, and who believed that nothing could save us all from the dogs but getting back with all speed to a tax on corn - "that field I have known to grow five and six quarters of wheat to the acre. Now look at it." Certainly such an expanse of seeding docks I never saw. "Afore now," said a working man later in the day, "I have thrashed out corn as didn't yield more than five or six sacks to the acre." I saw yesterday hundreds upon hundreds of acres of wheat and barley that could hardly yield much more. Thousands of more I saw yielding nothing at all, but just such vegetation as grown upon land when it is abandoned. Such an expanse of thistledown as stretched out before me at one point on my drive from Althorne to Chelmsford I never saw in my life. A good night's wind I should think might sow three or four counties from that field, while everywhere the hedges and ditches and roadside were choked with weeds. Yet there is no work for the villagers of Essex, and they are streaming into the big towns because miles and miles of land - inferior, no doubt, but which nevertheless might comfortably support a large population if they could be got to work upon it under such conditions as science could prescribe and capital secure - cannot be made to yield first three or four profits for other people. The land would support the actual workers on it, but that is nothing at all. It must give the clergyman his tithes, and the farmer his income, and the landowner his rent, and the Lord of the Manor his dues. It will not do that, however, therefore let it got out of cultivation, and let the people stream into the towns. Oh, the pity of it! As one flits along past their lowly homes, how near the people seem to an ideal life of simplicity and purity, comfort and contentment! How near they seem, and yet, alas! how far. I have seen few more pitiable objects than an old woman in a little hovel of a place - in a garden full of flowers - without kith or kin in the village, only a friendly old neighbour to look after her for charity occasionally, the worries of a lifetime gathered in her wrinkled face, and on her lips a desolate cry that it might soon please the good God to take her rather than let her go into the workhouse. But old people are left alone to grow decrepit in towns as well as villages. Well, yes, they are, no doubt; but here it looks as though it would be so natural and easy for some of the young ones to settle around and they all seem to go away - all but "the old people and fools." If there was a sadder sight confronted me yesterday it was that of another old woman who looked comfortably off, and who I was informed had actually furnished a cottage for her married daughter that she might live next door to a semi-imbecile village ruffian who had undertaken to support her.

There are dark depths to some of these villages. I was driven through one in which I was assured that till a few years ago marriage was quite the exception, and we called at one two-roomed cottage in which lived father and mother and a family of six, including two grown-up sons. It was a case of overcrowding, and pressure had been put upon them to reduce the number. One of the sons had been turned out. "But," whispered a neighbour, "they've took in a lodger." "It ain't a lodger," said a nice looking child of twelve or thereabouts, on inquiry at the cottage, "It's Lizzie So-and-So." "And who is Lizzie So-and-So?" The child's face dropped significantly. Evidently she was ashamed of it. "It's my brother's young woman," she said. But how pretty some of the places look! The philosopher who should leave out as of no account in considering the condition of the people, the subtle charms of the poorest of these cottages, nestling amid flowers and trees and gardens and green fields, would prove himself as shallow as he who overlooks the benefits that come of the friction and stir and stimulus of great populations and life in cities. Shall we never be able to secure for the benefit of the whole people some such combination of the two - the peace and beauty of the country with the moral and intellectual stimulus of the town, as at present is practicable only for the privileged few?

"But the land," exclaims my Tory friend the Rector, "won't support the people, and it can't support the people even if they had it for nothing." "Didn't you tell me it had yielded five and six quarters of wheat to the acre?" "That was when it had been fifty or sixty years under cultivation, and was in splendid condition. Look at it now. What can anybody do with that? It would take years to get that into paying condition again. Where's the capital to come from?" "Have you not allotments about here?" "My dear sir!" exclaims the rector with all the emphasis he could command, "it's the greatest humbug in the world to believe that prosperity is going to be brought back by giving these people allotments and small holdings." "Well, but haven't you tried them here?" "Yes, we have, and what good have they done, I should like to know!" - "But what is the reason they have done no good? Won't the people work at them, or haven't they time, or what is it?" Pressed in this way, the good man was a little vague and indefinite. I think his notions were rather mixed, and that when he repudiated allotments so vigorously he really had in mind small holdings for peasant farming - quite another matter. But he certainly led me to believe that the allotment holders wouldn't work at them with sufficient interest and vigour to make them good for anything. However, he proposed to look round the neighbourhood, and we were soon straddling over gates and stumping across fields telling of poverty and neglect, and crops hardly worth gathering in. A delightful old soul my friend the rector. How heartily he abused the Government that did nothing but the dirty work of the Liberals! Just wouldn't he like to scarify the "demoniac miscreants" who had framed that new Tithes Act, that would so cruelly rob the poor clergymen, himself among the number! What a hearty dislike he had for "Joe Chamberlain!" And we wrangled and laughed and discussed the universe at large and Essex in particular. Now he would clap me on the shoulder in hearty assent, and the next moment we tumbled apart to the political antipodes. But there were the allotments. I was fairly taken aback. I had expected to see them as barren and miserable-looking as the rest of the cultivation in that part of the world, and lo! they stood there like an oasis in the desert. I think the good rector could hardly have been round that way lately. He made the most he could of a few weeds, and declared the potato crop was all diseased. I flatly disputed it, and would have it they were not diseased but ripe and fit for digging. We pulled up a root, and the rector tried to find some specks of disease about the handsome little tubers, but couldn't find me one. With the doggedness inborn in the out-and-out Tory, he wouldn't admit that he was wrong, but the potatoes were certainly good, and every allotment was as full as it could hold of cabbages and beans, potatoes and carrots, onions and parsnips - all good valuable food produce - while all around were thousands of acres producing nothing but docks and thistles. It was the most luxuriant and thriving object I had seen in a morning's travel, except the cottage-gardens and the fruit-trees, which everywhere down here look as though they *will* grown plums and pears and apples, whether Mr. Raikes will give us a parcel post to bring them to our homes or not. Yes, the allotments certainly looked thoroughly inviting, and paid well even at the stiff rent of 2*l.* an acre. And yet that good man still, I have no doubt, believes that by no possibility of social readjustment can those broad acres be made to maintain more than the dozen or so of struggling and despondent peasants still left in his parish.

I ought to have stated that the rector told me some of this land had just been taken by a Scotchman; and since writing the above, I have heard that large lettings have been effected in the neighbourhood I have been describing. There seems to be quite an invasion of some parts of Essex by Scotchmen, who are coming down, I am told, in considerable numbers. I was informed at one point that for sixteen miles the road ran along land that had been taken by Scotchmen who were going in for dairy farming, somewhat after the fashion of the good old times. They will give no employment for Essex hands for they are bringing their families with them to help in the work, and I hear of bonnie lasses with short petticoats and bare feet, and a general muscular development worth a couple of the labourers, left on the soil. I don't know whether they have brought the pianos. The only house I have seen occupied by a North Briton was a nice, stylish, little, now brick farmhouse, which I was told was not furnished much better than the labourers' cottages around.

Friday, August 2I, *1891.*

SIR,- Few problems are more important and many-sided than life in our English villages. Finding myself in what may be called the Rothschild district or the Vale of Aylesbury since reading the first instalment by your Commissioner in the county of Essex, I noted many changes since the "good old days of forty years ago," when I resided there. No land had gone out of cultivation, but much had been "laid down" to grass; many an old familiar cottage had been deserted, and the population of the never populous sub-district has decreased 225 during the last decade (5,880 to 5,455), as other adjacent districts had in about the same proportion. The farming interest generally had more or less gone to the bad, but seems improving, though never anything like Essex. The great landlords in Bucks are among the best in England, including Lord Rothschild, Lord Carrington, Lord Rosebery, Baron Ferdinand de Rothschild, M. P., Lord Chesham, Sir Harry Verney, the Duke of Bedford, Earl Brownlow. Large holdings are said to be the more profitably cultivated, but with small ones the general prosperity seems bound up, since, if the conditions are right, the occupiers stick to their holdings and have a stake in the prosperity of the country.

Of course money in the country goes farther than in London, rent being low and vegetables, &c., cheap. "What might you pay in rent?" I inquired of the occupier of a house with outbuildings and large garden well stocked with fruit trees, formerly in my own possession. "Four pound ten a year." Not 1s. 9d. a week; but quite enough. In a town the rent of such a place would be two or three times as much. Pigs, ducks, poultry, fruit, vegetables, &c., may more or less be also reckoned on to produce something. Certainly the people generally live better and dress better than formerly, and wages for labourers are higher; generally intelligence has increased, but probably no one will deny that the average agricultural labourer is less trusty and efficient. On all hands we are told that they work shorter hours, have more money, and are very independent. The high-principled English farmer of the past seems to have deteriorated. They used formerly to go off to the Nonconformist Chapel on a Sunday, but now it is asserted that those who profess to be Churchmen have been preferred by landlords, which, I believe, cannot be true of those above mentioned. They are much fewer. Going to a village chapel connected with Dr. Clifford's persuasion, the only place of worship near, I was told that "fifteen farmers" used to attend there, and, though creditably supported now, most of the farmers go to church or nowhere. The God-fearing labourer who used to conduct or take part in a village prayer meeting seems to have had his day; albeit many a devoted man spends Sunday in the school and in Christian work. If Nonconformists, however, were true to themselves they would find others true to them. "We have but half a dozen Churchmen as tenants on our 5,000 acres," said·a gentleman to me some time since. "We don't care whether they are Churchmen or Dissenters, if they have capital and are good farmers - that is what we want, and the result is, we have not a shilling owing to us for rent." If the farmers could see their way to employ more labour, if the labourers could get a little more of their mother earth to cultivate on their own account, left less at the public-house on a Saturday night, and showed more self-respect, life with them would be better worth living. Probably the farmer will add, "If my rent was lowered I could do."- Yours truly,.

GEO. LOOSLEY, Great Berkhampstead,   August 19.

SIR. - Having recently spent fourteen days in the county of Essex on recreation bent, I have followed your Special Correspondent's letters with interest, but it has been somewhat qualified by pain and indignation. During my visit I was astounded to find how low are the wages paid not only to agricultural labourers, but to artisans as well, for the mechanics of the towns are in proportion little better paid. Eleven shillings is the standard wage for labourers, if by fine weather they are able to make a full week, all "wet time" being disallowed. I met with a splendid type of a man one Sunday, who, as lay preacher upon a Methodist Plan, had come 15 miles from home to preach the "Divine Word" to a village congregation, and this earnest and valuable member of society, a mechanic in a town, receives 18s. a week. He had been urged to leave home and remove his family to a large Midland town, where his services for the same class of work would bring him 30s. per week, but being impressed that he could be more useful in his public work where he was known, he had

39

decided from that high motive to stay and bear his limited means for the good of the people. Thus a low wage standard seems to affect wages throughout. But it is not just, and therefore not defensible. I am firmly of opinion that the stale excuse of "not being able to pay more" is no longer tenable. Farmers are doing better. The time has come when the workers from the bottom upwards should be paid wages in equitable proportions, having regard to the worth of the work they do and the cost of living, and if any shall do with less, let it be those who "neither toil nor spin."- Yours truly,

"SOUTH LINCOLN"   August 19.

SIR, - I have conversed with farmers and agricultural labourers in many of the Midland and Southern counties, and I entirely agree with the views of your correspondent who has a small farm, and signs himself "One of that Stamp." (page 30) What is wanted is a larger number of that stamp. It is the opinion of labourers with whom I have lately talked in Wiltshire and Dorsetshire that the land is not made the most of, and that when more labourers were employed the land bore twice, and in some cases even three times, the weight of corn that is now got from it. As one man shrewdly remarked, "If the farmers had reduced their farms, or taken smaller ones, instead of reducing the number of their men, they would have farmed the land better, and it would have paid better." It is impossible that farms can pay if the land is not made the most of; but a man like "One of that Stamp" will succeed if he can get a small farm at a fair rent, will work on it himself, and will also employ sufficient labour to get the most out of the land. As regards the condition of villages in the village where I now reside, wages average only 12s. a week, but every house has its garden, and nearly every man has his allotment, which varies in size from 20 to 100 roods - or lugs, as they are called in Dorset.

The consequence is that there is very little destitution; the old people are not compelled to go into the workhouse, except occasionally single old men or women who have no family to assist them. Many of the people make nearly enough out of their garden and allotment produce to keep them, and it is undoubtedly this which prevents destitution. The poor people visited by your Commissioner are without those advantages, hence the difference.

I am, Sir, yours &c.,

"WANDERER"   August 19.

SIR,- In answer to your correspondent "P" (page 19), will you permit me to say a few words concerning the labourer whose "stolid heart" has yet to be stirred by the undiscovered preacher. The personal experience of those who have lived among labourers during a long life, tends rather to show that the preacher mentioned has passed away, and there is little probability of revival; years spent in various rural parishes of Cambs., Essex, Herts, Kent, Devon, and Wales, ministering to the mental and bodily necessities of labourers and their families, teach a thoughtful observer that the stolid labourer may be stirred to reverence the clergy, when the man in charge of the parish has a heart that can "soothe and sympathise," when he has the good sense and keen observation to adapt himself to the wants of his parishioners, and by throwing aside red-tapeism, rubric, and ritual, can become the servant, that he may win many to Christ. Instances can be given of crowded churches in rural parishes fifty, forty, or even twenty years ago, when the clergyman was revered almost to superstition by the smock-frocked men and scarlet cloaked women who filled his church to listen to his teaching, not because he preached of the "Fathers," the "Saints," the "Sacraments," the "Holy Days," the "Church," "Church authority," "Church discipline," "Church ordination," but because he magnified his office by unfolding the character of his "Divine Master," and extolled the Creator, whose works of nature the labourer sees to perfection; not because surplices, choral services, eastward positions, crosses, candles, and concert room decorations were insisted on, but because every member was considered worthy to join in responses and singing, though not trained for elocution or platform music. Is it not correct to say that simple, practical country parson is an individual of the past? Is it not a fact that more zeal is spent now on millinery, music, repetition of services, offertories, statistical figures of communicants, confirmees, church decorations, and altar worship, than is bestowed on training the character, nurturing spiritual life, and winning the sympathy of the stolid labourer. Instance can be adduced where young men have succeeded in emptying all the benches of a country church in less than a

41

month by their persistent idolatry of forms and ceremonies. The stolid labourer is often gifted with a large share of good common sense, and he is keen in detecting the real from the sham. That he has been moved by many an earnest preacher is a fact beyond dispute - that he will be moved by artificial display and ceremony remains to be proved.- I am, &c.,

"CHURCHWOMAN".

Saturday, August 22, 1891

(FROM OUR SPECIAL COMMISSIONER)

In my last letter I described a part of Essex in which the land was poor, a vast proportion of it altogether out of cultivation, where crops were of the scantiest, where the cottages were bad, and almost everything wore a general aspect of poverty and depression. To-day I have walked for some hours through a locality in all respects different. Many of the crops I saw were first-rate. There had been room for more labour, but everything looked prosperous; and as to the cottages in the village of Stisted, which I found at the end of my walk, between three and four miles out from Braintree, they must be among the best labourers' cottages in all England. They were put up by the late squire, Mr. Onley Savill-Onley, to whose memory a handsome stained-glass window for the parish church is being subscribed for, and who seems to have endeared himself to everybody. The squire, I am told, was a man of cultivation, a clever landscape artist, and took great pride in designing cottages, not only healthy and commodious, but pretty and artistic. He was, by the account of the Rev. Canon Cromwell, Rector of Stisted, in all respects a model landowner - lived among his people, spent his money among them, won their esteem and confidence, and generally acted the part of an earthly Providence to them all to an extent that one cannot but fear must have tended seriously to sap independence of character in the village. Pensions have been so freely granted to widows that they have accumulated in Stisted in numbers sufficient to have deterred Mr. Weller, senior, from even venturing to drive his coach through the spick-and-span little place. To add to the prosperity of the village, allotment land has been let at twopence a rod and the farmers in the neighbourhood are men of capital, and have habitually kept on their hands all the year round. If the labourers under such circumstances are not to be kept on the land it is difficult to see what is likely to keep them, apart from some totally different economic system. Good and cheap cottages - 4*l*. a year is about the rent - permanent work, cheap allotments without stint, while in Canon Cromwell they have a large-hearted, liberal-minded friend, earnest in every effort to provide education, rational entertainment, and everything else that may be practicable for them.

Such a combination of advantages must be very rare, and yet from this model little village the young men are streaming away into the towns or the colonies, just as they appear to be in almost every other part I have visited, and nobody seems to be able even to suggest a possible remedy. The truth I am reluctantly driven to by my visit to Stisted, more than by anything I have seen yet, is that this question is one of wages, and wages alone, and that unless means can be found of bringing up the standard of wages to a point which every farmer in the kingdom would scout as utterly preposterous, this shifting of the population cannot be decidedly stopped, and can be retarded only in proportion as that standard is approached. I was attracted in this direction by a report in a local paper that the labourers at Stisted and Pattiswick had refused to set about harvesting till the farmers would come to their terms, and that virtually an agricultural strike was on foot. The men in this neighbourhood get ten shillings a week during the winter and during the summer eleven. When harvest comes round this arrangement is suspended, for it is the custom here for them to form companies and to make bargains with their masters to cut, bind, cart, and stack the crop at so much an acre. Fifteen shillings an acre is an ordinary figure, when the men find their own beer. Some masters prefer to pay the whole in money, but the common arrangement is for the farmer to pay twelve or twelve and sixpence an acre with a certain allowance - not of beer, for the Truck Act forbids that - but of malt and hops, which the men brew into beer for themselves. There is a small brewhouse in Stisted, where the men, for a payment of eighteenpence or so, may brew their beer, which they generally do in the night. It is an obvious infringement of the Truck Act in spirit, if not in letter. It ought to be stopped, and if need be the amended Truck Act should be amended again. I am told that some of the masters manage in this way to get rid of the bad barley they cannot otherwise find a market for, and those who are trying to promote temperance among the harvesters find it a difficulty and a discouragement. This beer-making material is worth about thirty shillings, and the men, one of them told me to-day, reckon to cut ten or twelve acres of wheat per man, the whole earnings being divided among the company. Suppose each man harvests eleven acres, at twelve and sixpence, his share will be between six and seven pounds for the harvest, to which must be added the thirty shillings' worth of malt and hops. Of course, if the crop is heavy, there is more work to the acre than when it is light, and the men and masters have to haggle until they can come to terms about it. This year there was a difference of a shilling or eighteenpence they couldn't get over, and the men refused to go to work. Two or three days appeared to have been wasted in this way, while one after another the masters gave in, the largest and probably the wealthiest holding out the longest. However, terms were eventually agreed on, and when I reached the locality, nothing but the drenching showers prevented the cutting of some very fine crops.

I jumped over a bank into a field, where a party of them were waiting, and had a long talk with the men, as well as with several others I met in the course of my walk, and their testimony was practically identical. It was with them all a question of wages. It is the big shilling, they told me. "But are there no other reasons why men are leaving the country?" I asked, "Do you dislike the work, or don't you like living in a village?" No; it wasn't that. They would stay in a village if the pay was right, and they didn't mind the work, but there was too much of it for the money. The masters had had them under their heels far too long, and unless things were changed there would be "ructions". If things weren't altered they would all go. "When you go back to Lon'on," said one brawny fellow ensconced deep in a shock of wheat, "tell them ironmongers up there they needn't make no more o' them things" - indicating the scythes - "we ain't a goin' to use 'em." "But don't you think men are better off down here at the pay you are getting than they would be in London at a higher rate? You know a man's expenses down here are very much lighter than they are in London." "There ain't much difference for single men," was the reply," and there's a lot o' difference in the pay." In the course of the morning I talked with a respectable-looking working woman, who afforded rather a telling illustration of this. "Well," I began," "and are the people leaving Stisted and going into the towns, as they are doing in other parts?" "No," said the woman; "I don't know as they are - except the young 'uns; they keep going!" "Except the young ones! But they are just the ones who ought to be staying to do the work." "Yes," laughed the woman, "that's true enough; but you see they like to better themselves if they can. I got a boy as has jest gone from here." "Ah, and why did he leave?" "Well, sir, he couldn't save nothing out of his pay. All through the winter he got ten shillings a week, and when he'd paid me for his board and lodging and had dressed himself - he is a young fellow of two-and-twenty, and dresses pretty well - there was nothing left. 'Mother,' he says, 'I shall never be better off at this game. I'm a-goin' to try my luck in London.'" "And did he find work when he went to London?" "Yes, he went over somewhere down Penge way and got on at once with a contractor or some't to drive a cart at a pound a week, but he soon gave that up and got on to the railway. I ain't quite sure what he gets there, but I know it's over a guinea." We talked of working hours, and I asked the woman what the people did with themselves in the winter evenings. "Some on 'em goes to the reading-room up in the village. That was where my boy used to go when he had had his tea and washed. He'd go up there and read the paper." "Ah, and I suppose it was there he picked up his idea of going to London?" "Oh, yes, sir. He see the advertisement about the place he got in the paper." "And does he like it? Wouldn't he like to come back again?" "No, sir; it suits him very well indeed. He's been down once or twice, and he looks hearty and well, and says he's very glad he went."

"Yes," said Mr. Cromwell afterwards, "I know the lad you are referring to. He and two friends of his used to come up to the rectory to educational classes. Those two friends made up their minds to go out to Canada, where they got employment immediately. I forget exactly what pay they got, but something like five times what they were getting here. And these young fellows have friends in the village, and these things are known by everybody." Can there be anything more natural than this exodus from the villages? Can there be anything more inevitable than the virtual depopulation of our agricultural districts unless some radical change can be effected? Some of the farmers will tell you that ten or eleven shillings a week is but the nominal wage, and that at times they earn considerably more. There is some truth in it. A labourer's wife and children will sometimes earn a little by picking stones off the land. For a month or six weeks a woman may earn as much as eighteenpence or a couple of shillins by pea-picking; so that the Tory rector may have been right when he told me that a cottager and wife and children sometimes had as much as a pound a week coming in. It is possible they may have just while the pea-picking lasts. But if you tell this to the men they are instantly down on you with a contra account. "They calls it eleven shillings a week,"·said the men in the harvest field to-day, " but what about the days o' pourin' rain when you can't get into the fields? Don't they stop yer pay for them?" "I should think they do!" cried the fellow buried deep down in the corn shock. "They'll say, 'hullo, here's a shower of rain. Go and send those fellows home. Darn 'em! They'll all be under the hedge.'" "Ah," said another, "many's the time as I've been home with five or six shillins for my week's pay."

Of course there is a great difference in masters, and things vary somewhat according to local circumstances, but in Essex, so far as I have seen it, I don't think it would be far wrong to put down the income of an able-bodied labourer as from five to ten pounds at harvest, and for the rest of the year ten or eleven shillings a week when in work. The best of the young men among agricultural labourers find no difficulty at all in getting employment in the towns. It is not they who drift to the dock gates and the casual wards, but they oust others who have to do so. Why should a young man stay down in his village when he is practically certain of finding employment at double wages, with all sorts of indefinite possibilities in the towns? As things are, he will not stay. The whole conditions of his life will have to be changed. The farmers down here can tell you why. As a rule, with very few exceptions, they have always been against education. With very few exceptions, they are dead against it now. If they speak candidly - as they will sometimes - they tell you that this restlessness and shifting are simply the results of education. And they are undoubtedly right. Schools and newspapers and ballot boxes and trade unions and penny postage and cheap travelling are all educating our peasantry. It is of no use to rely upon old remedies now that you have got new men with new cravings, new ideals, new sense of power and importance and new resolution to live a life a little more worth living. There is no going back. "The proper remedy for the evils of liberty," said Fox, "is more liberty." The proper remedy for the evils of education is more education. Every agency by which men can be made out of drudges and dolts and mere beasts of burden must be kept in operation with redoubled energy and they must be got back to the land which so sorely needs them under conditions affording some of the stimulus of hope, some little scope for enterprise and ambition.

TO THE EDITOR OF THE DAILY NEWS

Sir, - The letter of your Honiton correspondent of August 17 (page 32), suggesting more attention to English village life deserves special consideration; and, if through the effort of such writers and your Special Commissioner, the public mind of agricultural life can be aroused, it will help to a solution of some of the difficulties which exist. The last census disclosed the important fact that in most of the villages in the Eastern Counties population has decreased and, as a consequence, commercial as well as agricultural depression is severely felt. How to alter this state of things is a problem very hard to solve but it is one that certainly demands attention; and, if any plan can be suggested to keep more of the young life in villages and small towns, it will be the means of partly solving this problem. The question of allotments is one of much importance, as both political parties find it necessary, when seeking the support of the labourer, to make this a prominent feature of appeal; and there is no doubt where land can be obtained at a reasonable rent and near to cottage homes it is a means of help in supporting the family.

Many agriculturists are giving more attention to market gardening; and this when adopted gives additional employment to women and young persons at certain seasons of the year. But there is yet room for further effort to benefit such localities and that is by introducing manufacturing industries where young women as well as young men might find employment. There are few such in Suffolk, Essex, Cambs., also Norfolk and where they exist then improvement is found; and while even such efforts would not entirely check the immigration to large centres, it would materially prevent the quiet depreciation which has been going on the last 20 years.
I am, Sir, yours faithfully,

W.Pearson, Stapleford, Cambs.   August 20.

Sir, - Your Special Correspondent's letter in *The Daily News* of August 20 (page 33) gives an only too true account of the foul state of the land in East Anglia. Doubtless the moist season has been especially conducive to the growth of docks and thistles which have never within my recollection been so rampant as at present. It is not only on neglected farms where labour is scamped, but on farms like my own where no reasonable expense of labour is spared, that weeds prevail. But although I spare no expense now, the tenants off whose negligent hands I lately took my farms had unhappily allowed the seeds of weeds to accumulate in the land for years. The excessive moisture of the present season, alternating with half days of heat and sunshine, has resulted in a quite abnormal crop of weeds. If the land had not been labour-starved for the last dozen years, the seeds of the weeds would not have accumulated in the ground and we should have tided over the present season with comparative immunity. As it is, I fear the land must go from bad to worse as the lateness of the present harvest will exceptionally favour the seeding of the docks and thistles which abound, especially in the barley crops, generally the last to be cut.

No doubt the Education Acts, which have deprived our farmers of children's labour, are partly responsible for the triumph of the weeds. Most farmers of late years declare themselves unable to pay men's wages for doing boy's work. Although, as your correspondent truly points out, allotments are as a rule, if not exceeding half an acre, better farmed, it is unfortunately the fact, within my own not inconsiderable experience, that allotments of one or two acres are not better done by than the larger farms. It is therefore only a comparatively small area in each parish which can at present be profitably devoted to allotments. Having lately let off several fields in one, two, and three acre allotments, at the maximum rate of 30s. per acre, I am writing with the truth of the facts above stated before my eyes. I am as anxious as Mr. Jesse Collings can be to see small holdings established but unfortunately, candidates for small holdings are hardly to be found in my neighbourhood. In about twelve years I have only found about as many applicants who have all been accommodated. But only one or two of my small holders rose from the ranks of the agricultural labourers. The rest are publicans, millers, village tradesmen, &c. Yours faithfully,

W.H.Hall, Six Mile Bottom, near Newmarket.   August 21.

Tuesday, August 25, 1891.

LETTERS TO THE EDITOR

OUR VILLAGES.

SIR, - In his remarks concerning allotments, your Commissioner has hit the right nail on the head even if he has not quite driven it home. Consider a moment. Those allotments pay with a rent of 2*l.* per acre. Does that include rates, &c., I wonder? What is the average agricultural rent of the surrounding land? Is it 15s. or 1*l.*? Not that, I expect. And are those allotments handy to the labourers' cottages, or have they to walk a mile after their day's labour before they can get to work on them? Is the land, "the worst land in the parish at twice the rent of the best?" as Professor Thorold Rogers put it. Even if all these questions can be answered in favour of the labourer, consider the gain in productiveness on a large scale that the figures as given indicate. Well does a careful observer know the look of those "cases" in the desert of much of modern farming. The long and short of it is, Sir, this:- Let the labourers have a chance of getting hold of some land at a fair rent, with leave to build sheds, pigstyes. &c., upon it. with security of tenure and tenant right, by which I understand a right of property in his own improvements, and he will not only keep the land. but it will keep him. He will keep it in good order as it should be kept, and it will keep him in comfort in his native place.- I am, Sir, yours obediently,

ARNOLD D. TAYLOR, Churchstanton Rectory, Honiton,   August 22.

P.S. I purposely use the vague term "some land," as the amount desirable would of course vary with the circumstances of the labourer.

SIR. - Will you allow me to make a few remarks and suggestions on this subject? Your corespondent "W. H. Hall," (page 48) who appears to be a landowner in Cambridgeshire, tells us that he has offered small holdings for twelve years, and has only found about as many applicants. Now, the essential things to know are, firstly. whether there was any considerable choice of land offered, so that a man might have the quality and the quantity of land he required; secondly, whether it was offered at rents either the same or very little higher than those paid by farmers for similar land; thirdly, and most important of all, whether intending tenants were made clearly to understand that they would be legally secured in their holdings so long as they paid the rent - have, in fact, a practically perpetual lease with full power of transfer - that there would be no restriction of their use of the land (subject only to the law of nuisance), and that their rent could never be raised, thus giving them full security for their improvements. Without these essential conditions of the tenure it is absurd to expect that men will labour and struggle to make a home on another man's land; with these conditions I shall be very much surprised to hear that there are not applicants for all the land offered. To test this, allow me to suggest that your Special Commissioner, who is giving us so much interesting information on "Life in our Villages," should make it a point to ask every agricultural labourer he talks with whether, if he had land on the terms above indicated, making it clear to him that he would be as absolutely free and secure in its possession as if he were a freeholder, subject only to the payment of a fair rent- whether under these conditions he could make a good living for himself and family. He might also ask whether, if every young man could have land on these conditions in the vicinity of his home, it would not to a great extent stop the exodus from the villages. Allotments will never do this, because they offer none of the advantages and none of the security of a permanent holding.

John Stuart Mill was of opinion that allotments were similar in their effects to the old bad system of parish allowance enabling labourers to work for lower wages. He says: "This, too, is a contrivance to compensate the labourer for the insufficiency of his wages, by giving him something else as a supplement to them; but instead of having them made up from the poor rate he is enabled to make them up for himself by renting a small piece of ground, which he cultivates like a garden by spade labour." And, after showing that allotments have decided advantages over the system of money allowances, he adds: "But in their effect on wages and population, I see no reason why the two plans should essentially differ." (*Political Economy*, People's Ed., pp. 222-3.) This is, no doubt, the reason why farmers often favour allotments, but object strenuously to small holdings. The former keep down wages and leave the men

dependent; the latter make the men independent, because self-supporting, and therefore raise wages. In my opinion, therefore, all discussion as to allotments is time wasted, as.is also all idea of permanently raising agricultural wages and improving the condition of the labourers, except by the simple, direct, and natural method of enabling all workers who desire it to support themselves, either wholly or partially, by the cultivation of the soil under the most favourable conditions possible, these being such a secure and permanent tenure as I have above indicated.- Yours faithfully,
ALFRED R. WALLACE, President, Land Nationalisation Society.

SIR - Of what use is it to talk of "introducing manufacturing industries" into villages when there is not enough house-room for the existing people, if they were accommodated as they ought to be? As sanitary laws become better known by the country folk, and as education teaches them to think of "bettering" themselves, can the youth help leaving villages where in some cases they live in constant discomfort? What, for instance, can be expected where the woman has but one small room in which to cook, wash, dry clothes, and do everything, and perhaps a family of nine, of both sexes and all ages, to find sleeping room for in two small rooms? Then there is the question of water; will some one tell us what the law is on that subject? In some parts of this villages the water supply is shamefully deficient, even where it could easily be supplied from the pipes of a neighbouring waterworks, which run through the village. So long as there is no way of compelling country landlords to supply to their tenants what is requisite for the decencies of life, surely one cause of village depopulation is found. The people dare not complain openly, as it is often a case of "take it or leave it." The old folks must put up with the wind and the rain in their houses, or be forced to go into a worse shelter, or even into the union. A landlord may say, "The property I have bought is not worth repairing." Perhaps so; still rent is paid for the house, and there remains the fact that some human beings are housed infinitely worse than their landlords' horses. No speedy reform can be hoped for if the source of it is to be purely a local one. A "Parish Council" sounds pretty, but in practice would it not be futile? The best intentioned of the most prosperous of the village people would not stand against any possible damage to their business. They would tell you they could not afford it; in other word, they must not offend their best customers. In the meantime towns are getting too full, and increasing knowledge, which has given birth to a growing and righteous discontent among the agricultural labourers, calls for aid. Who will give it?- Yours faithfully,

"A COUNTRY VICAR'S WIFE".   August 22.

Thursday, August 27, 1891

(FROM OUR SPECIAL COMMISSIONER)

In my last letter I gave, I think, good reasons for believing that the one great cause of the flocking of the agricultural labourers into the towns is the poorness of their pay, and the further I inquire the more certain it appears to me that nothing will stop this disastrous influx but a very material advance in wages, or something equivalent to it. I have just been out eight or ten miles from Thurston Station on the Great Eastern line, in Suffolk, where I was met on all hands with pretty much the same story as in Essex - land labour starved, wages about 11s. a week, young men going into the towns. There were exceptions. Just close to Thurston Station lives a farmer who, I am told, farms thoroughly well. He is a coal merchant as well as an agriculturist, and can always find work for his men. There is, I was assured, no dissatisfaction on his land. It seemed to be an exception to the general rule, however. At one point in the road I found a large gang of men who had just done dinner and were snoozing or smoking their pipes, and I got into conversation with them. They talked quite freely to me, and several of the men very sensibly and intelligently. The impression they gave me was pretty much the same as that I had received from the other party of reapers I mentioned in a previous letter, the impression of deep dissatisfaction with existing conditions or life and a strong disposition to revolt against them. Men had been going off the land, and they would continue to do so, as fast as they could. Was it likely, they wanted to know, that they were going to stay there at ten or eleven shillings a week while they could get thirty in town? "Where do they get thirty shillings a week?" I inquired. "At the breweries." said the man. "Do you know anybody who did it?" "Yes, a

chap in our village went to a brewery and got thirty shillings straight off."
Apparently they all knew of somebody who had left the land and "bettered
themselves."

"Now, tell me," I said to them - I suppose there were about twenty
men there, a fairly representative gathering of Suffolk labourers in the heart of
the country - "now, tell me what you think would be likely to keep the
labourers on the land? What do you think would be satisfactory?" One man
though "twelve bob" would do, but his moderation was scouted. Others
candidly voted for all they could get. After a wrangle which, to an ear not
accustomed to Suffolk vernacular, was a little confusing, one solid-looking man
said he thought fifteen shillings a week would be fair wages. "Give me fifteen
shillings a week and a bit of ground," he said, "and I'll be content. You
wouldn't ketch me a'going into a town." Content, alas! is but a Will-o'-the-
wisp, and it would be rash to predict that a general rise in wages, even to that
extent, would finally settle the difficulty. But the suggestion of fifteen shillings
a week and a bit of ground seemed to be generally approved. "What do you
mean by a bit of ground?" I asked. "Well, say a quarter of an acre." "But some
of the men tell me that a day's work on the land is quite enough, and that they
don't care for more of it when they have done that." "Well, I got a quarter of a
acre myself, and I find I can do it very well." "And what is it worth to you
now, all the year round?" "Well, I reckons it's as good as two shillings a week
on to my wages." "Then fifteen shillings a week and a quarter of an acre of
ground would keep the men in the villages, you think?" Yes, that might do it,
and nothing much short of it would. What is the probability of any such
remedy being arrived at this point upon which the readers of *The Daily News*
may be left to form their own opinions. Some of the horse-keepers I have
found getting fourteen or fifteen shillings a week, and able to rent a bit of
ground. But the nearest approach to it by ordinary labourers in this locality
that I have heard of is in a village eight or nine miles out of Bury St. Edmunds,
where a short time before harvest began the men struck for twelve shillings,
and got it. How long they will keep it is a matter that may perhaps be
positively decided shortly after the completion of harvest. These men had been
getting ten shillings a week.

My charioteer was an intelligent man who knew the country all
round, and his conversation was instructive. He had no idea of my purpose

beyond the intimation that I was interested in the condition of the land and the labourers, and he talked very freely. Yonder was a village where lots of people went away last summer. Over there was another where the farmers last week wanted thirty men to begin harvest, and couldn't get them anywhere. Yes, there was no doubt things were in a bad way. There was land at Stanton that hadn't had a plough over it for five years, and Mr. So-and-so somewhere else had got so many acres of turnips you couldn't see for weeds. "I tell 'e what it is," said a man who had come up driving a van while our discussion was going on on the roadside, and pulled up to take his part in it, "the farmers ain't half doing the land." "No, that they hain't," broke in another. "Why there's five crops in that there field. There's thistles and docks and all sorts o' things besides the barley." "They don't do nothin' to the land," resumed the man up in the van. "What they mean to do is to get all they can out of it, and then when it's got down till it's good for nothin', they'll clench it up, and then where are you?"

This man had a good deal to say. He spoke like a capable, intelligent sort of person, but with a certain rancour I couldn't help noticing. When we moved on, my driver explained to me that that man had been in the employ of one of the farmers in the neighbourhood, but had left on some ground or other, intending to get employment with some other farmer. But he found it impossible. "If a man don't put up with whatever a master likes to do, and leaves him, there's no chance of his getting another job with any o' the others. They hang together," he said. I don't, of course, know the details of the case of this particular man, but I noticed that he was not driving a farmer's vehicle, and the remarks of my driver entirely tallied with what I had heard in other quarters. In many localities there seems to be a sort of league among the masters against the men, always ready to repress and punish any display of independence. "The masters," said a picturesque yokel a day or two ago, "ha' had we like that," striking a particularly ludicrous attitude, and bringing down a ponderous hob-nailed hoof on a clod of mould, supposed to represent the neck of the labourer. "The masters ha' had we like that; and now we mean to ha' they." One mustn't, I suppose, take too literally poor Hodge's rebellious expressions. My driver, as we jogged along, gave me very droll accounts of some of their attempts to get up strikes over the harvest work. As I have previously explained, the gang of labourers work together in getting in the crops, and before beginning they have to arrange terms. For this purpose one of their number is selected as "lord," and he has to conduct negotiations, trusting, of course, to the moral support of the rest. "Maybe there's ten of 'em and they'll all on 'em swear like fury as they won't do't under so much, and you'd think as they'd rather die fust. They be all agoin' to have it and no mistake. Well, they go to the master, and then p'r'aps there's two on 'em'll hold together and all the others'll give in without sayin' a word." The unlucky "lord" in such a case comes in for the brunt of the bullying - or "mobbing," as they call it here - which it seems to be generally allowed many farmers and bailiffs indulge in very freely on the smallest provocation.

"Yes," said a Nonconformist minister who had been working among the Suffolk labourers for seven or eight years - "Low wages is the first thing that makes these people so anxious to get off the land." "They are going then from here also?" "Oh, yes, continually going. Only a week or two ago I lost two of my young men." "Low wages the first point. And what is the second?" "The second - indeed, I am not quite sure whether it ought not to be put first - is independence." By this the speaker proceeds to explain that he means that these young men, who are continually leaving the villages, are largely actuated by the desire to get out of that serf-like condition in which they find themselves, and the abject subjection they are under to the farmer. "Unless you have lived among them," said this minister, "you can have no idea of the gulf that separates the two classes." The tyrannical, domineering, nigger-driving sort of treatment the men have to submit to I have heard about in many quarters. "And there's another thing," said the man up in the wagon, who, as I have explained, probably had specially good reasons for knowing what he was talking about, "eres many o' the men got to live in the farmer's cottages; they be on his land. If you offend him it ain't on'y yer work as you loses. It's a clear kick out - work and house and neighbourhood too. Very like there ain't another house to be had for miles, but out you must go. Is that right? Ought a man to be dependent on a master like that?" "No; he didn't," was the clamorous response all round. "O' course he didn't." It was this question of cottage accommodation that I had mainly come out here to inquire a little into. I have loitered so long on the way however that I must leave the subject for another letter. It might be supposed that as so many are continually evacuating the villages that deficiencies in cottage accommodation must be a difficulty rapidly solving itself. It does not appear to be so however. There are many of these villages in which there can have been no cottage building for years. Some of the houses become totally uninhabitable, and large numbers of them are far too closely packed, and if by chance a house is vacated there is a rush for it, while many of the people, as I have shown to some extent in a previous letter, are compelled to live in cottages that are a scandal and a disgrace to all who are responsible for them.

TO THE EDITOR OF THE DAILY NEWS

SIR, - I read your articles on Village Life as they appear to my labourers, and we discuss the various questions raised. The result of our talk seems to be that the deplorable state of agriculture in Essex may also be seen here in Oxfordshire on the numerous farms which of late years have been neglected from want of capital or otherwise; that the condition of the small farmer was never worse, but that the condition of the labouring man was never better than it is at present. The more people that go to the towns the better for those who are left behind. The only drawback is the distant view of the workhouse, for however great wages the labourer may receive, he puts by not a single farthing for old age. This prospect, however, might easily be averted if the enormous sum of money raised by the poor law in the village was kept in the village, instead of being sent away, who knows where? I believe, however, that the workhouse contains no one from this village. The only remedy I can think of in order to keep all the land in cultivation is for joint-stock companies to find capital and work the neglected farms, and utilise capital which might otherwise go to such places as Chili and the Argentine Republic. I have during the past two years taken to farming for amusement, certainly not for profit; and take great interest in agriculture. The rector your correspondent mentions ought to know that an allotment is of the greatest value to the labourer, and amply repays the labour expended on it (page 36). I have turned the fifth part of an acre of my farm to garden ground. This repays me 10 per cent, whilst the rest of my farm pays nothing.-Yours. &c.,

"AN OXFORDSHIRE LANDLORD"

.SIR, - I have read with much interest the series of papers on "Life in our Villages," but neither your "Own Commissioner" nor any of your correspondents suggests any adequate remedy for the evils portrayed. Our agricultural labourers are fast forsaking the land and overcrowding our towns. This is the fact. The cause is that their wages are inadequate, and the conditions of existence such as to make life not worth living. What is the remedy? Clearly we must secure for the labourer a better return for his toil; we must provide him with a wholesome and comfortable dwelling, and we must enable him to participate in the comforts, conveniences, and enjoyments of civilized life. Giving him a patch of land to eke out starvation wages will not accomplish this. By fixing him to the spot it will make him more absolutely dependent upon a particular employer. But the manner in which he uses an allotment when he gets it points clearly to the solution of the question. If, after toiling for a master he can in his overtime convert such a patch into an oasis as described by your Commissioner, what would he not do if he had land enough to occupy his whole time and under such conditions as would secure to him the full benefit of his labour? Add to this, instead of the "picturesque" cottage, surrounded by the beauties of nature which make the dark interior the more repulsive by contrast, a healthy and comfortable house with good water supply, light and heat, so situated that he can enjoy the social intercourse of his fellow men without resorting to the public-house, and education for his children without their trudging two or three miles through mud or snow, and the exodus from towns would be as marked and rapid as that from the country has been for several years past.

My suggestion is to establish throughout the country rural villages somewhat after this model: Let 1,000 acres of land be divided into 200 plots of five acres each. In the centre of the whole let a block of buildings be erected, containing at least 200 good sized rooms, a suite of public rooms, such as a dining hall, a reading room well supplied with suitable literature, a recreation or smoking room, a work-room for women, schools for the children, rooms for teachers, baths, washhouses, &c., the whole to be well supplied with water, lighted by gas or electricity, and warmed by hot-water, steam or flues; on each plot, a shed for stores and tools, a piggery and poultry pen, cow-houses and stables where required. The rent of each plot of land should include that of at least one private room, with free access to the public rooms, and use and enjoyment of all the conveniences provided. In such a colony numbering probably one thousand souls in all, men, women, and children, the inmates would have almost everything they could wish for within their own borders. The men would not be tied by the leg to each other as in co-operative farming; but, while perfectly free and independent would doubtless find many ways of co-operating for their mutual advantage. The life would be that of a club. No one need associate with another unless he pleased, but there would be the opportunity for social intercourse to any extent mutually agreeable. National credit would be much more usefully and profitably employed in establishing such colonies as these throughout the country than in buying out one set of Irish landlords to replace them by another set. But we must first "catch our hare." We must have the land. Nothing can be done while the land is under the control of individuals whose chief, if not only object is to draw the largest income therefrom at the least possible expense. The people must be aroused to a sense of their right, and demand it. The nation must awaken to a sense of its duty, and take the land under its own immediate administration. This does not mean that landlords are to be treated as they treat their tenants, turned out upon the roads to starve and die; they may be relieved of the control of the land and annuities guaranteed to them not exceeding the net income derived therefrom, with an equitable provision for their gradual diminution and ultimate extinction. This is the first essential step, not only for the amelioration of the people, the revival of trade and renewed prosperity, but to prevent decadence and decay and those consequences, fearful to contemplate, which sooner or later spring from a people exasperated by long continued oppression and suffering. - Yours truly.

F. L. SOPER, Highgate,   August 25.

SIR, - Your Special Commissioner's articles on village life are exciting widespread interest, and he is most certainly correct when he arrives at the conclusion that it is the poor wages which depopulate our villages. How many there are who long for a country life, but who cannot see their way to earn as good a living there as in town? What must the feelings of some of us be who feel perfectly confident they could make more money in the country if only they had the means to start? Farming I know little about; but fruit-growing, speaking broadly, is a field of labour not even entered on by our countrymen. If their trees have fruit on, very well; pull it off, put it in a hamper, and send it to market. In the country part I come from I have never even heard of any grower sorting his fruit. Fine and poor, speckled and deformed, it all goes together. What a field of labour, and paying labour, is open to anyone doing the thing properly. In this climate, where nothing can be relied on except changeable weather, it would be necessary to have a certain amount of glass to make sure of something in bad seasons. In a plentiful year I have seen tons of the finest apples piled in a long row rotting, because they would not pay for carriage. This crop was as much a loss as if there was none at all; nay worse, as labour had been expended in gathering it. Why could we not in England core, peel, ring, and dry apples in such years for a winter sale? They tell me the drying apparatus is inexpensive, and will also dry other fruit. The boxes for packing apple rings and picked fruit could be made on the premises; thousands upon thousands would be needed. They would cost much, but pay well. Properly managed, a small fruit farm would employ a large number of permanent heads, they would become skilled hands commanding high wages. Ordinary farm work requires but little brain (on the part of the hands), but fruit growing and culture, carpentering, painting (the glass houses), stoking, packing, sorting, &c., all require careful attention. There would be scope for good men, and the best men would be best paid. The countryman, farmer or what not, appears to me to have an easy joy-trot life so different to that of the city man. Yet here is a country occupation offering, I am sure, a grand reward, which would give a man endless work, but it would be work he could put his heart into. If he did not fear having too much on his hands, he could take a little farm land for a dairy, some sheep, pigs, and corn for his horses. It would mean more work, but save him buying a good deal of manure. Poultry also would help him against insect pests, as well as with eggs and chickens. What a glorious vista is here opened up! It would mean a working day of more than thirteen hours, but they would not be spent in a city warehouse. They would be spent in the country, where, I am sure, the bulk of the numerous countrymen in every town would like to live if only they could get the chance. - Yours, &c.,

"A COUNTRYMAN"   August 25.

59

LETTERS TO THE EDITOR

.

SIR - The problem of solving the difficulty connected with the hopelessness of a labourer's life is retarded by the fact that the labourer himself contributes so little towards forcing a change. Years of degrading slavery, and in many parishes abject dependence on the parson and squire, have effectually stamped out his manliness, and his patrons have done but little to improve his circumstances, being content merely to assure him that life in a workhouse is not nearly so bad as it is painted, and that after all a pauper's grave is of little moment; besides which, coals and blankets are provided by his more fortunate neighbours for needy cases, whereof the labourer ought to be glad, and exhibit real thankfulness for their consideration and kindness. Large farmers have done fairly well of late years. Their rents are less per acre, and their expenses proportionately lower, but farmers occupying from 80 to say 250 acres complain of their difficulties. Their rents in many cases are too high, and the local tax gatherer claims from such his full due, so that when rent, rates, taxes, and railway charges are paid there is too little left, and as a result those he employs are poorly paid, and exist permanently on the verge of starvation. For house provision the labourer depends upon an owner as a rule who has been schooled to think that the income received from the estate is now far below what it should be, and the encumbrances incurred from family charges render relief well nigh out of the question.

Thus it frequently happens that small farmers, unable to make a living, drift into the towns, and try their hands at business; and the more intelligent labourers become competitors for town employment, adding to the difficulty by forcing many of their weaker brethren into squalor and hopelessness. Trade Unions will still further improve the conditions under which town workers earn a living, and intensify this emigration from rural districts. This outcome seems inevitable until such time as the labourer becomes more intelligent and finds out his real worth as a worker, and the value of his vote. Then, and I am afraid not until, shall we find that our rural population will force their employers to solve the agricultural difficulty. The remedies so far suggested with authority come from the Liberal leaders, and include - equal division of the rates between the occupier and the owner, taxation of land values, compensation for improvements and disturbance, compulsory powers for providing allotments, compulsory powers to enable local authorities to acquire land and build decent homes for the working people. I presume the outcome would be that every owner of land would be required to declare its value with the knowledge that the local authority might select it as being suitable for their needs at the declared value. Thus the land tax levied on a more just basis, and at a fair sum, would produce a large amount in relief of taxation now levied upon industry.

It is admittedly unjust to tax the farmer upon the land used purely for agricultural purposes, and this gain of income would allow for the local rates being levied merely upon the house he occupied, and enable the farmer to pay the labourer the real value of his hire. Compensation must of necessity, when real, carry with it a secure tenure, and this should materially encourage better cultivation, giving more employment. Local councils could, if not hindered, buy costly machinery, provide decent houses built upon quarter and half-acre plots, for 2s. and 2s. 6d. per week rent, provided with pure water and proper sanitary requirements. Under such changes the workhouse should cease, except as a means of dealing with those who are disinclined to work, and orphan pauper children should be boarded out in suitable homes. The aged, who are deserving, will be dealt with in the full knowledge that they have for many years contributed to the requirements of the parish, and that their right is to be cared for as befits an enlightened and Christian community.

Yours faithfully,
A.W..   August 25.

SIR, - I feel indebted to you for publishing the correspondence that has appeared in *The Daily News*, which is, of course, only one part of a very great national question, that of the "Land" and its "Laws." I for one hope the next Parliament will grasp it fully. As far as I have observed, none of your correspondents have drawn attention to the comparative cost of living to a working man and his family in cities and villages, and I suggest to you that your Correspondent would do a great service if he will prosecute an inquiry into this subject and publish it in your columns, my impression being distinctly that most of our working men have little, if any, knowledge of it until they find by bitter experience they are no better, if so well, off after leaving the villages, and perhaps without the means of returning to them. A case came under my own observation in Wiltshire some time back of an intelligent, well-conducted working man, who had a wife and five or six young children and 10s. a week wages, with a cottage free, garden and ground to grow all vegetables and potatoes, and kept a pig, and earned extra wages during turnip sowing and harvesting. I asked him what he expected to get if he went to Bristol, as he was talking of doing. He thought, 18s. a week. I asked him to consider what he would be better off for his change, when he would have to pay about 5s. a week rent, and buy all his potatoes and vegetables, and have no pig or extras, such as harvest money &c., &c. He did think it all over, and remained in the "village." If my theory be true, that a large portion of working men who leave our villages for cities are no better off for the change, I am none the less of opinion that there is room for very great improvement in the various conditions of their life, and hope the time is near when talking about reforming our land laws will cease and be replaced by action.- I am yours truly,

CHAS. WILLS, Bristol,   August 26.

Saturday, August 29, 1891.

EDITORIAL.

THE FUTURE OF OUR VILLAGES.

The letters of our Special Commissioner on Life in Our Villages have attracted and continue to attract a large amount of public interest and attention. The space which we can afford for correspondence on the subject shows as much as that, and what we publish is a very small part of what we receive. Many interesting communications have perforce to be sacrificed simply because the size and number of our columns are limited, if the interest and importance of the subject are not. The condition of the agricultural labourer and of that farming class with which he is at present inseparably connected appeals to every Englishman who has the slightest regard for the present and future welfare of his country. Notwithstanding doubtful seasons and inclement skies, agriculture is still the greatest of British industries and the resource upon which thousands of families habitually depend. Free trade and the development of steam power have made the consumer largely independent of the market at home, and have enabled the deficiencies of Russia to be supplied by the abundance of the United States. But there is still a large demand for native produce which, if it tends to encourage pasture at the expense of tillage, nevertheless affects every class which lives by the application of labour or capital to the soil.

Our Special Commissioner has brought out with especial prominence two main facts. The first is the constant, though gradual, migration from the country to the town, especially to London; the second is the deplorable state of those who remain in their native villages. The remedies suggested by our correspondents are various, and some of them are mutually incompatible. But almost all the writers agree that our Commissioner has correctly stated the facts, and that these facts are in the nature of public misfortunes. Overcrowding and the neglect of sanitary laws are morally as well as physically mischievous. The depletion of rural districts is only less to be regretted from the social point of view than the continual increase of a metropolis already swollen to an unmanageable size. There are obviously no more than two ways of checking a process which ought rather to be reversed than extended. One is to diminish the attraction of London. The other is to enhance the allurements of the country. It does not need much argument to show that the latter alternative is the more feasible of the two. Nothing will ever persuade a young fellow of pluck and spirit that stagnation is better than movement, that low wages are preferable to high ones, that freedom and independence are less to be desired than alms and patronage. The questions are why these unenviable characteristics adhere to our villages, and by what means they may be dissociated from them.

The state and prospects of the labourer are partly dependent upon the laws which regulate the tenure and distribution of land. It will be observed that in all this controversy we hear little or nothing about the Allotments Act of 1887. It may be an exaggeration to say that that statute is a wholly dead letter.

But at least its operation has been so slight, spasmodic, and fragmentary that it has not appreciably influenced the agricultural problem. Most economists of repute are agreed that, land being a natural monopoly, its use and ownership should, so far as is possible and convenient, be regulated by the State. If the present discussion has proved one thing more clearly than another, it is that the possession of land in small patches by labourers pays the proprietor, arrested the progress of rural depopulation, and results in profit to the community by encouraging the most productive form of agriculture. Our Commissioner has put forward with perfect fairness, and certainly without any hostile bias, the case for large as against small farming. There is no doubt a superiority, which mechanical inventions and chemical discoveries foster and promote, in farming on a big scale over farming on a little one. But the comparison is habitually and somewhat fallaciously drawn between the employer of fifty hands and the employer of five. It is the man who tills his own plot, who relies entirely upon his own energies, and does nothing by deputy, that reaps the largest proportionate return from agricultural land. An Allotments and Small Holdings Bill, if it is to be of any practical and calculable use, must contain the amplest compulsory powers, and be carried out in the easiest as well as the least costly manner. Nothing can be more absurd than to sneer at the Free Land League. The simplification of titles, the cheapening of transfer, the abolition of life interests and entails, are absolutely essential to the success of the small culture so many of our correspondents desire to see. But though necessary, they are not of course sufficient. Councils representing the people, and acting for the general good, must be empowered to obtain suitable land at a fair price for the labouring class if any improvement is to be made either in the lamentable lot of the manual cultivator or in the depressed condition of British agriculture. The old phrase "a stake in the country" was delusive because applied only to the rich. That the largest possible number of persons should be directly interested in the general prosperity is not only a legitimate aim, but should be a primary object with every genuine statesman.

The latest batch of county elections showed very clearly that the present leaning of the agricultural labourers is strongly Liberal. But of course they will very naturally and properly expect that if they help to put the Liberal leaders in office, the Liberal leaders shall do something for them. They want not only a real instead of a sham Allotments Bills, not merely such a Land Bill as all earnest reformers have demanded for a quarter of a century, but also, and above all things, a voice, and a decisive voice, in the management of their own affairs. The abuses which our Commissioner describes - social, a sanitary, and economic - are not, as things now stand, the fault of those who suffer the most from them. They are due often to the selfish apathy, sometimes to the actual misconduct, of irresponsible landlords who will not recognise that property has its duties as well as its rights, and who tell the inmates of a drainless hovel that if they do not like to live in it they may go elsewhere. We do not forget the existence of sanitary legislation, and of the Local Government Board. But, as Horace asked, *Quid leges sine moribus vance proficiunt?* Which may be roughly translated, What is the use of laws if they are not enforced? A Village Council, if it justified its existence, would take care that Parliament was not flouted and human life sacrificed to save the pockets of the wealthiest ratepayers or to protect nominated guardians against the necessity of exerting themselves. Many and loud are the complaints of the low wages paid to agricultural labourers. But farmers cannot always afford more. The times are very hard for the farmer. He has the greatest difficulty in making both ends meet, and his rent often swallows up what little interest he could otherwise make on his capital. Mr. Disraeli once laid it down as an economic axiom that the land had to find three profits. It had, he said, to support the owner, the occupier, and the labourer. Mr. Disraeli seemed to think, or at least wished to suggest, that these profits were inherent in the nature of things, and that if they were not divided among three persons, one person would be making three incomes. The whole argument is based on confusion of thought, the fact being that unless land more than pays for the trouble bestowed upon it, there is no surplus out of which rent can be provided. The farmer and the labourer are in the same predicament. It is the sleeping partner, the landlord, who swallows up what might keep them both.

Saturday, August 29, 1891

(FROM OUR SPECIAL COMMISSIONER)

Agitators are of course very dreadful people, but in moving about among the rural population of Essex and Suffolk one cannot help fervently wishing that he could let a few agitators loose among them. There is a stir among these dry bones, but oh! for a few prophets to breathe upon them and set them striking mightily! All sorts of things are wrong. To a large extent the land is not half cultivated. The people are not half paid, and consequently many of them are badly fed and abominably housed and ill supplied with water. Existence with them is a dull, dead-alive, hopeless sort of drudgery, without interest, without enjoyment, without any practical result except the mere keeping of body and soul together, and the end of it all is the workhouse, while the community at large is of course the loser of all the added wealth the land might have been made to yield. And yet you cannot talk with those people for a quarter of an hour without being impressed with a perception of the truth that all these evils might so easily be remedied if you could but kindle and sustain the energy and aspiration you clearly perceive within them. Put into these men just that same mainspring of legitimate and healthy self-interest which keeps going so many busy wheels all the world over, and at once you will fetch out of the soil the wealth to give them plenty of food and good water and comfortable houses and everything else they want to keep them on the land in contentment and prosperity. Why don't we turn our attention to the problem of fetching out of the men and the land what is really in them instead of vainly endeavouring to put things right on a wretched basis of ten shillings a week, supplemented by poor-law doles and rate-aided cottage buildings? In the mass of agricultural labourers we have got a great wealth-producing steam-engine. Set that steam-engine going, and all that is requisite will be produced. But instead of getting up steam we are shoving behind - painfully labouring to push round the wheels. Of course. if you are bent on getting your engine along, and can't raise the steam, you must push behind; but it is really weary and disheartening business. My meaning will become apparent, I think, to any one who will listen to a simple narrative of the attempt to get cottages for the poor people of Ixworth.

Ixworth is a considerable village about four miles from Bury St. Edmunds. Mr. W. F. H. Millington, whose extremely able essay on the Housing of the Poor won the Warburton Prize at Owens College, Manchester, last year, and who is resident here near the borders of Suffolk, tells me that it is not conspicuously worse in its sanitary condition than many other villages in this part of England; but it is fairly representative. I went over there a day or two ago, meeting by the way market-day carriers' carts one after the other laden with young country women with their boxes and bundles on their way to service in the towns. Ixworth strikes the stranger as a pleasant and prosperous village, and any one driving through it would certainly have no idea of overcrowding or ruinous homes or pestilential fever dens suggested by the appearance of the place. Tory guardians and Tory parsons, being of a caste altogether separate from the cottagers, would never have found out that anything was wrong in it. The Church living is a very poor one, I am told, and in the past, right poorly it seems to have been filled - if one may judge by results. About two years ago, however, the Rev. F. D. Perrott, a liberal-minded man of private means, took over the charge of the parish, and set about trying to get in touch with the cottagers. He found, I am told in other quarters - for Mr. Perrott has left home in ill-health - that the Church had scarcely anything to do with the people, and the people scarcely anything to do with the Church.

He soon got things on a better footing, however, and succeeded in forming the Ixworth Agricultural Labourers' Association. The labourers were brought together for the discussion of subjects bearing on their social welfare, and then, of course, came out the facts of their home life. Up till then the people had been 'hopeless and helpless, but now they began to make their troubles known, and in the depth of last winter men came in from villages miles away to meetings in Ixworth. I have before me particulars of some of the Ixworth cottages, got together by a house to house visitation of a resident in the place, and they are shocking enough. Numbers of houses have not so much as a back door, to say nothing of garden plots. Numbers of them are reported "not wind and water tight." "There is a row of houses in this lane; the total number of inhabitants is 44, and there are three closets for their use. In one house, consisting of two rooms, there are ten in family. In this row there are no back places at all." "Water comes into both bedrooms," in the report on another house, "and walls and roof are very bad." In another house "the wind and rain come in, and the rats. The woman showed me a bed quilt covered with holes made by the rats." In another case "Doors are very bad, and the walls tumbling down. When it rains much, the water runs from the back kitchen into the sitting room, and forms a pool in the centre." "I have asked several tenants to come forward and give evidence, but they are afraid to do so. They have told me they feared being turned out." Can anything be more abject and pitiable than the condition of people condemned to exist in such places, and afraid even to indulge in the satisfaction of a grumble about them? Dr. Thresh, whom I have mentioned before as the medical officer for the joint unions of Chelmsford and Maldon, was called in as a specialist to report on the state of things. After giving similar details, Dr. Thresh says, "These wretchedly small, overcrowded houses not only affect the morals but the health of the inhabitants. Rheumatism and chest affections are caused by sleeping and living in such damp, draughty dwellings. Infectious disease cannot be isolated, nor can any case of illness be properly treated in them. Apart from serious illness they are the cause of depression of vitality, generally affecting the bodily vigour, as well as the spirits, and rendering the system unable to withstand the actual onslaught of disease."

I myself visited several of the cottages and some of the people seemed quite scared by the few simple inquiries put to them, evidently regarding them as the preliminary to their being cleared out. One woman told me she had been on the look out for months for another cottage, but the only one she could find was four miles off. What was the good of a cottage four miles off your work? she wanted to know. "If they turn me out I'll die on the roadside," she said. "I wunt go into the work'us, I wunt, I wunt," she exclaimed, fiercely striking a stick she held in her hand on the seat of a chair beside her. While she spoke she stood beneath a beam in her low ceiling that looked as though it only wanted somebody to stumble in the room above to give way and bury her and her children. In one room not so bad but that it probably could be repaired, I found, by the way, a very interesting old man whose reminiscences quite belied the belief that the agricultural labourer is so much better off now than he was a generation or two ago. He sat by his broken fireplace shaking as if with the palsy. He had had a sunstroke, he said. He was incapacitated for work, and was dependent on the parish for his maintenance, after seventy-two years' work upon the land. "I be seventy-six," said the old man, "and I was set to work 'most soon as I could walk. There warn't no schoolin' much in them days." "It is a pity that there wasn't," I put in. "Ah! 'tis a pity. If I'd on'y learned to read and write, I could ha' done a good deal better nor I ha' done. Why, even now," continued the old fellow, bristling up with an energy that his seventy-two years of toil had not quite exhausted, "if I could on'y write, I could do some't or other." "Nonsense," grunted the old dame on the other side of the fireplace, "what could you do, I should like to know?" "Do!" retorted the shaky old fellow, resenting this disparagement of his capabilities. "Why, if I could write down names and figures, couldn't I go round wi' coal or some't?" and he looked as though, even now, it wouldn't take much to persuade him to try for as much scholarship as would suffice for the coal business. "They talk about labourers bein' so much better off nor they used to be," he said, in response to a remark of mine, "Why, when I was a boy we used to do t'thrashing wi' the flail; and we'd be at it in the barns all the winter through. There was one pun' notes in them days, and many's the time when I was a boy o' fourteen and worked wi' the flail wi' my feyther we'd take home a one pun' note for our week's work. Why, if they were to pay'e a one pun' note now, they'd think as they were goin' to be bust up." Perhaps the old man's memory was at fault, but on another point he was confirmed by his wife, and I think he spoke the truth. "So you've really been at work seventy-two years?" I said. "Aye, that I hev, and for years I used to walk eleven miles a day in goin' to and from my work. The walkin' takes it out of 'e wus nor the work." Nothing is commoner than to find cases in which men walk two and three miles to their work.

One of the cleanest and most beautifully kept little homes ever seen in a village, was one in which a delicate looking elderly woman said she was never well. She showed me the brick floor and walls all reeking with moisture, and she took me out at the back to see the source of a terrible smell which when the wind was in a certain quarter rendered her cottage almost unbearable and made her feel sick and ill. It was the cesspool of an old closet, slightly boarded over, and within ten or twelve feet of her back door. She would give the world to get out of the house if she could only find another. Like scores of others in the village, however, she was condemned to live in this pestilential place, where any day fever or cholera might quite naturally break out.

69

All this clearly tends to hasten the influx into the towns. The proper and radical remedy would of course be to improve the earning power of the people. If by any modification of our agricultural system we could bring science and capital to bear on these labour-starved fields of Suffolk, and give the people such an interest in their occupation as would really make them work, all the evils would remedy themselves. No doubt we should require an Act of Parliament for obtaining plots of ground by some simple and inexpensive procedure. That is an urgent necessity in any case. But we should want no Act of Parliament for putting up houses if the people could pay for them, and if they can't pay for them there must be something radically wrong. Why do not we fearlessly face this radical wrong? Why doesn't that land support these people? That is the question, but we do not squarely face it. We shirk the question, and we pass Acts of Parliament for shoving the engine along without getting up the steam. Last year Parliament passed the Housing of the Working Classes Act, on the whole an admirable measure, and under our existing social circumstances very necessary. In the towns it was especially desirable. But in these rural districts the problem of housing the people is quite a different one, and the provisions it contains for the providing of agricultural labourers' cottages have at Ixworth so far broken down, and will, I fear, prove a dismal failure.

First the "Rural Sanitary Authority" had to be prodded on to action, that is to say the Thingoe Board of Guardians - every man of whom I am told, by the way, is a Tory - had to be induced to do something for the poor at the expense of the rates. Mainly, as it would seem, by the alarming result of the Stowmarket election they were got to move in the matter. They applied to the County Council for leave to put the Act in force. In accordance with the provisions of the Act, the County Council appointed one of their number, Lord Francis Hervey, M.P., to go to Ixworth and hold a formal inquiry whether new cottages were necessary, whether there was no probability of their being provided without the operation of the Act, and whether all things considered it would be financially prudent to undertake the business. Well, this was all done. Mr. Theodore Dodd represented the labourers. Mr. J.J. Spark was for the Guardians, Mr. R.H. Wilson for the Lord of the Manor, and Lord Francis Hervey made by universal admission an excellent president of the court. Overwhelming evidence was adduced; the case was abundantly made out, and the Council were ready to issue their certificate, and then - the whole thing collapsed. It had been proposed to build I believe a dozen poor cottages for people exposed to wind and rain and foul stenches. Probably two-thirds of the cost would have been represented by the rents the people would pay. The other third would have had to come out of the rates. At the last moment the Guardians were horrified to find that this frightful expense, owing to their having omitted to make an application to the Council to the contrary, would have to be spread over the whole of their district instead of being limited to the place immediately benefited. They therefore begged that the Council would not grant their certificate, and that they might not be permitted to put up the cottages. They still pretend they want to do it, and they are going to begin the business all over again, and I hear that over this question of the incidence of the rate, there will be a dogged and determined fight. When they have held their inquiry and settled about the rate, and the Council have authorised them to proceed, then it will become a question whether they had better proceed. If they decide that they will, the landowners may refuse to let them have the land at a reasonable rate, and they may have to put in force compulsory powers, ruinously expensive and provokingly dilatory. And all this because the people working on the land for ten hours and a half a day can't fetch out of it enough to pay for a decent roof over their heads, and enough food to keep body and soul together. It is quite time that the day of the democracy had begun to dawn upon us.

TO THE EDITOR OF THE DAILY NEWS

SIR, - The interesting articles in your recent numbers on the above subject reminds me of the night when some twenty years ago on my return from a meeting held in a country village in Warwickshire Mr. Archibald Forbes - then your Special Correspondent - was awaiting me for the purpose of eliciting some information with reference to the agitation just then commenced, and which led up to the formation of the National Agricultural Labourers' Union, of which for the first few years I was the general secretary. I do not forget the many thrilling letters from Mr. Forbes's pen which awakened such immense enthusiasm throughout the country, and to your successfully appealing for pecuniary aid was largely due the success which for some years attended that organization; and I can only hope that your new efforts may also stir up the general public to the most pressing and important consideration of the question of land and the labourer. Since the day I drove through the Warwickshire villages with Mr. Forbes many things have happened. I have travelled through the States and Canada, and have elicited information from the log shanty in the forest and the huts of the prairies; and for the past ten years I have lived in Australia, and have had good opportunities of observing life in its relations to land settlements in all its phases. I have now returned for a short season to revisit the scenes of my old labours, and for all the little improvements which may possibly obtain, I am not particularly gratified with the progress. So far as my observations have led me, I have come to the conclusion that in material prosperity there is little indeed of which the farmers or labourers may congratulate themselves or the country at large claim much credit. But to my mind there is a silver lining to the cloud. There has been a decided awakening in the intelligence of the rural mind, and an inquiry - as indicated in the letters of your Special Correspondent .

What must he do to be saved? It may seem strange to the people of this, generally considered, overcrowded country to be told that the same phases of relationship between land and labour which exist here also obtain in greater or less degree in those sparsely-populated hundreds of millions of acres in Australia - the overcrowding of towns and cities, and the privations of agriculturists. South Australia, with its 313,000 population and its area of 900,000 square miles of territory - millions of acres of which are unused, notwithstanding their favourable situation and advantages of soil and climate - are still held against the use of the would-be industrial land-user. And I doubt if it will scarcely be credited that in this vast country, with its scanty population, there is the same political cry from the people for "working-men's blocks" as here for village allotments, and that to get a living hundreds and sometimes thousands of the people are driven to and fro, migrating and immigrating from one colony to the other, driven to all sorts of expedients, such as "protection," and divers other class expedients of restriction and taxation to enable them to live. In fact, all the old world evils are fast being reproduced in the new, from the poverty of the field, to the revolt of the factory, and down to the dirty little unfortunate half-clad match children who infest the entrances of our theatres, and this in a country which, in its own experience, should scarcely understand the meaning of the terms out of work, strikes, lock-outs, or poverty. As in England, so in Australia, and from the same causes; and it will be well if the efforts of your Correspondent with those of others who have the seriousness of the work at heart may lead to a careful investigation of the causes, and lead up to the discovery of the remedies. I rejoice in saying that this investigation is being earnestly pursued in at least some parts of my adopted land, and I venture to hope that already the axe is laid at the root of the tree of evil - the bane not of Australia alone, but of the greater part of the civilised world - landlordism.

In your leader of August 14 (page 12) in which you suggest the direction in which possible remedies may be looked for, there is a good deal which the people of England should well ponder over. As you very truthfully say - "We want a social Woburn and a social Rothamstead to teach us how the land should be held, as well as how it should be farmed." Moreover, it will be a sorry day for the English toilers if, as you suggest, the competition of American agriculture should cease. It may be true that a temporary advantage might be gained by the tenant farmer and even the labourer, but it would last but a short time, and under our present system would soon be overtaken by the landowner. And the agriculturist - farmers and labourers - are not a whit more interested in the solution of the land system, and the placing of it on a just basis, than are the manufacturer - capitalists and artisans - of our manufacturing districts. But my purpose in this epistle is not so much to discuss the problem as to stir up inquiry and to appeal to my old friends the trades organisations. I am of opinion that there is a vast amount of latent intelligence and energy in and throughout the numerous labour unions to undertake the revival and consolidation of agricultural labour unions in the country districts, a work the importance of which can scarcely be over-estimated, not merely as it relates to the farm labourers themselves, but in its effects on the labour organisations of the towns and cities. From the evidence adduced before the Royal Commission recently it appears that the straitened circumstances of production as it relates to both employer and employed are by no means confined to the rural and agricultural districts. Nor does a greater scientific skill in either field or factory bring any but a mere transitory advantage to either the skilled artisan or labourer; for by our present political and social system the immense extra values accruing from science, inventive skill, or dexterity in handicraft, speedily find their way in one form or another into that immense and voracious vortex - the breadth and depths of which are as yet, I fear, but faintly perceived by the masses of the people - rent. And so the ever-increasing values created and earned by all sorts and conditions of producers are quietly absorbed by those who earn them not. Only a comparatively few years ago, and at the time when it was my privilege to attend the Trades' Union Congress, it was considered a thing improper to deal with any matters in those assemblies which partook of a political character. I am pleased to observe that that old prejudice has been largely discarded of late years, and that the leaders of the people now see very plainly the impossibility of securing justice so long as our social system is based in injustice. Strikes and lock outs - those interminable conflicts of capital and labour - can serve but little purpose so long as the main profits of their united industry are swallowed by the common enemy of both.

There are great questions before the newly enfranchised of this country; and the one great question why it is that the material prosperity of the industrial community does not keep pace with the ever expanding wealth of the nation must be put forward and answered. And in my humble opinion here is a wide field for prospecting for the great Liberal party. It is touched by a few in a very gingerly style; but if the Liberal party are to hold their own, to say nothing of advance, they will have to take a decided stand, and put forth a programme in which there are some elements of hope for the people. It is a little wearisome at present to attend the meetings and listen to the speeches of the leaders of Liberal opinions - men who claim for themselves that they are not merely "Liberal," but "Radical," in politics - to hear little more than a mere play on words of the failings and eccentricities of the opposite party. These things may be a very agreeable pastime as a sort of light comedy, but the country is requiring more of the leaders than this. Really the programmes put forward by the two parties are at present so very similar that it seems to be but a toss up as to who can establish the prior claim for allegiance; and I believe that the county is ready for a policy - a new and progressive policy - in which the people may join with heart and hope as containing the germs of a future prosperity. My only fear is that the so-called Liberal leaders are not alive to the circumstances of the position, and that it will be necessary for a new party to spring up. This need not be, and I fervently hope that the necessity may not

arise. In any case it seems to me that there is a pressing obligation on the present labour unions to leave no stone unturned to secure the organisation of the rural labourers. I am glad to know that something is already being done in this direction, but which is only small in relation to the whole. The Liberal party must not overlook the fact that although they may claim the credit of enfranchising the village labourer that will count for little in the face of a disorganized people ever at the mercy and under the influence of the Tory parsons, squires, and Primrose dames. The constitution of the normal village life of England is already three parts Tory, and Liberal principles can only be diffused and maintained in the rural districts with considerable and sustained effort. Since the enfranchisement of the farm labourers is largely due to the efforts of the workers in the towns, it seems to me that it is not less the duty of the urban associations to direct the organization of their protégés in the country - a work clearly as necessary and important to the one as to the other.
Yours, &c.,

HENRY TAYLOR, S. Reddish, Stockport

SIR, - I have read your articles and letters on "Our Villages." I am a tenant farmer myself, the son of a tenant farmer, and the great part of my life has been spent on farms. Perhaps you will therefore allow me to say a little on the subject. Mr. Alfred Wallace (page 49), of whom I should wish to speak with the greatest respect, as a partner with the great Darwin in the splendid theory of the origin of species, is in favour of some scheme of what is rather vaguely called "land nationalization." Mr. Gladstone has spoken of this, I believe, as either a "folly or robbery," and it seems to me that such a gigantic operation will not be likely to come for may years, and if passed its blessings will be doubtful. So I will not occupy your space with the many reasons there are against it, but to show how it seems to me moderate prosperity and content can be secured to rural England. In the first place the farmer is always blamed that he does not pay a higher wage than he can get a profit on, for I take it men only pay for labour in industrial concerns in the hope of getting some profit. Land, however, from which all must get their food, is allowed in this country to be held as a monopoly and let at competition rents, and low competitive wages follow. Now suppose that Parliament gave to every tenant the right to sit at a fair rent, with fixity of tenure and free sale, things hardly any tenant enjoys now, what would be the result but a great development of energy and higher cultivation, which should raise wages by the increased demand.

Writers like your Correspondent must bear in mind that farmers have in England always farmed to a certain extent in leading strings; they had to take care to please two exacting masters, the landlord and agent. It is creditable to them that English farming is what it is. Make them free men, and they will not be behind any one. Let them have scope to exert their different abilities and not force them to go in one rut because that is the one that the landlord or agent thinks best. As a class, their own talents will do better for them than the kind of little Providence which a good landlord, as he is called, thinks he makes his estate and those who dwell upon it. When he is not good he is simply a curse. And after all to give the present race of tenants this is only giving what Mr. Alfred Wallace advocates for the small holders he would set up. Why condemn the present farmers till they have had a fair chance under fair conditions? With regard to the wage-earners, their position is worse than the farmers. I could write much on it. But a remedy should be tried at once. I advocate placing all rural dwellers under a fair rent, and as long as that fair rent is paid, the occupier should not be liable to be turned out because the house belonged to farmer B, and occupier C refused to work for B. This would do something to stay the unsettlement; and for those who could show they were willing to put some capital on the land (a small sum fixed as a minimum) from one to three acres should be added at the fair rent of the district, which if possible should be at his house. For I do not believe that an allotment is much good to the agricultural worker unless it is at his back door. This land he should be able to feel he could improve to its utmost capacity without being in danger of being robbed by increase of rent. But the great thing to help and content the agricultural workman would be to let him buy his own cottage and garden by a system of deferred purchase on the lines of the Ashbourne Act. Those who dream of an agricultural millennium by what is called free trade in land I can only call fools. It only means shifting the liabilities of the rural dweller from one more or less wealthy man to another. The vast bulk of Englishmen are not investors, they only live from hand to mouth; and farmers and tradesmen have rarely enough capital for their businesses, but they do and can pay their yearly rent, and if this rent can be made to buy their dwellings it will solve one of the hard problems. If the Liberal party will take up this matter in a spirit of fairness to the tenant farmers and generosity to the workmen, I, for one, though I dislike and doubt the wisdom of a Dublin Parliament, will do my little best for one to see them back in office. But of this be assured it is a policy, properly advocated which would at once bring its reward.

"WESTERN COUNTIES" August 26.

SIR, - (1) Can farming in England be made to pay? (2) Can village life be made attractive? It is necessary to prove the former before it is worth while to consider the latter. On the former point my experience, mainly of Yorkshire, is the reverse of your Commissioner's. Among the farmers of Yorkshire has taken place a process of artificial selection, and under it the small farmers have proved themselves on the whole the fittest. Of course many large farmers have survived, but they are mainly of two classes; Those who have had sufficient reserve capital to outlast their losses, and those who, originally of the class of small farmers, have taken larger farms, having sufficient capital for them, but have retained the habits of the class from which they have sprung. The small farmer has these advantages in the struggle. He himself works and saves a man. He knows the amount of work to be expected from every man he employs, and he sees that he gets it, being about his farm when the larger farmer is in bed or at the market town, or engaged in social amenities. He understands the values of all stock he buys and sells, and he does the buying and selling in person, and so keeps acquainted with the fluctuations of the markets. And in doing his own stock buying and selling, he perhaps saves the commission which in one form or another many foremen get from those they deal with, and in any case he has the advantage of the keenness a man exercises in his own interest beyond that a man shows who is dealing with another's pocket. He spends no money in luxuries nor in going to two or three markets a week for the sake of meeting friends. When he goes to market he goes to buy or sell. He has not to starve his farm from shortness of capital. He makes the most of small culture - chickens, ducks, eggs, butter. He has

77

practically no house expenses. His sons and daughters either help, or go out to service, or other employment. He has no servants, no groom, no horse which is not absolutely necessary for working the farm or as stock. In pointing out these advantages which the small has over the larger farmer, I by no means deprecate the social and domestic requirements of the latter. I simply point to the fact that farming in this country will not bear them. I believe that farming must, and will, again fall into the hands of a socially lower grade than the large farmer - one more accustomed to manual labour, less desirous of luxuries. The inflated prices of some years ago did harm in introducing the wrong man to the land, in tempting men to take farms beyond their capital, and in forcing up rents. In the main farming is likely to fall into the hands of the man able and willing to carry it on with the most modest requirements from its results. But even the fittest small farmer has in these times serious difficulties to contend with. Prices are low, rents are high. The landowners' contribution of capital in the shape of buildings is deplorably deficient. Buildings ruinous, cold and inconvenient, no proper arrangements for stall feeding, none for saving manure from rain and sun. The ammonia runs down the village street to find its way into the village well, or it finds a nearer receptacle in the house well, conveniently placed between the house and the immediately adjoining farmyard. He is too far from a market to make the best of his small culture without increased facilities for its transmission, and when he does reach the nearest railway station, rates are ruinously high.

Apart from more radical nostrums, I think his best hope lies in improved facilities for transmission to market centres, reduced railway rates, co-operative collection and distribution, co-operative retailing. These and steam tramways are all suggestions well worth careful consideration and discussion. I know districts where a railway would not pay, but which a light steam tramway would amply serve and bring into touch with a good market. Then, again, local co-operative cheese and butter factories offer to the small farmer advantages in enabling him to make the best prices. I have lately had the opportunity of making observations in the counties of Somerset and Dorset, and it is deplorable to see land so well fitted for small culture, at no great distance from the best market in the world, producing not a fourth of what it might do if facilities for transmission were afforded and a little better knowledge and method exercised. I find rich grass land, villages buried in

orchards and luxurious vegetation of every kind, dependent for their market on hucksters from a neighbouring small town. I find orchards of trees neglected, unpruned, old, scarcely ever a young tree to be seen, and when seen ill-planted, untrained, unstaked, already showing signs of disease from want of knowledge or of care in the way it has been, not planted, but stuck into the ground. Apples and plums of inferior kinds only such as will not command a good price by the side of better fruit. I find fowls of inferior strains, bad for table, poor layers. I find stock, implements, and knowledge at a low ebb. Even in Kent I have ransacked some of its fruit districts, and looked in vain for fruit to compare with that with which it will have to compete in the market. I find a total want of knowledge of drying and canning fruit, with the result that all the fruit of a district is rushed at one time upon the market, with the inevitable effect upon prices. It is easy to find fault, but with your permission, I will in another letter enter into some discussion of remedies, and also touch upon the second of the two questions with which I began this letter.-
Your obedient servant.

A.H.J.

SIR - A slight printer's error in my letter of the 25th instant (page 60), which appears in your issue of to-day, makes me say "Local Councils could, if not hindered, *buy* costly machinery, .provide decent homes built upon quarter and half-acre plots, for 2s. and 2s. 6d. per week rent," &c. My letter should read, "Local Councils could, if not hindered *by* costly machinery, provide decent homes," &c. If parish councils are given compulsory powers to purchase land and erect dwellings for working men, which is very desirable, the application of the Act must be made simple, and free from the need of heavy costs being paid to lawyers, surveyors, &c., or we shall have another sham Act of Parliament added to the Allotment failure.- Yours faithfully,

A.W.   August 28.

SIR, - The letter you kindly published on the 29th (page 75) suggested a plan, which would keep ordinary farm workfolks on our west country lands. The method indicated could be carried out by influential people without legislative interference. To retain another important class on the land - pushing, energetic, and ambitious, but without capital - legislative change is essential. The "acres," are now clearly ear-marked by the splendid cadastral survey of England just completed, and these "acres" should be made as readily saleable as a house, a horse, or a shipload of corn. Old lawyers will not like this, but the new ones will glean handsome fortunes as of yore. At present a farm worker, with a brain, heart, and muscles perhaps as good as George Stephenson's learns the good trade of farming by the time he has turned twenty or twenty-five. If he follows his trade, at it he must stay till he dies of old age in the workhouse. There is no stepping stone close to his foot, as there should be, by which he may rise in his vocation, so he chucks up his wholesome work and goes to a stuffy town, too often to sink to the bottom of it. If land were easily bought and sold plots of all sizes would filter into the hands of many owners, and farmers' men would see chances of hiring land in quantities to suit their growing needs.

Instead of blank despair, hope would tempt the farm worker to stick to his trade, and many a barren-looking wasted acre would smile with a harvest. This would be no small comfort to landowners, who are now too often hide-bound with a false social expenditure entailed by the nominal ownership of inalienable land. Allotments, as the law now makes them, are little better than an expensive bribe to keep the farm labourer "in his proper position," as the vile old phrase has it, and are often a clog instead of a help to him. Unless near a town, allotment produce has hardly any commercial value at all. Everybody around has enough of the things it offers, and if allotment-holders only received for their produce the wholesale market prices, minus carriage, for their garden stuffs, they would never be paid for rent, see, and labour. Mechanics, artisans, mill hands revel in allotments, for they afford them a relief from their work, an outlet for their energies, and if they live near thickly populated parts, a premium price for their produce. The easier and cheaper they can get them the better, and all honour to the generous souls who make them attainable, in spite of the clumsy, bad allotment laws. But for the purpose of improving "Life in Our Villages" by bridging the huge gap between farm workmen and tenant farmer or yeoman, allotments are a "delusion and a snare." After this it seems a contradiction to assert that tenant farmers can manage to live on the small profits of small farms when allotments can hardly be made to pay. The solution is a practical one. The soil of England pays for manuring, and will not pay without it. Manure comes, bone, body, and blood, from animals. Small farmers keep animals, allotment-holders do not - the occasional and evanescent pig assisting the garden only. So in small farms, as in larger agricultural holdings, the arable (corn) farmer fails, where the pasture (cattle) farmer rubs contentedly along. Small versus large farms I must not here discuss, though "Life in Our Villages" must include life in cottage, dairy, house, farmstead, and hall, and should graduate easily from one to the other. Yours faithfully,

JOHN HIGGINS, Pylle, Somerset

(FROM "THE SPEAKER.")

The studies of "Village Life" drawn in a series of gloomy and instructive letters which have been appearing in *The Daily News*, will rank as true portraiture with every student of modern rural England. Dr. Jessop has painted the same picture, in different perspective, in his "Return to Arcady," and any man who will give up a few months of his life to interment in an East Anglian village can verify it for himself. Briefly, it represent a melancholy death in life, a population divided into four neatly defined sections, and separated from each other, in sentiment and interest, as completely as was Robinson Crusoe from his surrounding islets of savages. The landlord, the parson, and the farmer can, and do, unite against their common foe, the labourer, but the time has long passed when the three possessing classes in the country can be said to own any abiding bond of sympathy. All four are more or less involved in the common economic decay which has overtaken the fabric of country society, though, paradoxical as it seems, it is probably at this moment true that the labourers have not, save in such counties as Wilts - the very purgatory of the rural working man - sunk much below the level of more prosperous years, but that is due to the fact that Hodge, having nothing to lose,

81

has run away from the fields to the town, and left, in may districts at least, only such a supply of labour as barely suffices the farmer for his annual husbandry. Not that the remnant - which, as might be expected, is the older, the less progressive, the less valuable element in its class - is in the least degree satisfied with its lot. Counting all the "extras" in Hodge's takings - his "haysel" and harvest money, his allowance for hoeing turnips, his bit of kitchen garden, his wife's occasional earnings in field work - it is doubtful whether his yearly average amounts to 14s. a week. Under the best conditions he saves nothing, and the Union remains and will remain the inevitable asylum for old age, the rough stepmother of the deserted or orphaned village youth, and the winter retreat of the older and less efficient members of the working community. Save in those rare spots where employment in a mill or factory is available, it is impossible to find an East Anglian settlement where the smallest signs of social progress exist. Life is maintained; that is all. The spiritual aspect of these *morae* habitations of men is a desolate as their material outlook. With the decay of the village industries, the absorption of the village shops in the town "emporium," and the decay of the old picturesque fairs and their attendant merry-makings - the remembrance of which stirs vaguely in the hearts of old workhouse inmates, but is fast slipping from the memories of the mass of the people - has disappeared most of the colour in rural life.

(FROM "THE GRAPHIC.")

An admirable series of letters on village life in England is being published in *The Daily News*. The writer is not content, as so many writers on the same subject have been, to evolve an imaginary rural world from the depths of his own consciousness. He is studying for himself the places and people he describes, and the consequence is that he presents a remarkably vivid and truthful picture of the circumstances amid which country folk pass their lives. The fact by which he has been most impressed is that our villages are being rapidly deserted by the younger generation. Everywhere in the districts he has visited young men are quitting their homes for the towns, where they hope to "better themselves." The phenomenon is not peculiar to England. All over the

European Continent and in America exactly the same tendency is exhibited, and, no doubt, the causes are in most parts of the world essentially the same. Young men do not feel that the country provides them with adequate scope for ambition and the exercise of their best energies; and they are irresistibly attracted by the chances of promotion which they believe to exist in big cities. To some extent the process is not unwholesome, but in England it has assumed proportions which make it a national danger. There is only one way out of the difficulty, and that, as the able writer in *The Daily News* urges, is to improve the conditions of life for our rural population. It is not enough that landlords should build better cottages, or even that farmers should give higher wages. Young men must have an opportunity of obtaining on reasonable terms land which they may cultivate at a profit, and in the cultivation of which they will not be arbitrarily disturbed. If they had such an opportunity, there are still very many of them who would prefer rural to urban life; and their prosperity would be good, no only for themselves and their families, but for the entire nation, great landowners included.

COTTAGE DWELLINGS,- Dr. Morris, the medical officer of the Wellingborough rural sanitary authority, has made some extraordinary revelations in a report to the authority. He states amongst the shocking cases of overcrowding that a man, wife, and eleven children lived in a house that had only one bedroom. In another case a man, wife, and five children, the eldest sixteen, slept in one room; and in a third case eight people slept in one room. These revelations, however, were mild compared with what the doctor had to say as to the condition of cottage property in the villages of Ferndish and Wymington. With regard to these, he said he had read of the condition of the Indian in his wigwam, and of the negroes, but the state of these people was worse than the savage or the slave.

LETTERS TO THE EDITOR

SIR, - I have been much interested in your letters "Life in our Villages." As a member of the Technical Instruction Committee of the Herts. County Council I may say that we have had a great difficulty in helping the villagers, especially those who work on the land. The questions are how to retain them on the land, and to improve their dull lot. I will not stay to define the word technical, but I notice that all subjects are regarded as technical that are included in the directory of the Science and Art Department. These subjects are at present 25 in number. They are constantly being added to when there is a demand for any fresh subject. Hertfordshire has 6,400*l.* to devote to technical instruction of what, for brevity, I call our beer-money. How can we best spend, or rather invest, this so as to get a return of 25 per cent.? The towns have been well considered, and they can look after themselves. What we want is a systematic plan to help our villagers and agricultural labourers. In my opinion, the best thing to do, or one of the best, is to set up in every village of the county, or wherever 12 or 15 earnest students can be collected, some class in connection with the Science and Art Department. Some subjects are well adapted for town or country - such as animal physiology, botany, the principles of agriculture. I prefer this last. The course would be 30 demonstrations, and should be begun before October 15th. All that is required is a teacher, a chairman, a secretary, and three members of a committee, men or women. The secretary writes to the Department to get a form. All the students who pass might earn 1*l.* or 2*l.* each. This money should go to the teacher, also half the grant from the County Council; the other half for expenses, plant, &c. I should like to say more on the advantages of setting up in each village such an institution for secondary education and for making the lives of our labourers healthier, happier, and brighter, but I fear your patience and space.- Yours truly,

ALFRED THOS. BRETT, Watford House, Herts.,　　　　　　　　　August 29.

SIR, - I have carefully read the interesting accounts of your Special Commissioner of "Life in Our Villages." Perhaps a few lines from this part of the kingdom may not be uninteresting to your readers. I am a farmer in South Leicestershire, occupying a small dairy farm. Living in the heart of the Midlands, we have many industries around us - collieries, ironworks, and various kinds of factories. The wage paid to our agricultural labourers is considerably higher than in the more southern parts. I pay my waggoner 19s. per week, my cowman, 18s., labourers 16s. and 17s all the year round, exclusive of overtime in harvest. A lad who lives in the house has 9*l*. 10s. per annum and his board. The hours of work are from half-past five morning to six at night. These wages would be considered excessive in some counties, but I am quite sure that for good wages men will give good honest work, and I can say that my men take as much interest in and are as anxious about my stock and crops as I am myself. I always discuss any important work to be done on the farm freely with them, and often profit by their sound experience. I do find that they are ever to the minute with regard to time - freely rising at any hour of the night, or sitting up all night sometimes with a sick animal, &c. I always try to treat them with the same courtesy and respect as they do me. I think my neighbours pay rather less than I do for the winter months and more for the summer, often setting piecework, which I do not approve of. My cowman also hires a pasture field of about four acres in the village; and keeps two cows and some pigs. He has also a large garden. The waggoner also has a very good garden, with a large and productive orchard. I believe they are content and happy.

Now I come to the younger generation. Although our villages are not deserted to anything like the same extent to which they appear to be in the south and east, yet the pick of our young men do go off to other employments which offer higher wages and many advantages which we have not in the country, especially society and free libraries, and they also escape the patronage and attention of the parson (meant in all good will) and the parson's wife, and the weariness of attending services at church which they do not understand. The old country parson is gone. The Dissenting chapels do not attract as once they did. Perhaps this migration has its advantages, bringing fresh blood and vigour and muscles into the towns. I am convinced that by paying wages on, which a man can live and bring up a family respectably, farmers will always obtain all the help they require. Farmers complain that times are bad and that they cannot afford more wages. Times are bad, very bad, but why are wages always to be attacked? What about rents? Are those who toil not nor spin to bear no share of the bad times except a paltry return of 10 per cent.? Are those who have borne the heat of the day alone to be the sufferers and their hard lot made still harder? But landlords cannot afford to reduce rents; in numberless cases they are receiving not more than 2 or 3 per cent. on the money invested. Well, those men have speculated in land. Some speculate in brewery shares. They must take the consequences of having paid too much. But few landlords are in this case. I know a village not many miles from here where the average rent 70 years ago was 20s. per acre. It is now 45s. per acre. Why do farmers persistently and stubbornly support that part in the State which never yet as a party did anything for them or anybody else, unless compelled, except themselves? The party which upholds the Game Laws, and is now doing its best to make the Ground Game Act a nullity. Why do they not (recognising the red herring of a duty on wheat), shoulder to shoulder with their workpeople, send up representatives who will uphold agriculture, reform the land laws, and establish where necessary land courts with power to fix fair rents, with fixity of tenure, &c. The time was when they did so and the farmers who fought at Naseby and Marston Moor "never were beaten," and I am proud to trace my descent from one of these.- Yours, &c.,

"A LEICESTERSHIRE FARMER"

SIR. - If your Special Commissioner should extend his travels as far as Norfolk, I would beg him to pay a visit to the village of Little Melton. In this village, which is 4½ miles from Norwich, he will be able to see the working of the allotment system, which has been in operation for 51 years. The late vicar let his glebe in half-acre patches at a rent of 30s. an acre - no tithes - to such men as, from the number of mouths they had to feed, seemed most in need of help. The present vicar has carried out the same plan. That the land has been no benefit to the holders, I am far from saying; that it has been as advantageous as it is generally assumed that it ought to be, I doubt. In no case does a tenant live more than half a mile from his land, but this distance is sufficient to take from it the greater-part of its value. To keep the labourer on the land, I would suggest that what is wanted are acre allotments with houses on them. You cannot bring the land to the houses, so houses must be taken to the land. As your Commissioner truly says, there is no such thing as an empty cottage in the Eastern Counties. Population increases, and young men and maidens will marry. How, without houses, can they remain on the land? Yours faithfully,

E.B.   August 28.

SIR - In this Oxfordshire village 12s. a week is the ordinary pay which the farm labourer receives all the year round; besides this he gets 3*l*. 4s. for haymaking and harvest. His sons, when they arrive at the age of 18, get nearly the same amount, and the "boy chaps" get quite enough to give them ample food and respectable clothing in which to "arm about" their girls on Sunday. Every labourer also can get a quarter of an acre of allotment, which supplies the family with vegetables all the year round, and I believe your Commissioner would exclaim if he were not ashamed of uttering so well-worn a quotation:

O fortunatos nimium sua si bona norint
Agricolas.   Georgic II., l. 458

I dare say, however, that many labourers here think that they ought to get more money as their share in the produce which their labour has raised. They see perhaps 100*l*. worth of hay go to the station en route to the London market, or they see a cow sold for 20*l*. which they reared up when it was a calf. Counting the hits and taking no notice of the misses, they are apt to believe that the farmer is making no end of money, which, as a man remarked to me, is all spent in sherry wine and croquet lawns. Very few farmers appear to keep accounts. If they followed my plan of handing a balance-sheet of my farm accounts to my labourers it would put a stop to all idea of striking for higher wages. I tell my labourers here, and I believe truly, that their lot is a better one than that of most gentlemen. They are brought up in their native villages and are educated free, whilst the young gentleman passes most of his time at a boarding school. The labourer passes the best years of his life - manhood - in

England, and marries the girl of his choice, whilst the gentleman is generally forced to go abroad, where his bones are not unfrequently left. The labourer also gets his children off his hands directly they can go to work, whilst the young gentleman, if he can't pass a competitive examination, remains loafing about, a miserable man without anything to do. I work with my labourers, and, with the exception of mowing and reaping, they are very seldom called on to do work which is painful on account of its severity. I often tell my rich neighbours that there is nothing pleasanter than a good day's work in the field. If they really wish to appreciate a garden or a farm, they should cultivate or help to cultivate it themselves. The only fault I find with my labourers is that they appear to eat too much rich food and consume too much beer. Ah! but there is that beastly workhouse. Well, let us only keep the poor-law money which is raised in sufficient quantity in the village to supply our aged paupers in venison and salmon, and then our labourers would be left without any reasonable cause of complaint.

"AN OXFORDSHIRE LANDLORD"

SIR, - During the past few months I have been residing in an agricultural district, and in this time have met with poverty and distress on every hand. Having had especial opportunities for noticing and examining into the causes of this, I have come to the firm conviction that only a thorough revision of the Land Laws will remove the evils. Mr. Taylor has hit the nail on the head (page 49) when he advocates the right of the labourer to have land at a fair rent. But here we have another difficulty to contend with. The labourer may get his land at a fair rent, but the Board of Guardians assesses him at 2*l*. 10s. and acre, while the large farmer, who rents the next field, is only assessed at 1*l*. or 1*l*. 5s. an acre. I ask, sir, is this fair or just? By the present system of assessment the poor many is paying the rates for the rich one, and the Board of Guardians are doing their best to drive the small farmers and the labourers from the district. I would invite the attention of your readers to the following cases which came under my notice last week. They relate to the wages paid to labourers in this neighbourhood, the average wage being 10s. 6d. a week at the outside. Thomas, aged 38 years old, has a wife and six children, the eldest of which is

11 years of age. He gets 12s. a week, but has not been in work for the last six weeks; and pays 1s. 6d. a week for the rent of a tumble-down cottage. His wife is about to be confined. They are on the point of entering the workhouse. Fred has a wife and four children, ranging from three to 12 years of age. He gets 11s. a week, and pays 1s. 6d. for rent a week. His eldest son, 16 years of age, is now earning five shillings a week; but neither father nor son have constant employment, and often the family are without a crust of bread in the house. These are ordinary cases, met with every day; while the wage, 11s. or 12s., is considered a good one. These people have nothing before them if they stop in the country but the workhouse. A young fellow, 23 years of age, got married a week or two ago. His wage was 7s. a week. He has since received a rise of 1s. On asking his master, a wealthy gardener and florist, for an advance of wages, he was told that if he did not like what he got he could go. The only remedy, besides amending the land laws, for keeping the people in the country, is to introduce into the villages manufacturing industries. True, in some quarters this would cause overcrowding, for I found at Somerton, one of the few parishes in this union where the population has increased during the last ten years, and where a collar factory has been lately introduced, houses where seven people slept in one room, and the sanitary arrangements worse than pig-styes. If these houses were condemned, no new one would be erected, and the people would naturally leave the district and flock to the towns. Something must be done for these poor wretches - I can scarcely call them people, so broken down in spirits they seem to be - and unless that is done quickly we shall find that the farmers will be without competent men altogether. Unless some remedy is immediately found to keep the people on the land, and by which they can share its benefits and live in comfort and ease without the thoughts of the workhouse continually haunting them, no one can blame the people for going where they receive wages that will keep body and soul together.

Yours faithfully,

"REPORTER", Langport. Somerset.

SIR, - Your valuable articles on this subject have brought to public notice a matter of importance to those Londoners who like to take their holiday in the real country. Every year the demand for country houses, villas, cottages, and farm apartments increases. But one thing keeps many people away, and that is the difficulty of getting good drinking water. At present we are within twenty miles of London, and the only water we can get is either stored rain water or well water from a drain-soaked soil. There are, I believe, two authorities who could give us this necessary of life. The Cobham Vestry is one of these, the District Sanitary Board the other. But Cobham itself is well off for water, and the sanitary authority will do anything to bring the water except undertake the financial responsibility, which amounts to doing nothing. So we get to the familiar English dead-lock. The situation is rendered comic by the recent action of a landlord whose father had water brought to his cottages on the common, and had a pump put up for the use of "the cottagers at Downside," to quote the inscription. For some days the pump-handle was chained up, now it has been taken away. I have referred to the inscription, but do not find that the word "my" has yet been inserted before "cottagers at Downside." This should be done, or the pump-handle returned unchained or his beneficent family should cease to take public credit to themselves for what is at the present merely an ordinary act of business. One would think that it would be to the general interest if some portion of the large sum of money spent in the holiday season could be expended in our English villages, but so far as my experience goes, neither the landlords nor the authorities will do anything to provide visitors with drinkable water or do anything to induce people to stay in the country.- I remain, yours truly,

C.G.C, Downside, Surrey.

SIR,- I fear most of the suggestions for checking this evil are little better than "pills for the earthquake." Allotments and pension schemes are good as far as they go, which is but a little way. Land nationalisation may or may not be desirable; either way, it is out of the range of practical politics. Phalansteries will not work, while individualism continues to be an element in human nature. But surely there is a way of escape, if the people would but see and utilise it, namely, the restoration of the all but extinct yeomanry, statesmen, or cultivating proprietors. Suppose a farm capable of producing, with high culture, crops, the sale of which will provide for seed, manure, wear of permanent stock, all public charges, and plenty of well-paid labour, and leave a net profit of 200*l.* The cultivating owner will be, not a rich, but a fairly prosperous man; and, if manly and genial, a natural leader and a social blessing to his little circle of employés. But if that farm be loaded with a rent of 150*l.*, the tenant-farmer must make out the difference between 50*l.* a year and a livelihood for his family by employing less and cheaper labour - in short, by labour-starving the land and sweating the labourers. It is not his fault, nor the fault of his class. Yet the whole tendency of legislation and social custom, for ages past, has been to exterminate cultivating owners, replace them with labour-starving and sweating tenant-farmers, and continually stimulate the national tendency towards the agglomeration of huge estates, whose life-owners are rich enough rather to leave the land untilled than allow it to be cultivated, on terms that will afford a decent maintenance to the labourers. It would be worth while to face a temporary doubling of the National Debt - say for the next 25 years, if by that means half the territorial magnates in the country could be expropriated, and their overgrown estates divided into cultivators' freeholds, ranging from 30 to 300 acres. The cost should be chiefly met by a graduated income or property tax.

RICHARD, of Taunton Dean.

(FROM THE "SUNDAY SUN.")

The Daily News has performed an important service in publishing its descriptions of "Life in Our Villages," by its very able and painstaking Special Commissioner. The letters are singularly free from redundancy; and, although strong feeling has been aroused in the writer by what he has seen, there is nothing melodramatic or unreal in his way of telling the story. He would not himself, perhaps, claim that the gloom he depicts hangs with equal impenetrableness over every part of rural England. In some districts, notably in the Midlands, where small auxiliary sources of income - such as glove-stitching and the sale of garden produce - are drawn from the large towns, the standard of comfort is much higher. The readiness with which in these more favoured places the villagers rise to the level of their improved surroundings is altogether encouraging. The cottages are kept with great care, and there is generally some little attempt at daintiness in the arrangement of the window curtain. The gardens in front are in the season a small paradise of scent and colour. The men and women lose that look of settled vacancy which is often only one remove from imbecility, and a little variety - scarlet by preference - is introduced into the dresses of the children. These exceptions, however, are only just numerous enough to prove that the soul of Hodge has not been kept under the clay long enough to become mere clod, and that he soon shows himself amenable to refining influences. The broad fact is that in other parts he is leading a life that is not worth living; that the collier deep in the mine has a merry existence compared with his; and that the little gutter child who dances to the grinding of the street organ in a Drury-lane purlieu represents *L'Allegro* as contrasted with the *Penseroso* of the village child in its sullen loneliness.

(FROM THE "ESSEX COUNTY CHRONICLE.")

In another column we publish a further extract from the letters of the Special Commissioner of *The Daily News* on Life in Our Villages. The writer gives a graphic and evidently impartial and accurate account of a visit to the Stisted district. What he saw there seems to have produced upon his mind the impression that the one real grievance of the agricultural labourer is the low rate of wages. All that has been told the Commissioner elsewhere about the effect of the dullness of rural villages, the absence of society, and the size of farms, has been swept clean away by finding that, while every provision has been made at Stisted for the comfort and happiness of the people, the young men desert the place for London almost as readily as they would desert a village which had never known a large-hearted and philanthropic landlord like the late Mr. Onley Savill Onley.

(FROM OUR SPECIAL COMMISSIONER)

I have to-day travelled for some hours through the by-ways and villages of that part of Suffolk that borders on Norfolk. The country is much of it very pretty. It is beautifully wooded, here and there traversed by small streams, dotted about by the most charming little cottage houses, with now and then a pleasant rectory, a picturesque old church, a lordly-looking mansion, and undulating park, or a richly-laden orchard. From such a round as I have taken to-day, one brings home with him a mental panorama made up of almost everything that is peaceful and pleasant in rural life. Here is a vicarage garden with a party of lawn tennis; yonder through that woody vista is a little company of harvesters; now you have a rosy-looking woman shaking down the plums for a fair haired child, and further on you see a venerable-looking dame sitting by the open door amid flowers and bee-hives. Peace and quiet, beauty and fruitfulness, prevail everywhere. The village shoemaker is deliberately stitching away in a breezy little workshop, with the scarlet blossoms of kidney beans glowing in at the open door, and hollyhocks and rosy apples peering in at the window, out of which the good man now and again gazes as though in heart he is out with the reapers yonder in the waving cornfield.

We push our way through the stalwart, standing corn down towards a cottage clad in grape vine and half-buried in the brown rustling wheat, where stands the village blacksmith, not under a spreading chestnut tree, but, better still, within the shadow of a well-laden pear tree, planted knee deep on the margin of the blacksmith's own cornfield. Sickle in hand, and with two or three young men about him, the burly smith, with his cornsheaves and his pear tree and the cosy cottage just over the hedge there all combine to make a picture such as, one cannot but think, must often haunt the memory of the emigrants from rural England into the docks and railways depots and warehouses of London. "A good deal more fresh air 'ere than in Lon'on," says the blacksmith, as he mops round his brow, wet with honest sweat and looking with pride on the splendid sheaves of corn he and his assistants have just bound up. "Aye, aye; they keeps on going off," and then like everybody else the village blacksmith proceeds to explain the depletion of the villages by s'posing they want to better themselves and suggesting as the only possible means of preventing it the payment of better wages. There's no doubt he thinks the farmers are very short-handed. He laughingly mentions one man who has four hundred acres of corn and has got four men to cut it - a hundred acres apiece before them.

In this village of Barnham wages for a considerable proportion of the men are slightly better than in any other neighbourhood I have gone through. They are getting twelve shillings a week - a fraction over twopence farthing an hour it comes to - and seven pound ten for the harvest. One cannot but suspect, in moving about three rural districts, that the wages received by the people really have little or no relation either to what they earn or what the master can afford to pay. As Mr. H.L. Smith says, in his paper on the "Migration of Labour," read at the National Liberal Club last year, the rates of wage in rural districts are largely customary, and every here and there it strikes one very forcibly that if the people were strong enough to form a good strong union among themselves the whole situation would undergo a total change. In this village of Barnham the monarch of pretty nearly all the surveys is the Duke of Grafton. He pays, as I have said, seven pounds ten for the harvest. Why does he pay that? Is it a sum based on any calculation of the quantity of corn to be cut, the number of hands to be employed, the chances of weather, and so on? I suppose there must have been some sort of calculation some time or other, but, so far as I am informed, such considerations enter very little into the matter. It seems to be assumed that at harvest time an agricultural labourer ought to earn from five to ten pounds during the time within which the corn is fit for cutting and carrying, and the Duke of Grafton chooses to pay seven pounds ten for some weeks of incessant toil from sunrise till sunset, and very often a spell of work by the light of the harvest moon. The Duke sits up at Euston Hall and offers seven pounds ten, the men down in the fields want eight pounds, and the agent runs backward and forwards between the negotiators. The harvest certainly is great, and the labourers few, and if they only had the pluck to hold out they would probably get ten pounds, but not one of them dares to take the lead in insistence on a material advance upon what is customary - though by the way I think I was told that in previous years the payment has been seven pounds - and they meekly give in and go to work. "If you offend the Duke and his agent in this parts," said one, "you may as well go to the devil at once." Not that, so far as I can learn, the Duke of Grafton is open to much criticism. His labourers are better off than those of most landowners in this neighbourhood, his cottages are good and cheap, and the general conditions of life among his people are unquestionably good. As John Bright would have said, he is a very respectable Duke.

By the way, there is a very interesting little relic of the regime of the last Duke of Grafton standing by the roadside in Barnham. It is a little wooden Primitive Methodist chapel on wheels; at least, that is what it has been, though it appears now to have been turned to some industrial purpose, having been purchased, I am told, for the sum of five pounds. I talked yesterday with a shrewd-eyed, ruddy-faced, stubbly-chinned old villager whose share in putting up the little conventicle had cost him some years of exile from the place. They wanted the Duke to let them have a bit of land to put up a Primitive Methodist chapel, but he refused them. So they built this wooden shanty, and put it on wheels in one of their gardens. The agent remonstrated, and tried to persuade my old friend here to take his conventicle to one of the "free villages." But no, said the sturdy peasant, all villages were free to worship God as they thought proper, and he wouldn't budge. He found alas! that the freedom was only theoretical, and in the end he lost his employment, and had to clear out, leaving the little schism shop behind him. Eventually, however, after some years, he found his way back, and now looks a hale and hearty old man, about whose brow one fancies there are the marks of troublous times, softened, however by an eventide of comfort and prosperity. I am told that the obduracy of the Duke was ultimately overcome by the prayers of the Primitives, who couldn't and wouldn't pray for the death of the man who thwarted their evangelizing efforts in the villages but were very earnest in their supplications to Heaven that "every obstacle might be removed." The Duke seems to have got an intimation of what was going on, and thought it prudent to answer the prayer himself.

In this village of Barnham the cottagers seem to be as comfortable and prosperous as good management of the property and considerate treatment can make them. They have good cottages, gardens, allotments, good water, and as things go, good wages. Yet the population of the place has slightly gone down since the last census, and the universal testimony is that "the young 'uns all go." An intelligent villager - not a labourer, but a man of the working class

- gave very emphatic evidence to that effect. He was a member of some Nonconformist Church - now freely tolerated - in the village, and he said they found invariably that as soon as they got hold of a young man and set him thinking a bit, he began to think of going. They lost all their young men that way he said. It strikes one as curious that all the farmers - even those who may reasonably be presumed to have plenty of capital - seem inclined to pinch and save in the matter of labour. I had mentioned to me 2,000 acres of land on which, upon the highest reckoning, not more than seven men were regularly employed, and as one spins along through miles of cornfields you see every here and there unmistakable evidence of the labour-starving of the land, and men will tell you of the reductions that have been made within their recollection. When I drove from Thetford through Barnham, Livermere, Troston, Honington, and Euston into Thetford again, the day was breezy and dry, and thousands of acres of corn stood ready for cutting. With the men actually at work it looked as though the harvest wouldn't be got in till Christmas. Here and there reaping machines were going, and I hear that the American reaping and binding machines are gaining extended use in some parts of the Eastern Counties. Every innovation of this kind, of course, tends to the immediate displacement of hands.

Some of the little glimpses one gets into life in the remoter villages are really very curious. In one place a woman incidentally alluded to the blankets that were lent to the people. I was surprised that she should have the loan of a blanket, for she seemed a respectable and spirited little body, who might have been supposed above it. But it appeared that everybody in the village had the loan of a blanket. "But," I said, "are there no people in the place who are unwilling to borrow bed-clothing?" "No, Sir; everybody has 'em - unless it is the estate bricklayers, I dunno' whether they have one. They seal 'em up in the spring, and they unseal 'em in the autumn." "Seal them up?" I said, in perplexity. "Yes, sir; I'll show you mine," and the vivacious little woman whisked up stairs and brought down a calico bag, the mouth of which was sewn up with string, the ends being sealed with black wax. She proceeded to explain that in the spring they all had to trudge up to the rector's wife with their charity blanket folded up in its bag to have it tied up and sealed. They took their bags back home till October, when they again went to the good lady to have their seals broken and the blankets released for winter use. Every cottager in the village had the loan of a blanket and seven hundred-weight of coal. There was a clothing club too, to which they all contributed, but everybody who went to town to buy clothing had to take the parcel from the shop straight away to the parson's wife, who would minutely inspect them to see if they were suitable for persons in their state of life. There is the clerical beneficent domination on the one hand, and on the other there is the squire who owns all the cottages, and whose agent requires them to mind their P's and Q's if they want to remain. They pay their rent yearly, but they all sign an agreement that an eight days' notice to quit shall be sufficient. They have to be very careful. Their children musn't wander from the pathway in the park, and dreadful things would happen if they were known to bring home a few dry sticks.

Now, I know nothing of the clergyman or his wife, or of Lord De Soumarez, the owner of the property, and I have not the least desire to represent them as oppressors or tyrants. They may be the most amiable of their race. I can quite conceive that the vicar's wife may be actuated by the kindest and best of motives in going to the trouble of minutely inspecting their purchases and sealing up their blankets. It keeps them clean and ensures fair usage and proper storage when they are not wanted. The woman certainly had one point on which, evidently, her mind was a good deal exercised. They used to have nine hundredweight of coal when the population was larger. But latterly it had been only seven, and although the population of the village had gone down recently and there were several houses empty the coal still kept at seven hundredweight. If there were fewer to have it, surely there ought to be more to have. How it was she couldn't make out. Apparently these things are all managed over their heads. But I dare say it is all right. Nobody of course ever heard of charity funds going to pay the organ-blower at church, or to wash the choir surplices. The thing is inconceivable, and no doubt some satisfactory explanation would have been forthcoming if I had had the enterprise and the time to look into the matter. But suppose that all these things are just as they should be, can one conceive anything more pauperising and degrading than the kind of tutelage under which these villagers live? Can you wonder that young men of spirit are eager to clear out of such an atmosphere of serfdom? As to such "charity," a clean sweep ought to be made of it. It is a mere relief to the wages list of the employers. I am not quite sure, but I think I was told that ten shillings a week was the rate of pay prevailing here, and I was certainly informed that young men - "quite grown chaps" - had been working for five and six shillings a week and eight shillings had been paid to a young man of 20. Only last week two of them left the place. In the next village all the houses and all the land, except one small plot on which a chapel had just been built, belonged to one man who has consolidated several farms, putting his labourers into the farm houses and pulling down the cottages. He and his labourers had entered into a compact for ten shillings a week from Michaelmas to Michaelmas. The men had tried to get a revision of the bargain recently but without avail. "When a says a thing," observed a buxom dame, "you can't move'n and," she added emphatically, "I like'n all the better for't."

TO THE EDITOR OF THE DAILY NEWS

SIR, - Speaking with some little knowledge of the land question, I venture to say that life in our villages may be made very comfortable in the near future. If the Liberal party when it next comes into power does its best to improve the legislation of the present Government, and in two directions merely. 1. By making the existing Allotments' Act a Small Holdings Act. 2. By creating parish councils and giving to these the administration of the above amended Act. It is important to bear in mind that the Allotment Act asserts the principle that land may be taken, against the wish of the landlord, for the creation of allotments. Of course the machinery for giving effect to this is so bad that scarcely any land has at present been obtained by labourers in despite of the landlords. Parish councils, however, would be likely to do what sanitary authorities only hesitate about. But to use a homely phrase, "the game must be worth the candle." Now, half an acre or an acre of land, far away from a man's home, is not game worth the candle. On the other hand, could he get as much as five acres, if he liked, and make his home thereon, and pay rent for this, not to a capricious or grasping landlord, but to a parish council of which he was a constituent, it is evident, surely, that the parish council would have the strongest motives for acting energetically. For step by step its constituents would become independent both of farmer and landlord. A constant alternative to wage-service would be open to all who till the soil. The economic consequences of this need scarcely be dwelt upon. Wages in villages would go up. People who had sought precarious employment in towns would have a motive for returning to the place of their birth. Comfortable villages, in short, would prove an effective solution of the terrible labour problems of our big cities. Of course the landlords would suffer in the end; but who cares? They have had a rare time of it at the expense of the people.

Yours obediently,

WILLIAM JAMESON, Manor Park, Essex.

SIR,- I beg to submit copy of a letter just received from a village in the Midlands, showing that the state of the agricultural labourer in that locality is similar to that described by your Special Correspondent in Essex. The names I suppress, as their publication might be detrimental to the writer.- Yours, &c.,

"A FARMER'S SON"

.

"Dear Sir, - I have to thank you for sending me *The Daily News.* The articles on 'Life in our Villages' are most interesting to me; especially as some of the statements are strikingly true of this village. I often wonder what will become of the village if the decrease of population continues as of late. The pith of our young people leave us. At this I do not wonder. What is there in a place like this to keep a young man of average intelligence? The highest position to be reached is that of a carter or shepherd at a wage of 12s. or 14s. per week, the ordinary labourer getting only 10s. or 11s., and this with the prospect of being out of work some of the winter months. This is the case of some of the few left here. I do not wonder at the young people leaving. I have had a great desire to get away for years, but having a family and other ties has prevented me. The only remedy, so far as I can see, is the one suggested by one of the writers, namely, put the working man on the land. Give him a nice little plot to cultivate, and I don't think he would then run off. But there is another thing which we Dissenters have to look at. The modern Church clergyman, as a rule, is bent on the overthrow of Dissent in the country villages. I am sorry to say that we have such a one in our village. He has been here a few months, and his chief work seems to be to hind Dissent. He is just the type of man referred to by the correspondent signed 'Church Woman' (page 41). He is seeking to rob the chapel and Sunday-school all he can. As soon as he was settled here he went round the parish, from house to house, taking care to find out those who went to chapel, also the children attending Chapel Sunday-school. We had in our school two or three who had been baptised at church, and he claimed them, telling the parents that the children belonged to the Church, and that it was quite wrong for them to go to a Dissenting Sunday-school. I am sorry to say the parents have yielded, and have taken the children away. He also circulates a book on 'Church and Dissent,' in which the writer tries to prove that Dissent is a great sin!- I am yours, respectfully,

"A.B."

SIR, - I have read with interest many letters, and heard many speeches upon this subject, but I have yet to learn how houses for the labourers can be built so that the rent can return an interest to the owners of even 4 per cent. net per annum. And I should be exceedingly glad if any one of your readers can instruct me how to do it. In doing so he must not forget to take into account the bye-laws which are in force in many or most of the rural districts, which means extra cost for building in accordance with such stipulations. Your correspondent "A.W." (pages 60 and 79) says that "Local Councils could, if not hindered by costly machinery, provide decent houses built upon quarter and half-acre plots, for 2s. and 2s. 6d. per week rent'" by which I suppose he means the rent would be interest upon the cost. All I ask is, show me the way to do it.

B.W.   August 30.

LETTERS TO THE EDITOR

OUR VILLAGES.

SIR, - In common with many thousands of your readers whose early associations were "truly rural," I have followed the correspondence which has appeared in your columns lately with considerable interest. My old friend Hodge appears to me in some danger now of being over-coddled. Time was when his "friends were few." A couple of decades back, *The Daily News* stood out very conspicuously as the champion of his cause, and I could almost fancy that the same gifted pen that is now portraying his vicissitudes in Essex lifted the veil then to the astonishment of those who wondered what the agitator, Joseph Arch, was about. A good many things have happened since then, and the most important, as far as the labourer is concerned, has been the opening up to him of a new world in the shape of the British Colonies. The whilom English village encumbrance has become the eagerly sought for and amply remunerated necessity of the Canadian and Australian farmer. It has been my great felicity to see the men who were treated as criminals by their besotted British employers for daring to question the adequacy of an eighteenpence a day wage, receiving from their New Zealand masters seven and eight shillings for a two hours shorter day's work.

      I am unable any longer to pity men whom I have thus seen so amply remunerated when they have had the pluck to avail themselves of the circumstances of life. There is not a British colony at this moment that would not gladly welcome any number of good field workers. Why then should I be called upon to waste my sympathy on such valued members of society? If any of them are still underpaid it is surely their own fault. I have never seen a poor farm labourer abroad. He is ever master of the position. Hundreds of the Berkshire, Oxfordshire, Wiltshire, and Warwickshire men, whose severe hardships your Correspondent of 1872-3 so graphically narrated, are to-day prosperous colonial farmers, and there is nothing to hinder hundreds more from becoming such. I therefore venture to enter a protest against any longer regarding Hodge as an object of pity. If we have any pity to spare let it be displayed towards the unfortunate London clerks and other genteel fraternity whom no one wants, and whom every colony spurns from its door. I shrewdly suspect that it is the British farmer rather than his labourer who is to-day "up a tree." The low price of produce generally, while it has spelt ruin to the master, has meant a twenty-five per cent. increase of the purchasing power of the labourer's wage. I was glad to find that Mr. George Loosley (page 38), who knows rural life as well as most men, endorses this view of the labourers' present case. "They work shorter hours, have more money, and are very independent," he told us lately in his letter. I hope, however, he is incorrect in saying that "the average agricultural labourer is less trusty and efficient" than he used to be. I am afraid this is only a stingy employer's estimate of the case. Certainly the higher colonial wage and shorter hours of work have no such result. One of the most striking revelations of my extensive travels during the last decade has been the vast improvement in the morale of the workmen consequent on their improved circumstances. The slouching, obsequious, shuffling fellow of the English village I have met in New Zealand transformed into a smart, self-reliant, energetic citizen, full of "go," and not wanting in political enthusiasm. The conclusion of the whole matter, therefore, appeals to me to be somewhat thus: there must be no more coddling of the farm labourer. If he cannot stand up let him fall down. If, with the world before him, he elects to vegetate in such vile quarters as your Correspondent has described, let him do so. No maudlin sympathy can permanently help those who will not help themselves.

I am, &c.,

ARTHUR CLAYDEN.

SIR, - As one who has been until lately a country parson in Dorsetshire, I have taken the deepest interest in your timely and accurate articles on "Life in Our Villages." The great evil of the agricultural labourer's life is that it is a life without hope. Between the labourer and the classes above him a great gulf is fixed. In old age he can only look forward to the workhouse. To remedy this sad state of things nothing is more necessary than more small holdings, which men with small capital could take and become, in a certain measure, independent. Let me give two cases which lately came under my notice in the same village. Not long ago a young man came to me to arrange about his wedding. He had put off marriage until he was about thirty, and had always lived with his parents and been of a saving disposition. He told me that on his marriage he intended to invest his savings, about one hundred pounds, in taking a small beer-house with a few acres of land attached to it. I expressed regret at this. He answered, "Well, it is the only way I can get a bit of land," and I had to acknowledge that his plea was true. Another case. An agricultural labourer some years ago was given a little heifer in lieu of wages owed him by a semi-bankrupt farmer. The heifer for some time was fed by his wife at the wayside. It became a cow, and, in due time, the parent of other cows. The labourer took a field. Now he is a small holder. He cultivates about twenty acres of land under every possible disadvantage. It is situated in the next parish to that in which his own cottage stands. He pays a very high rent for it. He has to go more than a mile twice a day with his pony-cart to milk his cows. He has no proper buildings; but he makes his little bit of land pay. He is far more independent than the ordinary labourer, and has no reason to fear the workhouse in his old age. The question of "Life in Our Villages" will not be solved by small holdings, but they will go some way towards it. Small holdings will also in an indirect way have a beneficial effect on the physique of the labouring population. They will make it possible for the poor to get milk readily and cheaply for their children. The small holders will sell milk in small quantities. It is too much trouble for the large farmers to do so. Ordinarily, the children of the rural poor are brought up without milk from the time they are weaned. The affect on the growth and health of the children is very bad. Again, the agricultural labourers need union. They are the most disunited of all the battalions of this great army of labour. They are helpless in the hands of their employers.

More and more, I regret to say, it is becoming the custom to turn men off during winter on the plea that there is no work for them to do. If the rent is to be paid the labour bill must be kept down. I have come home from an afternoon visiting during which I have again and again come across instances of the breadwinner being thrown out of work for six or eight weeks in the midst of a bitter winter, and have marvelled at the heroic patience of the agricultural labourer. He suffers in silence. If he was violent, politicians would at once recognise that something must be done. A strong agricultural labourers' union, a multiplication of small holdings, and something in the shape of a national pension fund for old age would transform the hard and dreary lot of the rural labourer.- I am, &c.,

W. S. SWAYNE.

SIR - In reply to the letter of "B. W." dated August 30th (page 99), which appears in your issue of to-day, and in which he asks to be shown how houses for labourers can be built so that the rent shall return an interest to the owners of 4 per cent. per annum, I should be pleased to show B.W., or any one else interested in the matter, how to build labourers' cottages (containing three bedrooms, two living rooms, wash-house, coals, and closet) to let at a rental of 2s. 6d. per week, and still return a certain 4½ per cent. per annum on the total outlay incurred. I have built a number of these cottages myself, and can show B. W. a row of well-constructed, convenient, and picturesque cottages in a village in Essex which return the owners more than 4½ per cent. per annum.- I am, &c.

W.G.   Sept 1.

SIR, - By far the most sensible bit that has been written yet on this subject is to be found in the last line of the brief letter by "B. W." (page 100) in your issue of yesterday, viz., "All I ask is, show me the way to do it." The lamentable condition of British agriculture and village life is notorious, and therefore it is no use whining over the hard lot either of the farmer or of his work people, or to make absurdly unworkable suggestions to render confusion worse confounded, which is being done by the talk and writings of over zealous friends. There is a way out of the difficulty, no doubt, but the vital question now is, have we the qualified men living capable of attaining this? If so, then I for one, a member of one of the oldest agricultural families in the kingdom, am most anxious that such qualified men only should be entrusted with the duties to formulate a scheme for the salvation of British agriculture and village life.

G.Nicholls   Sept 1.

"A Devonshire Squire" writes:- Possibly better house accommodation and a bit of land held in certain possession may help the labourer to eke out his wages by labour of his own, and may reconcile him to the conditions of a country life. Still this would not cure the evil, for the temptation would remain as strong for the young men, the life and stay of a village, to wander off wherever the inducement of better wages or a less monotonous existence may attract them. May not, however, a solution be found in making agricultural labour itself more attractive, more scientific, more up to date, offering greater inducements for advancement. Already there is a move in this direction, by offering premiums to country schools to enable them to impart some technical and scientific agricultural instruction, something a degree beyond the rule-of-thumb method that has heretofore been the only one possible.

The first and greatest difficulty that stands in the way of scientific farming is the want of capital. Agriculture demands capital as much or even more than most businesses. A large capital must be sunk in stocking a farm, in the purchase of implements and manures, in wages, in rent, before any return can be expected. Capital is required to stand the luck of bad seasons and low prices, and to wait for slow returns. But capital is just what the small farmer lacks. How can he be expected to possess it, when the stages of his advancement have been from the position of a labourer to that of a dairyman, and from the dairyman to the small farmer? But lack of capital implies low wages, land dirty and impoverished from lack of labour or manure, and generally bad results. And so the whole concern - landlord, tenant, farm, and labourer - go to the bad. The first remedy, then, would seem to be farming over a larger area, under the superintendence of a man of acknowledged ability, and having the command of a large capital. If no one person can be found to possess both the · latter qualifications, why should not farming be brought within the operation of a limited company - be put under the control of a properly-qualified manager - subject to a competent directorate, who should overlook and regulate the expenditure. Agriculture with large capital to depend upon, would occupy a different position; there would be a general improvement along the line. Wages would go up, a better class of labourers would be employed who could afford to pay a better house rent, better cottages would be built because it would pay to build them; and even if the prices of agricultural produce did not go up, the profits of farming would, because of the greater returns, from the land due to the better method of working it. It may be that the new motive power of the present day may have as great a work to do in the field of agriculture as in lighting our streets and houses, driving our engines, or propelling our boats.

Mr. Thomas Pickworth, Loughborough, writes: "I know no men who have so little to cheer them as the agricultural labourers. Incessant work, day after day, week after week, year after year - the same dully, dreary mode of life, without a chance of bettering their condition. Hope has not a ray of comfort for them. They dare not look to the future; for what is the prospect? Death or the workhouse. During a considerable portion of the year they leave home before it is light and return not until it is dark. Their children's faces they only see once in seven days. Walking probably three or four miles to work, under a hedge or a haystack they eat their cold victuals. Drudging all day in all weathers, they return at night weary and wet, carrying on their backs a few gathered sticks, the only means they probably have of drying their dripping garments or preparing their scanty meal. Can nothing be done to remove this blot on humanity? Has benevolence no resource? Is Wisdom at her wit's end? I cannot believe it. Build cottages - no, not cottages - build houses, comfortable houses, on the land the labourers work on. Attach to their homes a good piece of garden ground, and give - yes, give - them one day in the week to cultivate it. No reduction of wages. I believe more work would be done in five days than is now done in six. The long, weary walk to and from work is labour utterly lost. Two hours per day, twelve hours per week, or nearly two months a year, are spent in a task unprofitable, unnecessary, and exhausting."

"L." writes:- From all accounts, it appears that the condition of life in the villages is what it is with the connivance at least of the gentleman considered to have the spiritual which must more or less include the material care of the villagers - the clergyman of the established church. He, if any one, is supposed to have influence with the landlords and the ruling powers. The decadence of dissent, referred to by some of your correspondents, too, has an important bearing on life in the villages, since it is usually the most independent and enterprising who leave the villages for big towns. Apart from the nature of the tenets imparted by the Dissenters to the people, it should be remembered that the Dissenters break the monopoly of the Church parson, which in itself must have a wholesome influence, and if that influence fails the look out is dark. More and more the clergyman aspires to have the rule in matters not only religious, which to a great extent means sectarian, but in the disbursement of charities and the management of everything, notably the village schools. By all that is holy, free, and progressive, let there be combination for the purpose of freeing life in the villages from the despotic control of the clergy, who, though sometimes kind and good, ought never to "rule the roost." "Would not so and so help you?" I remarked to a poor woman who consulted me on getting her invalid husband into an infirmary. "We go to chapel," was her significant reply.

"J. F. S.," noticing that some of our correspondents, and notably "B. W." (page 100) appear to doubt whether labourers' cottages can be built so as to pay even a small percentage upon the cost says: "Almost anywhere it is possible to erect plain but substantial four-roomed cottages with the local building materials, and in strict conformity to the bye-laws of the local authority at 200*l.* per pair, or less if several pairs are erected in the same neighbourhood at the same time. Taking the rent of such cottages to be 2s. 3d. per week each, the income (5*l.* 17s. per annum) is sufficient to pay 4 per cent. upon the cost o f building: 4*l.* rent of half acre of land, say 15s., leaving a surplus of 1*l.* 2s. for repairs and empties. But why should not the local council (whenever it is established) endeavour to satisfy the land hunger of the labourer, endeavouring to make him a freeholder as building societies, with all their faults, have made many working men in towns leaseholders to the great advantage of the man and the community. Surely what is done by a trading society for the benefit primarily of the shareholders, must also be possible (and much more besides) to the local council, so that a slightly enhanced rental may make the occupier the owner in a term of years. Why should not the labourer be able to get his cottage and garden plot - and a fair size plot too - in the same way that the class above him get their pianos.

Mr. James Rayner, Aldington Hythe, thinks there is only one solution, and that is the municipalisation of the land. He says, "Western Counties" (page 75) asks for fair rents as the one panacea, but what is a "fair rent"? A fair rent for land, like a fair price for potatoes or fish or leading articles is precisely what it will fetch. Why should "Western Counties" expect landlords in a world where everyone else's conduct is to sell in the dearest market, to run their business on philanthropic lines with the Beatitudes for their sole guide? Once admit the justice of private property in land it is simply robbing the landlord for the benefit of the tenant to fix a lower rent than the former could get in the open market. If one thinks the matter down to the bottom it is clearly seen that all land value is community value; intrinsically land has no economic value whatever apart from population. Labour and capital are the two factors in the production of all wealth but they do not enjoy the full fruitions of their ratios because private property in land permits a third extraneous party, who has contributed nothing to the result, to step in and claim a huge slice of the produce. The difference between what "Western Counties" calls a "good" landlord and a "bad" is simply this: The former takes a rather more generous view of the standard of comfort due to his tenants or his labourers. When he has satisfied himself in that respect he, like all the others, wants the rest of the produce for himself. Ownership of the land confers the power to poll-tax the human race, and we cannot buy a loaf of bread without paying tribute to this insatiable Caesar.

Mr. John Higgins, Pylle, Somerset, says:- The touchstone of "Life in our Villages" is the condition and ownership of the cottages. The best built new cottages show that some landowners are as kind and considerate as other classes, but their great possessions compel them to act through various agencies. This sifts the money for even ordered repairs. The farmer's steading must be patched up or he will leave the farm or ask for reduction of rent, but if a cottager complains of his windy, leaking den he is voted a nuisance. The agent cannot be bothered, the cottage is neglected, and the workman, with his just complaint, either gets his discharge or takes the neglect as only another addition to the miseries of his life. This must not be left so. The condition of the country side is the outgrowth of all the millions who have lived and died upon it. Yet as the taint of evil is not wholly the work of any one class, all should help to sweep aside a little of that misery, the true pedigree of which is "Greed" by "Criminality." out of "Ignorance" by "Sloth."

(FROM OUR SPECIAL COMMISSIONER)

During my rambles in the Eastern Counties I have found the general state of things - the condition of land and crops, labourers' wages, hours of work, cottage accommodation, facilities for getting allotments, and so on - all varying from place to place. But two things I have found almost invariable. Wherever I have been I have found, as I have repeatedly said, that as a rule almost without exception population has been dwindling, and small farms have been consolidating into large ones. This increase in the scale of farming operations I find to be quite as striking a feature of the agricultural situation wherever I have been as the decrease in the population and, as I have shown, it is indeed to a great extent the cause of that decrease. This consolidation of farms is not, of course, always a voluntary proceeding. In some instances I find it attributed to the folly and infatuation of landowners. Only yesterday a gentleman told me of a case within his own knowledge in which a farmer was giving thirty shillings an acre for land. At that rate it was impossible to get on.

He went to his landlord, told him that his difficulties were such that it was impossible he should continue to pay that rent. He offered eighteen shillings as the utmost he could afford. The offer was refused, the tenant left his farm, or, at all events, took steps for securing another, and then apparently the landlord discovered his mistake, and sent to say that he would accept the eighteen shillings. But it was too late, and eventually the land was let at twelve and sixpence. Several persons have said to me that if landlords would be content to take from small farmers rents as low as they are continually having to take from large ones, the small man would not have to give up. No doubt that is often the case; but it is safe to assume that in a general way landowners know their own business best. Here and there the short-sighted folly of an individual may drive out a small farmer, and hand over his land to a large one; but we may rest assured that wide-spread movements - general changes such as this from small farms to large ones - are not brought about by individual folly, but by the operation of great economic forces. To a very large extent at least it is the landowners who are assuming occupation of land for their own farming. With the price of wheat low, and seasons unfavourable, many small farmers will tell you that during the past few seasons they could do no good for themselves, even though they were rent free. Small farms have been given up because they could not be made to pay. Fresh tenants could not be found for them, and landlords, rather than let them go to ruin, have taken them into their own hands. In Essex and Suffolk I have again and again shown that the migration of labour into the towns has been very largely due to the reduction of the staff of men consequent on such changes. In a short incursion I have made into Southern and Central Norfolk I have found just the same thing going on. "This joining of one farm to another has been the curse of Norfolk," said Mr. George Rix, a rather remarkable leader of the agricultural labourers in the Eastern Counties, to whom I may have to refer again, and who I may mention, by the way, in 1849 got married on one-and-twopence a day. "It has been the curse of Norfolk," he repeated. "It has made a difference of a man to every hundred acres of land." It has done here, in fact, pretty much what it has done everywhere else. It has reduced the number of hands employed, it has in some localities overstocked the labour market, and of course, has tended to keep down wages. From the agricultural labourer's point of view, it has been an unmitigated curse. The shopkeepers in the small towns have complained bitterly of it too. They say that instead of four or five households coming into a little town with their orders for farm implements, and household necessaries, and groceries and clothing, there is but one family, and that one as often as not gets supplied from the big co-operative stores in town. I have heard this again and again from shopkeepers. At the same time there is, of course, general complaint that instead of the rural population increasing and growing more profitable, it is continually dribbling away.

At present, then, this consolidation of farming is extinction for the yeoman class, it is bad for the agricultural labourer, it is bad for the provincial shopkeeper, and it is bad for the community at large, not only because it is, as things stand, against the interests of entire classes of great importance, but because very commonly this large scale farming fails to produce as much as the land is capable of producing. A large farm wants an immense amount of oversight. The farmer cannot see to it himself. He has to trust to others, and he does not get good work out of his men, and his land is not well tilled. Another argument I have heard against extensive farming is that stock is not bred upon such farms to anything like the extent it should be.

Animals at certain times require special attention which they do not get because they are not under the master's eye. Losses are very frequent, and those who farm on a large scale prefer the branches of the business which are attended with fewer risks. I have already quoted the opinions of those who speak favourably of extensive operations. They say that as a man of capital - and in many cases with private resources quite apart from his land - the big farmer can buy largely; he can get the best machinery, he can fully employ his horses and his men all the year round, and if the market for his produce is bad, he can wait till it improves. All this is universally admitted. But even with all his advantages, it is contended that for the large farmer himself the system is not entirely satisfactory, while for everybody else concerned it is absolutely bad.

All this is seen more or less clearly, and there is an intense and widespread feeling that something ought to be done by way of remedy. All sorts of speculations and suggestions are rife. Let us have technical education say some who appear to think that if Hodge could only be persuaded to do his turnip-hoeing on scientific principles his enjoyment of the work might make all the difference between ten shillings in the country and five-and-twenty in town. Certainly let us have technical education. Educate, educate, educate, by all means in your power. It will all help on towards the final solution of the question. But do not let us be simple enough to suppose that that alone will do it. By general consent it is the many-sided education of the rural districts that is emptying our fields and selling the huge population of our towns. The agricultural labourers must have better cottages say others. Of course they must. For us as a community to rest content that either in town or country people shall be penned up in such pig-styes, as many of them are forced to put up with, would be a foul disgrace to us. We democrats must keep hammering away at this question of the housing of the working classes without pause or intermission, until every working-man's family has a house that is fit to live in. But as I have already shown young men are streaming away from villages in which the cottages are beautiful, absolutely all that could be desired for them, and allotments to boot. Cottage building will not do it alone. Others say let the law be altered that compels the hopeless fathers of families struggling to exist on eleven shillings a week to contribute a shilling or eighteenpence of their week's earnings for the maintenance of their old fathers and mothers. Aye - something is wrong here, too. It is right and proper that a man should help his old parents when they can no longer help themselves; but it is pushing a right principle to a brutal application when half-starved peasants have 10 or 14 per cent. of their scanty earnings wrung out of them every week of their lives to save the pockets of ratepayers. Nor is the cash payment the whole of the matter. Pitiful tales could be told of days of lost labour and weary tramps over long miles, and of fruitless appeals to Boards of Guardians to relieve poor wretches of burdens they are not able to bear. Everywhere the labouring poor speak bitterly of this demand upon them. "I stuck to th' old man as long as I could," said a labourer, "and I 'ould do it. Th' old 'un 'ad a seat by my fireside and a bit o' some't to eat while I could gi't to 'n. But when he went into the 'ouse 'cause I couldn't afford to keep'n at 'ome and feed the young'ns, they didn't aughter a come down on me for a shil'n a week, and I told 'em so." "You went before the guardians?" "Yes, and I 'ad to walk five mile through a drenching rain and five mile back over it, and then they wouldn't let me off. They said as I must pay, and I wa'n't workin' above half time, and they know'd it." In the abstract principle the law is right; the practical application of it by rural boards of guardians - largely, of course, composed of rate-paying farmers - is often a cruel wrong. There is urgent need for alteration here. But here again I fear amendments are not likely to have any material effect on the solution of the agricultural question.

Yet another suggestion is made in a letter which has reached me from a gentleman who is strongly of opinion that, "whatever the Liberal party may do in the future, unless the curse of drink is stayed in some manner, you can never do any.permanent good for the people of the villages." I sincerely hope that the Liberal party will do whatever may be thought wise and practicable to "stay the curse of drink" in the villages, and the towns too. I cannot say that in the course of these rambles I have come across much evidence of it. In some of the villages there have been no public-houses. I went through three in one afternoon, in which my attention was called to the fact that there was no public-house. I must not pretend to say that I take this to be evidence that all the people were teetotallers. In many parts they are given to brewing their own beer, and, for cheapness at all events, they quite cut out the brewer and the publican. They give, I am told, four-and-six or five shillings for a bushel of malt, and a shilling a pound for hops, and out of this they brew eighteen gallons of beer, for which at the public-house they would have to pay twopence-ha'penny a pint. But, apart from this, some of the big landowners won't have a public-house on their estates, and I was told more than once in answer to inquiries that drunkenness was not very rife among the villages. How could it be, I was asked, on village incomes? Now let me entreat the teetotal readers of *The Daily News*, whom I already see in imagination sitting down as one man to pen an indignant protest against my gross misrepresentation of village life in this respect - let me entreat them to observe that I am not speaking of village life in general, but only of so much of it as has come under my own observation. I know that in other localities it may be different, and even here there may be more of the evil of it than meets the casual eye or the chance inquiry. I am fully alive to the grave difficulty that is presented in the drinking habits of the labouring class to every advance of social progress. We must battle with this difficulty by every means in our power, especially by means of intelligent recreation and opportunities of social intercourse apart from the public-house. We have got to battle with drink and all its evils, but do not let us delude ourselves with any idea that the putting down of drink and making the people sober is a solution of the agricultural problem by which we are now confronted. All these points I have alluded to are worthy of the most earnest consideration; but something more will have to be done, or the agricultural problem must remain unsolved.

TO THE EDITOR OF THE DAILY NEWS

SIR, - The extreme importance to the whole country of this question of village life induces me to write to you again on the subject, as I think that those who are in possession of any facts which may throw light on the matter, or who have been able from actual personal experience to form some definite judgment as to what might be done, ought to do all they can to put these facts and opinions before the public. There seems to be much doubt as to the efficacy of the allotment system, even if it were thoroughly carried out, as a means of retaining labourers in the country. I believe myself in allotments as a temporary stopgap, but to that extent only. They are a help if certain conditions of convenience, fair rent and so forth are present; but much more is needed. To put the matter into a nutshell - it is the prospects (or the absence of

113

them) of the labourer that present the difficulty. The skilful, energetic worker in any other line "gets on," his prospects improve, he has something to look forward to. The labourer has nothing of the kind. Be he as skilful and industrious as he may, he is only worth the more to his employer; his own wages remain the same. It is the prospect of reaping some increasing reward for industry and skill, as life goes on, that is the attraction in the towns. Can the labourer be given some such hope in his own particular business? Certainly; if he can be given access to the land on fair terms, and with security that he will be allowed to reap all the fruits of his own industry thereon. There are in my own parish men who afford examples of this. They rent land on which their predecessors (generally their fathers or other relations) had "squatted" before the enclosure of the commons. The excellent cottages (in comparison with many others about the place) in which they live, the fruitful, well-drained gardens which they cultivate, are the product of their own and their predecessors' spare labour through many years. They pay rent to the parish; rent which even now is double that of the average rent of the whole parish. I say "even now" because I had a hard fight soon after my arrival in the parish against a proposed large increase of the rentals of these plots, and succeeded in preventing it. I need not enter into details, but the fight was obstinate. I only succeeded by adopting the "Plan of Campaign." The point is: Do these men leave the place? No, Sir, they don't. They stick like limpets to their base, and it would take a good deal to move them now. Where there is one such holding there ought to be fifty. Yet these men have no real security - only such security as the common-sense and justice of the parish officials may give them. Notice they are tenants, not freeholders. The great objection to a peasant proprietary is the constant temptation to mortgage the land. By means of these expensive mortgages the petty local money-lender gets hold of the plot after plot, he grows into a landowner and his son into a squire - perhaps a defender of the Church and a Primrose "knight," or whatever they call themselves. If parish councils are to be any good you must abolish the property vote. It is that which has rendered the vestry a nullity as a means of expressing the popular will. There is a great deal more to be said and done. The Liberals must take it in hand in downright earnest. For myself, I am sick of half-measures and counsels of expediency. We want village councils, with one man one vote; we want village co-operative stores, in which every villagers should be a shareholder, so that the poor man need not pay more than any one else for his tea and sugar; we want an improved system of houses of public refreshment and amusement under parochial management, and served by salaried officials, the profits going towards public improvements; we want a good system of intermediate schools to which our cleverest boys can go free of expense to their parents; we want technical education in every parish; we want - oh! lots of things; and more power to the elbows of the men who will try to get them for us!-

Your obedient servant,

.

ARNOLD D. TAYLOR, Churchstanton Rectory, Honiton,   August 31.

SIR - I hope you will see your way to reprinting in pamphlet or book form your Special Commissioner's articles on "Our Villages," together with the letters which have been evoked by them. I like "A Leicestershire Farmer's" letter (page 85). It is pleasant, kind, and breezy, but surely he is wrong when he says that "those who toil not nor spin" reap their 10 per cent. Certainly the landlords, to whom he refers, do not. I myself believe from close observation that the land-owning classes are face to face with a crisis to which the whole financial calamities of South America are but a flea-bite. Take East Kent, for instance. Land there in any quantity is unsaleable. The weight of it is dragging down the unfortunate owners to beggary. They simply can't sell, though most of them would wish to. In my opinion there is hardly an agricultural property in East Kent that would at the hammer realise the money for which it is mortgaged, and most country properties are mortgaged, or, as some could call it, "charged." Properties are put up after long advertisement, and are withdrawn without a bid or at a price which no doubt the mortgagee (not the owner) is unwilling to accept. I could give chapter and verse for this statement. I know now a large and fertile farm let at 2s. 6d. an acre, and as for landlords "not affording to reduce rents," they are no more superior to economic laws than any other class, and there is no difference to my mind in "not reducing rents" and in not getting them at all. "A Leicestershire Farmer" must remember that the state of things in his county (as he himself shows) and the increased rents are owing entirely to the increase in population and

115

consequent demand for supplies from the manufacturing neighbourhoods.-
Yours truly,

"AN OUT-AND-OUT RADICAL."

SIR, - In your Monday's issue "An Oxfordshire Landlord" (page 87)
commences his letter with this sentence: "In this village 12s. a week is the
ordinary pay which the farm labourer receives all the year round; besides this
he gets 3*l.* 4s. for haymaking and harvest; every labourer also can get a quarter
of an acre of allotment." This is a weekly average of 13s. 3d., and "Landlord"
complains that his men "appear to eat too much rich food and consume too
much beer"; in fact, according to "Landlord's" letter, the lot of the agricultural
labourer seems to be well-nigh all beer and skittles. No work which is painful
on account of its severity, rich and ample food, respectable clothing for the boy
chaps, girls to arm about on Sundays, educated free in their native villages,
able to marry the girl of his choice, better off than most gentlemen, leisure to
sit under his own vine and plum tree quaffing ambrosial nectar in the form of
Bass's pale ale, &c. Well, Sir, I am thankful that "Landlord" has wisely
refrained from naming this El Dorado, which seems to be a veritable Land of
Goshen, with Cannan thrown in, for the labourer. Had he done so I fear that
the way to this paradisiacal abode would ere now be thronged like the road to
Epsom on a Derby day, with men anxious to better their condition. But one
story is good, &c. I only hope that your Special Commissioner, when he has
finished in Essex, will itinerate to Berks., Bucks., and Oxon., and he will send
you letters which will "wring the heart; if it be made of penetrable stuff."
Wretched, tumble-down shanties, winter wages 9s., summer, 10s., homes
where a small quantity of fresh meat is an unknown luxury, respectable
clothing for their children an impossibility, quarter acre allotments
conspicuous by their absence, 10 to 20 poles being the limit, bread, lard, and
potatoes being the "rich food" upon which the children are raised (I speak that
I do know, and testify that which I have lived upon), a life of toil and drudgery,
a continual struggle to make both ends meet, getting behind in winter, the few
shillings extra earned during the harvest not sufficing to rub off the "score" at
the baker and grocer's; work and struggle, struggle and work, and the hated,

Oxfordshire village where the average wage of the tiller of the soil is 13s. 3d., but if there is it is the historical exception that proves the rule. I have inquired diligently, but I can find no one who can locate it, and it has never been heard of by, yours, &c.,

FREDERIC C. RIVERS, Oxford.

SIR, - Is farming as unremunerative as other businesses? Decidedly not, as shown by the insufficient capital taken into it, and the inability of farmers to pay comparatively adequate manual wages. Men farming their own lands are generally in a worse position than tenants, their farms having come to them, or been bought by them at much higher prices than land can be rented at, the tenant being in the position of a hirer, or in another sense a borrower (if Mr. Walter Bagehot's theory is correct, which is not disputed), then as a hirer he is better off, or makes a better return on his capital than the man having the land his own. The small owner and occupier never could hold his own - it was always a downward course. Circumstances are not altered to make his lot in any way more hopeful. In a somewhat remote Berkshire parish of arable and meadow land from which I write, twenty-five years ago there were no garden allotments, and very little attached garden to any of the cottages. At different times during that period there have been laid out in convenient and different parts of the village about 100 garden allotments, from 10 to 15 poles, at differing rents, up to about 3*l.* per acre, free of all taxes, admirably cultivated, and no one unlet. In the early days of laying out a plot, the observation of one of the after occupiers at the time was, don't make them too large or they will not be half done. The day pay of men in this parish is 2s., a weekly average for overtime and piecework of about 17s.; carters and shepherds about 2s. or 3s. in addition. Cottage rents from 1s. to 2s. 6d. weekly. A good many of the young men go away to London or large towns, into the police or on the railways. In point of numbers we remain in statu quo. There is a good natural increase to keep up the supply - considering "only the old and fools are left behind," it does them credit. If any truth attaches to what we read is going on in Canada and the States, it is much the same as here - people flocking into the towns, at the same time large tracts of land are to be had almost for the asking. At present there is no feasible suggestion how we are to keep the labourer upon the land. In this parish there has been a revolution in my time amongst the labourers in the way of dress, living, food, education, sanitary matters; and in the village street on a Sunday one would wonder where all the ladies and gentlemen came from.- Yours, &c.,

ONE WHO HAS LIVED IN THE PARISH SIXTY YEARS AND FARMED IN IT OVER THIRTY YEARS AS BOTH TENANT AND OWNER.

Mr. John Chandler, Stonor-road, West Kensington, writes: The only remedy for the present disastrous state of agriculture will, I venture to submit, be found sooner or later in the purchase of land by the State and the subsequent letting by the same to such tenants as by their antecedents and knowledge can till it to the best advantage. In Mill's "Principles of Political Economy" he sums up the advantages and disadvantages of farming on a large or small scale to the advantage, I think, or the latter. There should be a Minister and Board of Agriculture to oversee the State farms, that the tenants should produce as much from the land as possible, and to settle all disputes, and no man should be permitted to hold a farm who did not and was not able personally to superintend it.

Mr. R.W. Perkins, King Stanley, Gloucestershire, regards all proposals to reform the present system by methods which would have the effect of absolutely depriving the landholders of the great power which under improved conditions they would be capable of exercising to the general advantage, and which many of them would only be too glad to exert, as mischievous. The object, he says, of the Legislature should be to induce the possessors of the land-surface of the country to fulfil the obligations, duties, and responsibilities which, as the holders of land (for owners, in the absolute sense, they are not), they constitutionally owe to the State, and not, by the purchase of their holderships, to pay them for their neglect, and at the same time to deprive them of the great opportunities which they would enjoy of being useful. He proposes the following as a test-question for the industrial electorate to submit to Parliamentary candidates, viz.: "Will you pledge yourself to support a demand for the institution of properly-constituted authorities fairly representing industrial interests, and armed with the necessary powers to compel, as occasion shall arise, the holders of land to let, for any approved purposes, to any suitable and approved applicants such portions of the soil as they (the authorities) shall deem it expedient to demand, at a permanently-fixed annual charge for the use of such portions of land respectively, and which annual charge shall in no case exceed the rental value of such land immediately antecedent to the time of any such letting?" Mr. Perkins believes these propositions to contain the true principle of land nationalisation.

Mr. Andrew Reid, Leyton, writes: It would be a most happy conclusion to the interesting and powerful articles by your Correspondent in *The Daily News* if we could establish some strong organization of the liberation of the rural population. The agricultural labourers are at present powerless to associate together effectively. They are not in the position of the working men of the towns, who can form their trade unions. I should like to see formed the "Peasants' National Emancipation League," and before the general election. Its programme should be the parishisation of the land. These should be its objects - 1st, to make a fair wage a first charge upon the land; 2nd, to establish parish councils with facile powers - (a) to take land compulsorily and to let it out permanently to the labourers in large quantities and convenient situations, (b) to loan timber and materials for building homesteads, and seeds, plants, trees, pumps, implements for using the land; (c) to free villages and hamlets by paying out rackrenting and overbearing landlords owning the same; (d) to build and equip agricultural and technical libraries and schools, threshing mills, jam factories, &c.; 3rd, to establish a free bench of justice.

(FROM "THE LEEDS MERCURY.")

The articles on "Village Life" appearing in *The Daily News* continue to throw an interesting light on the habits and pursuits of our rural population, and the temperate, almost restrained, tone in which they are written will not detract in the least from their value. The magnates of rural England, spiritual and temporal, are on the whole dealt with tenderly, and the reader, who might perhaps have looked for a little political declamation, is left to judge for himself as to how far existing things justify the demand which is being made for parish self-government. Pleasantly anecdotal, too, is the writer

119

occasionally. He tells of one village where he came across a relic of ancient intolerance in the shape of a little wooden Primitive Methodist Chapel on wheels. Years ago a little company of humble worshippers desired the then lord of the soil to' grant them a site for a chapel, and when refused they built themselves this moveable conventicle. Such audacity did not pass without remonstrance from high quarters, and means were found, it is asserted, to punish the most refractory of the Methodists. The incident, however, is only a memory now, and the chapel on wheels has since fallen into commercial hands. There is another amusing little story with regard to village charities. The writer came across a remote hamlet where everybody had the loan of a blanket, and he was very much astonished to discover that every spring they were sealed up in a calico bag by the rector's wife, and unsealed y the same benevolent individual on the return of the cold winter nights. In many of these places, the writer assures us, the domination of the parsonage and the hall is complete, and the villagers, to use his words, "have to be very careful." At a time when the lot of our rural population is exciting such anxious concern, these articles are highly interesting and instructive.

Friday, September 4, 1891

SIR, - My ancestors were cultivators of the soil, as tenants, in one village, for more than four hundred years. In all that time none of them ever became the owners of a single acre of land. They were continually improving for the landlord, although they must have paid for it many times over; and this condition of things has prevailed in all our agricultural villages for ages, and still continues, as if the only possible method of life in the best of all worlds. As ordinary freehold agricultural land is now selling in this district at from 20*l.* to 30*l.* per acre, the tenant who pays 30s. per acre rent pays the full value of the land every twenty years; and yet everybody wonders why the labourer and the tenant farmer leave their native soil and seek their fortunes elsewhere. The wonder is that such a system, of adding to the wealth of the rich by the impoverishment of the poor, should have held its own for so long. Surely our impoverishment of the poor, should have held its own for so long. Surely our tenant-farmers will soon see that the perpetual ownership of the land without occupation or cultivation is the crying evil of our time, and demand some equitable law whereby the cultivator of the soil shall become the owner at the end of a lease of thirty years or so. The price and period could be calculated to the fraction of a penny and a day, and then, whether a man cultivated an acre or ten thousand acres, he would have every inducement to get the most from his holding, and at the same time self-interest would prevent him from beggaring the soil. It is astounding to me that this principle has not been adopted by the Farmers' Alliance, or that some union of tenants for their own defence against the owners of the land has not yet been formed in this country. I am, Sir, yours &c.,

"A FARMER'S SON", Banbury   Sept. 2.

SIR,- Although in a measure prepared for the revelations of your able Special Commissioner on the subject of the depopulation of the villages in the Eastern counties, it will perhaps come as a surprise to your readers that the recent census shows a similar condition of things in some of the more purely agricultural portions of Kent. In canvassing these districts, I have found the following points in a village programme meet with considerable support from the labourers:

> 1. Village Parliaments.
> 2. Power for the Village Parliament (a) to acquire land compulsorily for public purposes; (b) to let allotments and small holdings at a fair rental, with fixity of tenure; (c) to build labourers' cottages.
> 3. A Village Métropole, with free reading rooms, facilities for recreation and amusement, entertainments, &c. The class of refreshment to be supplied to be the subject of local option. Free baths to be attached to the métropole.-

Yours, &c.,
Sydney Hallifax   Sept.2.

SIR - I have read with much interest the letters in your columns on this important subject, and venture to offer a suggestion as to one of the many causes that operate to send the young people to the towns - viz., the education given to the boys and girls in the Board and other schools. Surely the object of education should be to fit men and women for their sphere in life, and to enable them to do better work than their fathers and mothers who had not the same advantages. But is this the case? One hears on all hands that the boys are too idle to work when they leave school, and the girls refuse to soil their hands with work that their mothers did when they were young; and as they cannot live in idleness on their parents, they prefer to go into the towns in the hopes of finding some more genteel employment than hoeing and weeding, &c.

Now if these boys and girls were given a knowledge of botany and natural history, if they were taught during part of their school life the best way of rearing poultry and keeping bees, the newest way of making butter and cheese, and how to turn plots of ground to the best advantage with the spade, they would have an interest in the life of the country which they now completely lack. In villages where the cottagers are able to keep a cow or two there might be started co-operative dairies, where the milk would be received and the girls employed in the manufacture of butter and cheese and the potting of cream for market under a competent manager. Nothing could be more pleasant than the work of a well-conducted dairy; deftness of hand, and great cleanliness are needed, and the enormous demand for the above-mentioned commodities on our large towns would keep the girls constantly employed, besides giving their fathers an incentive for keeping cows. Where the maidens are comely and intelligent the youths will be content to stay as a rule. It seems to me that great possibilities lie dormant throughout the rural districts of England, and that if knowledge and capital were brought to bear our villages might supply the dairy produce that now comes from France and Belgium, and happiness and plenty reign throughout the land.- Yours, &c.,

"A TOWN-DWELLER IN THE COUNTRY,"   Sept. 2.

"A Lover of Suffolk," as one well-acquainted with the neighbourhood of Ixworth for more than 30 years, sends a few comments on our Special

Commissioner's letter of August 29th (page 66). "It is terribly true," "A Lover of Suffolk" says, "that Suffolk labourers are badly paid, badly housed, and badly fed; that there is a dreary absence of outlook for those who remain on the land, and that the population is diminishing by migration to the towns. But, bad as things are now, they were worse twenty or thirty years ago. In one house I knew a boy who amused himself as he lay in bed with a broken leg by counting the stars through the roof. In another the wind used to come in at a hole in the wall and blow the candle out as the mother sat sewing. Both these houses are gone. A third, whose indignant mistress went to tell the landlord that if the thatch was not mended 'she'd be raised out of her bed,' was made watertight years ago. Nowadays, if lack of energy or love of the old place, or special difficulties in finding a new cottage cause people to stay on in a house which is tumbling to pieces, the opinion is freely expressed among the neighbours that some one is to blame. Formerly bad houses were looked on as a matter of course. If your Commissioner were a resident in these parts instead of a visitor, he would probably distribute his blame somewhat differently. In the village which I know best (and I am told in others) the greater part of the bad houses belong not to large landlords, nor to farmers, but to small owners of various shades of politics - men who have little money to spare, little enlightenment in sanitary matters, and (to judge by the petty tyranny some of them practise) little sense that the position of landlord brings with it duties as well as rights. Some insist on their tenants dealing at their shops, and take care that the bills are pretty closely paid up, while the rent is allowed to run because the furniture is security for that; and so the tenant has to be content with the goods the landlord chooses to supply and the price he chooses to put on them. Rent here is paid once a year, at Michaelmas, with six months notice on either side - an arrangement which has its good and its evil side, but probably on the whole tells in favour of the tenant.

As to bad water, I could tell a pitiful tale of typhoid in one place and diphtheria in another from drinking pond water, but this is on the decrease. Landlords can now be compelled by law to dig a well where more than a certain number of people are without proper water supply. Your Commissioner speaks of the workhouse as the final goal of a labourer's life. In this I think he is mistaken, as regards this part of the country. Out-door relief is the rule for the aged, the 'house' being a very rare exception. Whether out-door relief at the rate of half a stone of flour and from 6d. to 1s. 6d. per week is to be preferred to life in the union may be doubted, but as a matter of fact it is preferred, though how the old people contrive to exist on it they probably could not tell you themselves, and one of the saddest things about a labourer's life is that he has nothing better to look forward to than this. Allotments are happily plentiful and answer well for those who are strong enough to work them themselves. Even those who have to pay a neighbour to dig and reap reckon that something is left for themselves after the crop is sold and the rent paid, so that parish pay is eked out in this way to some small extent in some cases. But the problem of how to care for the aged, without taking away all incentive to thrift in the young, is undoubtedly one of the most difficult connected with country life. It is some comfort that things are not so bad as once they were, but it is sad to think that the improvement is mainly due to the thinning of the population by migration to the towns. The country physique tells in town life and the villagers more than hold their own there. They rise perhaps to better positions, but are they not helping to crush down by their competition the 'submerged tenth,' helping, if not directly, in their own persons, then indirectly to swell the number of the unemployed? And the improvement, such as it is, is hardly maintained, it has not increased during the last few years. Wages are lower now than they were just before the agricultural depression began. A strike would be useless, the farmers can give no more as things are now. One farmer after another goes bankrupt, and gives up his farm. What wonder that the weeds, this rainy season, are gaining on us? The farmer must employ as little labour as he can if he is to keep his head above water, and to look at some of the fields one would think the wholesome saying was forgotten which we heard quoted in the time of a 'look-out' in the neighbourhood: 'Once let the weeds get ahead, and they sit down with ye to ivery meal and eat the victuals out of your mouths.' Neither is it any use blaming the landowners. Many of them have let the family house and shooting, and gone away to economise. One farm was let to a hardworking man, of good reputation as a farmer, for no rent. The last tenant had let it down, and the landlord was glad to have it farmed on any terms sooner than have it on his hands. But, in spite of its being rent free, the tenant found himself sinking deeper and deeper into difficulties, and before the year was out he committed suicide. For such a state of things as this it is difficult indeed to find a remedy, but it is something to know the facts."

"B.W.", in a rejoinder to correspondents who have replied to his letter of the 30th ult.(page 100), says: As to building houses to pay a clear 4 per cent., I repeat I have yet to learn, and shall be glad if either "W.G." (page 104) or "J.F.S." (page 107) will show me the way to do it. The latter quotes figures to show that four-roofed cottages, "plain, but substantial," can be built for 200*l.* per pair, but he omits to add the cost of the land and the sundry rates. I have had some experience in building, and have now two small cottages nearly completed, each containing on ground floor two rooms, 12ft. by 11ft.; scullery, 9ft. by 7ft., coal place, and w.c., and three bedrooms. Depth of land, about 110ft. Houses built with stocks and place, 34s. and 25s. per 1,000 delivered. Three cupboards, one closet over stairs, one ditto under stairs, copper, sink, water tank, and waste preventer to each house, with one cesspool for the pair, gardens fenced in and furnished in a plain way. These, I am sorry to say, will not return 4 per cent., clear, after paying poor, highway, and water rates, if I let them at 2s. 6d. per week. I may not be so clever as some people at building cheaply; although I buy for cash first hand, and at the best market I can find. My experience is that houses built in country places cost more for labour than if built in the town, owing to workmen walking to and fro and extra carting, &c. of material and let for less rent than if in the town. I should esteem it a favour if either "J.F.S." or "W.G." would "show me how to do it," either through your columns or privately. With regard to the condition of many of our labourers, I may be allowed to say that, having travelled to the States and in South Africa, I can fully endorse what Mr. Arthur Clayden says (page 101) respecting the bright prospects of an agricultural labourer as compared with the "unfortunate London clerks," who, to their credit it be said, keep themselves clean and respectable. It is useless attempting to shut our eyes to the want of thrift amongst our rural population. The labourers as a rule have no idea of saving during their best times, and when in good health. If our labourer cannot exert himself in his own country as he does when he is out of reach of charity and the poor relief he must expect to suffer.

"A Villager" says: The villagers of Yorkshire regard the following as the best advantages that could be granted them. He asks whether the Liberals are prepared to give them these: 1. Village councils chosen by one man one vote. 2. Allotments. 3. Free libraries and reading rooms in every village. 4. Labour-paid candidates for Parliament. 5. Magistrates chosen by the people.

"A Cornish Farmer's Son" writes:- It is estimated that we are wasting annually over fifty millions' worth of manure. If put upon the land and raised in the shape of food it would give a return of two hundred millions. This surely would enable the British farmer to pay all charges incumbent upon it, and would place him in one of the first and foremost ranks of commerce. The future farmer must be a well-trained scientist, and the future labourer must be taught the best principles of husbandry and maintenance of health, and the future female servants must be properly instructed in all domestic duties previous to becoming wives and mothers, so that there shall be no waste, no want, no illness in the house (this implies that they must have proper houses to live in), as the true economy of nature affords ample and sufficient for everybody, providing nothing is wasted. On the contrary, as sure as anything is wasted, so sure will want overtake us. The cards will now have to be re-shuffled and the game commenced anew - the farmer first, the labourer next, and the landowner last.

Mr. Daniel Rogers, The Welcome, Wimbledon, is in favour of allowing farmers to work out their freehold in twenty years.

"A Lover of the Old Country" writes from Wales that the land does not support the people because the land does not belong to the people. With free trade in land we should be able to get at the commercial value of land, which in the present state of monopoly is utterly impossible.

A.W. says: Your correspondent "B.W." appears (page 100) to have read my correction of a previous letter, and questions the statements I made concerning the possible rentals of labourers' cottages from a financial point of view. If he will refer to my letter which appeared in your issue of the 28th ult. (page 79), he will find that I drew attention to the need of a properly constituted local authority being given compulsory powers to obtain land by a simple and inexpensive process for parochial requirements, amongst others the building of labourers' cottages upon allotments. With compulsory powers we may safely say that in almost every rural parish ten acres of suitable land for such a purpose could be obtained for 500*l.* (in many parishes possibly for half this amount): that six pairs of cottages may be built upon half-acre plots, allowing half an acre for each cottage. The twelve cottages with a quarter of an acre of land each and the fourteen cottages with half an acre of land each can be built with the necessary sanitary arrangements for 2,600*l*., an average of 200*l*. for each pair of cottages, the total cost 3,100*l*. Money has usually been borrowed for local requirements at 3½ per cent., but interest has been reduced generally, and 2*l*. 12s. 6d. per cent. is about the sum paid by the Government, so I am within the mark when I say that the money required ought not to cost more than 3 per cent. The County Councils could borrow it at this rate, thus the interest on the cost of the land and cottages would be 93*l*., rates 18*l*., repairs and insurance 12*l*. 5s.; total, 120*l*. 5s. The income from twelve cottages at 2s. per week, 82*l*. 9s.; and fourteen cottages at 2s. 6d. per week, 91*l*.; total, 153*l*. 8s.. The balance in hand each year towards contingencies or the repayment of the principal, 33*l*. 3s.

"One From the Plough" says:- The very best thanks of the agricultural labourer are due to you for opening up his lot and giving to the world a faint idea of how he lives, what his hardships are, and last but not least the uncertainty of his employment. What is wanted is smaller holdings, with longer leases, and then we shall get a better class of farmers, for very many good men are shut out of farms on account of the size and the want of sufficient capital to work them. A better class of cottages to live in is also wanted. Whoever takes an acre of land must work upon it, and not (following the example of too many of our large farmers) be continually running away to the fox hunt, the race course, and the drink shops, or their experience will be the same - bad crops, full of rubbish, in place of a good clean crop.

"Bedfordshire" writes: Thanks to your kindness in giving a few columns daily for the discussion of the question, many good suggestions have been made. There is no doubt that the small holding plan and the better housing of the labourer would be steps in the right direction, but we also want recreation for the young men, something beyond sitting in the village beerhouse listening to tales of imaginary battles by one of the community who has been a soldier or sailor, or to unmusical songs by one who is known as a "jolly good fellow, but fond of his beer."

Saturday, September 5, 1891

SIR, - I have read with great interest the letters of your Special Commissioner respecting the depletion of our agricultural population. He has, I am sure, endeavoured to state the case fairly, but as a landlord I do not think that he fully realises that after all it is the landlords who have suffered far more from the depressed state of agriculture than the farmers or labourers. Indeed the latter class are far better off in many respects than they ever were, they have better houses, cheaper clothes, better food, and (thanks to the present Government) free education. The farmers have suffered severely, but their rents have been greatly reduced all over the country. But the unfortunate landlords must still go on, in spite of reduced rents, increased taxation, and more expenditure on their properties, so as to keep them up to the status of modern ideas. No doubt many are in the same position as I am, possessors of estates from which their fathers and grandfathers derived a fair or substantial income, but now actually losers every year. Take, e.g. a farm of 600 acres which my father used to let at 1*l.* per acre, but which I now cannot let at all, and have to farm myself at a loss. Of course the real reason is plain enough, viz. - the great fall in the price of corn, inevitable, I daresay from the Free Trade principles which we have adopted, and which have resulted on the whole in such great benefits to the people at large. Still, the fact remains, our farming and agricultural interests are terribly depreciated. It no longer pays to grow corn, and we lay down our land in grass, thereby throwing out of employ thousands of men whom we used to employ on our farms. Everyone who has a practical knowledge of the subject knows that "Village Parliaments, &c.," would all be perfectly useless to remedy the present state of things in our purely agricultural districts, and until some way is found of making farming pay as it used the labourers having no employment will of course go off to the towns. The only chance a farmer now has of making his living is by keeping his "labour" account as low as possible.

"A WILTSHIRE LANDLORD"   Sept. 4.

SIR, - X, is a little village in the Midlands, beautifully situated on a river. All the land, houses, &c., in the place belong to the squire. There are only old men, children, and married labourers in it. The houses are, with very few exceptions, old, beautifully picturesque, with roses and other flowers creeping over them, but far from being perfect as regards comfort and sanitation. The squire looks after his people well in times of sickness, sending them many delicacies. The people are absolutely and completely under his thumb. He interferes in the most private affairs of each household, and his word is law in all cases and to everyone. He is a very High Churchman, and he compels his people to be the same. The yell of the Boothite preacher and the jingle of the tambourining poke-bonneted lass have never disturbed the quiet of this sleepy village. It would be no good their parading X, for none would dare to come and listen to their vehement harangues, although virtually bound to attend the meetings of the E.C.U. The labourers are expected to attend services on Saints' days, and the squire pays those present as if at their work. He himself collects in church, so that all are observed, and most naturally hesitate to let the plate pass without some contribution. No unmarried girl fit for service is allowed to stay at home with her parents without permission from the squire. One poor thing had a misfortune, and the parents were bound to send her out of the village, on penalty, doubtless, of being turned out of their old home; and she was not permitted to return to that village to see her parents except by permission of the squire. The miller was a man of independent means and mind. He left, and the mill was advertised in a Church paper, and amongst the inducements held out to tenants were "Church Privileges." There are no allotments, for such might make the labourers somewhat independent. Now, who on earth is surprised at young men refusing to live under such a regime? The village school is under the direct management of the clergyman, who is nearly related to the squire. You may be sure that they are strictly educated in the doctrines of the Church of England. There was a meeting of churchmen held in the neighbouring town, under the chairmanship of the Bishop, who instanced, as one of the signs of the interest which the working men took in the Church, that eighteen villagers had come over from X specially to attend the meeting. The Squire of X had carted them over like sheep, so as to make a display. I should very much like to mention a matter of great interest to the ratepayers. During a scarlet fever epidemic I visited a labourer's family in this district. He was a waggoner earning 15 shillings per week, on which he kept a wife and five children. He was allowed to inhabit a kind of house consisting of a kitchen and two bedrooms - the latter really one room partitioned into two. In one slept the husband and wife, and the child with the fever; in the other the remainder of the family. This family was too poor to pay into a dispensary or club, and consequently fell on the parish for doctoring. The doctor orders extra nourishment required, and consequently the ratepayers are compelled to make up for the deficiency in the man's wages.

The relieving officer informs me that such cases are quite common. Now this deficiency in wages - for farmers give "just what life requires, and give no more" - causes our workhouses to be filled with labourers incapacitated from further work by reason of old age or rheumatism, and such like ailments. Even if they have saved sufficient to join a club to pay the doctor, their wages are hopelessly inadequate to providing for an old age of any length. Our social system is hopelessly wrong. If a man works hard for a number of years, there ought to be something better than the workhouse for old age. If clubs can be turned into superannuation societies it will be a great step in the right direction. From my experience as a medical man, I affirm that workhouses are such horrid over-regulated prisons that I don't wonder at the poor preferring death to years of endurance in such uncomfortable abodes. Of course it is in the interest of economical ratepayers to stop out-door relief; but such is far fairer to those who are paupers through no fault of theirs, but owing to a ridiculous system of wage slavery. Land nationalisation and Socialism for me.

M.B. RHYS

SIR - I think the suggestion of a "Devonshire Squire" (page 105) that farming may be brought within the operation of a limited company is worth consideration. There is something more tangible in it than in the worthless mining and other speculations in which such large sums have been squandered of late. I do not see any reason why a company with a good directorate should not carry on the business of farming successfully, but I would suggest the adoption of the profit-sharing system. Give the labourers a percentage of the profits in addition to their wages, and they will have a direct interest in their

work, and the listlessness and discontent now so prevalent would disappear.-
Your obedient servant.
W.H.P.   Sept. 3.

SIR - As I am one who has migrated from the country to the metropolis, your
Special Commissioner's letters have been read by me with more than ordinary
interest. I think the real reasons why so many young fellows leave the country
districts are the small - miserably small - wage earned on the farm, and too is
the result, at least to a great extent, of the improved educational facilities of the
last twenty years. May I give you my experience. I am the son of a
Gloucestershire farmer, and received my education at the village school. I left
school at fifteen. At the time of my father's decease he was farming a farm of
120 acres. This was in 1876. My mother kept on the farm until 1882, when,
owing to the disastrous seasons and depression in trade, she gave up her
holding. During this time I stayed at home and managed, with the assistance
of a relative, her farm. I then obtained a situation as working bailiff on a
vacant farm in the neighbourhood. At the end of nine months I was idle, the
farm having been re-let. However, I obtained a situation as head herdsman on
the farm of a well-known Wiltshire nobleman at a wage of 15s. weekly. I
remained there two years, and it was during this time that I determined to
obtain a situation in one of our large towns. With this view I spent my
evenings in study, and ultimately obtained a situation as labour master and
assistant schoolmaster in a reformatory school. I remained there eleven
months, when I removed to my present situation as schoolmaster in a London
school. When I go home on my annual holiday I see my former school
companions, some of whom have saved a trifle, and keep a small grocery or
other shop. A few others, like myself, have migrated to the towns, whilst the
majority are either tenants of small holdings, general hauliers, or are working
as carters, herdsmen, &c., in the neighbourhood. I don't envy them. Their
wages average about twelve or thirteen shillings weekly; the only recreation
they can find is in the nearest alehouse, where they meet to discuss village
gossip, weather, crops, &c. No, Sir, when once a young fellow has set foot in
London, where he can earn more money, find recreation and enjoyment of a
hearty nature, he is not likely to return to his native place to low wages and a
dull life. It is undoubtedly hard for the townsman to be compelled to make

room, for so many sturdy, well-built countrymen, who are determined to make a way in life, but it will have to be borne.

The large farmer is, I am convinced, a better man than his neighbour who occupies a smaller farm, for the reason your Correspondent gives. Besides, the various farmers' clubs, dairy conferences, and other gatherings of a like nature, which have recently sprung into existence, diffuse much valuable, technical and scientific information, especially as to crop requirements, dairying, and the economical use of feeding stuffs, which is only seized upon and put into practical application by the large farmer. He is shrewd enough to distinguish new fads from real sound advice - witness his reception of some remedies which have been preached at him during the last few years. But anything which will tell him how to produce larger crops, more butter, and cheese of a better quality; or how to produce meat of good quality at a minimum cost, is well thought over, and in the end applied. The small farmer, as a rule, does not interest himself in these matters; but plods on after the manner of his fathers. He may, and I grant does, employ more labour on his land, but the results are not so profitable as in the case of the large farmer; as if he grows more per acre, he is generally compelled to sell to meet his rent, tithes, rates, &c., when the other holds until the market rises. This I know from actual experience and observation. There is much yet to be done in our villages. Parochial councils will give to the villager the interest he should have, and would willingly take, in the management of the affairs of his locality. Better houses, instead of the wretched hovels one too often seen, and better wages; reading and recreation rooms - these are the antidote to the village pot-house; and if in the hands of the parishioners themselves, will do more to keep them temperate than any amount of temperance lectures, *per se*. By all means let us advocate temperance principles; but in order to secure results it is necessary there should be found suitable rooms where reading, games, discussions, &c., may be carried on. These, if entirely in the hands of the people themselves, will prosper and extend, and prove a real boon to hundreds of country lads, who find at present that the Pig and Whistle is now their only club. Yours &c.

W.J.M.

Mr. G. Gunnell, Lynn, writes:- I am very glad you have taken up in the columns of *The Daily News* the important problem of "Life in our Villages." The greatest difficulty, to my mind, in this matter is the getting of truly reliable information. Your able Correspondent is shedding a flood of light on the dark spots of rural England; but in its very nature it must, taking into consideration the enormous interests involved and distance to cover, be but fragmentary. I was afraid, from his first letters, that he intended pronouncing in favour of large farms; that, to my mind, would have been a misfortune. My experience of large and small villages, depending solely on casual labour on large farms (excepting those who are hired for the year), is that there is chronic and general poverty always in existence, accentuated to a greater degree in times between seasons. I know of one large village in North-west Norfolk, population about 1,400, district purely agricultural, principally large farms, where it is no uncommon thing for whole families in the winter season to drift into the workhouse, because they cannot get work in the winter time on these large farms to keep body and soul together, and in the spring emerge again to try and pick up a precarious living for another year. I should not like to say this is typical of village life in general. But that it exists at all shows that there is something radically wrong with existing things. I have personally an implicit faith in small farms, and think therein lies our social salvation from present evils. There are districts that I am conversant with not 20 miles from here where there are large numbers of small farms. The people are comparatively comfortable, and no evidence of poverty exists. Rents are not high; in fact much the same as the surrounding larger farms. Under conditions like these land produces more, is better cultivated, and spreads over a larger area the good things of life, and although the work is hard and constant, it is not so hard, nor are the hours so long as those engaged in the ordinary work of the large farms, while the remuneration is much better. I know several cases of labourers who began with small plots of land, and are now keeping themselves entirely by their own industry on about 50 acres and from their own confession doing well. If such results can come from the present existing condition of land-letting with the general depression and low prices of to-day, surely some experiment in this direction might be tried. Access to the land on fair and proper conditions is what the labourer of to-day wants, either direct from the State or with rents fixed by a Land Commission. Why should he not receive

133

from our legislation some consideration? If he was transported to the sister isle, millions would be lavished on him, anything he might ask for he would get. But being law-abiding, docile, and for centuries the slave of the parson and squire, he gets the kicks while his brothers get the ha'pence.

"J.F.S." writes:- As "B.W." has asked me (page 125) for further information, may I say that the cottages he describes are not such as are altogether suitable for our agricultural labourers? He has evidently taken for his model the small houses found by hundreds in the suburbs of large towns, which are frequently inhabited by two families, and generally produce a weekly rental of from 5s. to 7s. The cottages to cost 200*l.* per pair, and to pay 4 per cent on outlay, at a weekly rental of 2s. 3d. or 2s. 6d., would be arranged as follows: Two rooms on ground-floor, one fitted as kitchen, with range and dresser, with cupboard under, the other room having fireplace and one or two dwarf cupboards, which are used as sideboards. On upper floor two bedrooms - one having a fireplace, and both having a large cupboard over stairs; w.c. and rain-water butt to each house, and a washhouse fitted with copper, common to the two houses. Earth closets are best; the product is a valuable fertiliser, and there being no cesspool, the wells are not liable to be contaminated. "B.W." has overlooked the fact that in my previous statement I allowed 15s. ground rent per house. The water supply "B.W." mentions, and consequent water rates, are almost unknown in the villages, but wherever a good water service can be had, it should be used for sanitary reasons, though probably an additional 25*l.* per pair will be required for plumbing work.

"A Kentish Man" says:- Perhaps just a few facts as to the life of agricultural labourers from two quite different districts may be of interest to your readers. One place is in the Weald of Kent. Wages, including harvest, haying, and hop-picking, average about 17s. per week the year round, out of which rent has to be paid - none too much. But my parish and the adjoining one, each of which has about 1,400 inhabitants, support 13 public-houses, and this at the expense of the wives and families and trade of the two places. The second district is in Devon, where my son has a farm. Five men are employed regularly on 60 acres arable and 130 of pasture and orchard, in all 180 acres. Four have 13s. per week, a cottage and garden, cider or its equivalent, 20 perch of ready cultivated potato ground, and scald milk and wood at very low figure, and one is kept in the house. I think this quite as good as Kent. I don't know much about the drink there, but I think that having cider, there is not so much spent. One reason why population decreases is that the girls are nearly all in service in towns, where they marry and remain, female servants being much in demand. While the above is not very roseate, it is certainly better than Essex and Suffolk.

"T.W.C.," Leicester, says:- I have followed with the keenest interest the series of articles on village life so skilfully rendered by your Special Commissioner, and can testify to their perfect accuracy. I passed twenty years of my life in an agricultural village in Norfolk, and have witnessed the constant and painful struggle for existence by the labourer, whose only goal is a pauper's grave. My object in writing is to corroborate your Commissioner's statement that drunkenness is not rife in the villages. If your Commissioner in his rambles should penetrate the wilds of Norfolk as far as a little village named Shouldham, he will find my statement correct. And he will also find there one of the best and largest-hearted clergymen that the Church of England contains. He is a man whose first care is the welfare of his people, and his life has been a series of pitched battles with Poor Law guardians, parish doctors, and landowners on the labourers' behalf. I should like to give one example to show his character. Some years ago a virulent kind of smallpox broke out in his village. The natives were naturally frightened, and the husband of a poor woman was unable to get anyone to perform the last offices to his dead wife. The kindly vicar, hearing of this, without hesitation, without fear of consequences, did his duty. He obtained the coffin, he placed the corpse within, closed it, removed the bedding and bed clothes into the garden and burnt them, and did all in his power to disinfect the dwelling. Was not that an act of sacrificial heroism? Would not the condition of the labourer be better could such men be multiplied? And yet such men, liberal as they may be, can bestow no permanent relief. Ground down by the farmer, who in turn is ground down by the grasping landlord, the labourer's only hope for a living in any degree of comfort is to escape to the town. "A few swedes (turnips) and a bit of fat or a ha'penny herring is quite good enough for a poor man's dinner," was the expression of a farmer living not far from the village I have mentioned to his labourers when they complained that his wages were insufficient to provide the bare necessaries of life. With any chance of a competency the labourers would remain in the villages. What they want is the land, and the land they must have if they are to be benefited, and through them the community.

(FROM "THE BRITISH WEEKLY.")

As widespread interest is taken at present in the conditions of rural life and has been stimulated by the remarkable series of letters in *The Daily News*, we have addressed to a few experienced Nonconformist ministers a letter asking the following question: "What immediate legislation do you consider practicable and expedient to arrest the exodus of the people from the villages and rural districts?" We print this week a first instalment of the replies received. From some of these replies in *The British Weekly* we make the following extracts:

The Rev. Walker Legerton, Brentwood, says:- "The account given by the Special Correspondent in *The Daily News* is a true picture of the state of things; there is an exodus from well-nigh every village in the country, as the recent census reveals. I must say I do not see how it is to be prevented. Village life is dull. Young people like life, hence they go to large centres. The pay is small, but under present circumstances it cannot be more. Farming does not pay. In many cases the farmers are worse off than the men, while the men have nothing to lose. I know of many once well-to-do farmers who have been brought to almost want. The tithe, tax, and rent more than swallow up what the crops realise; there is little left for labour. I wish I could see a brighter outlook for our village life. I am glad the subject is claiming public attention."

The Rev. E.J. Dukes, Bridgwater, says: Nonconformity teaches young people to have a sagacious and independent mind which they use to run away to broader fields and pastures new. The schismatic spirit of the Establishment has also helped to deplete the villages of multitudes of their most intelligent and active inhabitants. He has seen great numbers leave for towns and colonies because there was no chance at home for Dissenters. Mere disestablishment will do little to amend this thing, but perhaps parish councils, or village councils, to which the national property, such as tithes, churches, schools, &c., could be handed over, would do much to bring about the happy day when every steady and capable man and woman would have a fair chance in the race for a living. A Wiltshire minister says: We want a class of small freeholders in our villages, cultivating their own land and gradually effecting on it such improvements as the right of ownership alone can encourage.

The Rev. D.R. Morgan (Stroud) wants the Allotment Act, which he says is at present worse than useless, made workable, and he also suggests that farmers should be enabled by legislation to purchase their own land.

The Rev. Thos. G. Crippen, Milverton, Somerset, also desires among other things the improvement of the Allotments and Housing of the Working Classes Acts, and he adds: "In agriculture the landlord, if not exactly a middleman, is a prolific manufacturer of middlemen. Agriculture will pay when its proceeds are fairly divided between the cultivating owner and the labourer. Usually it will not pay as it ought with the landlord for a sleeping partner. The great need of the nation, without which all other efforts can have but very limited success, is to restore the all but extinct race of yeomen, statesmen, or cultivating owners. If, by some means analogous to the Ashbourne Acts, we could break up half the huge landed estates into small freeholds, ranging in extent from 30 to 300 acres, we should soon see the regeneration, yes, the social salvation, of rural England."

Monday, September 7, 1891

LETTERS TO THE EDITOR

SIR, - Every Liberal is indebted to you for the admirable articles and correspondence in your columns on this question. The exodus of the rural population is a fact which everyone professes to deplore. The causes which produce the evil have been at work for centuries, and only by a variety of remedies will a cure be obtained. The result to be secured is the re-peopling of our country districts, and this can only be done by making it worth the while of the people to live there. This you will not do unless it is possible for a labourer to make up his income to 1*l.* a week. An ordinary allotment will not do this. South of the River Trent, it is doubtful if the income of the labourer averages 12s. a week throughout the year, and it is a total mistake to suppose that the extension of large farms, with improved machinery, will be any help to him. The valuable letter of your correspondent "A Leicestershire Farmer" (page 85) conclusively shows how much more likely small farmers are than large to pay good wages, from the fact that they work amongst their men, and, nothing being wasted, they have a much larger surplus out of which wages can be paid.

What is wanted is that farms should be cultivated by labourers in the prime of life, looking forward by means of hard work and thrift to occupying small holdings on their own account as they get older. They cannot get the means of doing this unless in addition to their work they have an acre of land and upwards at a fair rent and with security of tenure - in fact, roughly speaking, the three F's of Ulster fame. The advocates of large farms will tell you that this system will prevent their getting labourers. What it will doubtless do will be to secure for the labourers the alternative of either getting work all the year round and a livelihood of 1*l.* a week or of spending their time partly on their own land and partly on the farmer's. I venture to say it will be better for both farmer and labourer when this is the case. Everyone is familiar with the complaint of farmers that labourers do not work now as they used to. Other employers, I believe, do not make similar complaints. The fact is a man does not see why he should for twelve shillings a week be giving as much hard work as he can get 1*l.* for if he sold it in the town market. Where the men are well paid you can secure a good day's work without great grumbling.

Far reaching reforms will be needed to bring this state of things about. The power of preventing the sale of land by settlement must be abolished. Village Councils, with one man one vote, will have to be created, with compulsory powers for hiring land for allotments subject to the approval of a supervising authority, and if needs be for afterwards providing land for the purpose of small holdings. A good system of allotments followed by the abolition of the Law of Settlement, together with a system of land transfer based on the example of our Colonies, would speedily provide an outlet for the energies and hopes of the working people of our rural districts. The South Division of Worcestershire, where I am fighting the Liberal battle, would furnish numbers of instances where men have made good progress by means of small cultivation, but where, owing to our land laws, their further progress is impossible. So long as the prejudices of the few are allowed to prevail over the interests of the majority, and the House of Lords and the great landowners and the lawyers are permitted to uphold our present ridiculous semi-feudal land system, our villages will be deserted and poverty stricken. There is nothing which the good of our countrymen more imperatively calls for than the sweeping away of our present land system and the building up of a more righteous and popular law in its place. This work the Liberal party must strenuously enter upon or forfeit the confidence of the rural population.- Yours, &c.,

FREDERICK IMPEY, Hon. Sec. Allotments and Small Holdings Association
Longbridge, Worcestershire,   Sept. 4.

SIR, - Through your valuable columns a great deal has been said upon this subject, but very few practical suggestions have been made. In Gloucestershire we find farm labourers very scarce, although liberal wages are paid, and in most instances very good cottages with large gardens are provided rent free. I am not going to attempt to give any elaborate plan for the alleviation of the distress which many of your correspondents speak of, but I would suggest that situations should be found for those out of work in districts where men are required. I contend that a little practice is worth a great deal of theory, therefore I will only add that I am taking a farm at Michaelmas, where I shall require a cowman and a carter. I have two excellent cottages, with large gardens, which my men will have free, and I am willing to give liberal wages to good men, and I could also find many such situations. Thanking you for opening your columns upon such an interesting subject,
I remain yours very obediently,

T.H. PHELPS, Tibberton, near Gloucester.

(FROM "THE SPECTATOR.")

The Daily News is to be congratulated on its "Village Commissioner," the writer whom it has sent into the Eastern Counties to report on the condition of the labourers, and the reasons which are inducing them to desert the countryside. He is a man wholly free from the rancour which so frequently impairs the judgment of such "Commissioners." He is indignant, of course, at many of the facts which he describes, and full of pity for sufferers; but he can see other facts, and he is not full also of hatred for those who do not suffer. He can see an employer happy and a labourer miserable, without assuming that the happiness is a robbery and the misery a consciously inflicted wrong. The parson who is a Tory and a pessimist does not strike him as a sort of monster, but as a worthy old gentleman rather belated in his views; and when the clergywoman compels her parishioners to pack their loaned blankets in sealed canvas bags, he understands, while condemning such excessive interference, that it is dictated by sanitary wisdom rather than mere meddlesomeness. That is the temper which produces confidence in a writer's testimony, and it is therefore with keen regret that we read letters which, from the literary point of view, ought to inspire only pleasure. *The Daily News'* Commissioner confirms completely the impression which anyone must derive from the reports of the census-takers. The village labourer is going away from the village, and no other labourer takes his place. The strong men, the adventurous, and the young, all migrate to the towns, leaving behind them only the old, the weaklings, and the few, who, for one reason or another, cannot afford to depart. "Good" village or "bad" village, village with rotten and picturesque cottages, or village just rebuilt at endless expense by the landlord, the story is always the same. The indraft of the towns is irresistible, and usually in silence, but with decision, and "for good," the capable young men abandon country labour. If they are blacksmiths, or wheelwrights, or thatchers - that is, in fact, skilled artisans - they may stop; but they will not plough, or dig, or reap, or make roads willingly any more.

They go, and there are none to take their places; so that there are parishes where harvesting is already a matter of grave anxiety, and where, by the testimony of both farmers and men, the regular supply of labour is hopelessly insufficient. It really appears as if in a few years more, when the generation which still unwillingly remains on "the land" has passed away, the fields must either be left untilled, or must be cultivated on some system of which as yet none of the immense classes interested in the problem have so much as thought ... Is, then, the country to be deserted, restored to the wilderness, as parts of Massachusetts are, or laid down, throughout in grass, the process which each census shows to be slowly going on in England? Probably not; at least, no such calamity is yet recorded of any fertile land undevastated by conquest, drought, or famine; but the remedy may not be any of those as yet suggested. It may be found in a total change of tenure such as would attract to the soil all those to whom independence and a certain inexhausting sameness of life seem more than compensations for the feverish life of cities. It may be that, owing to some changes in the course of trade, our cities will decay, and become as unattractive to the peasantry as the decayed cities of Belgium or North Holland now are. It may be that the new motive-power, now almost in sight, may disperse instead of concentrating labour, and so bestow on agriculture everywhere the conditions under which it is carried on without difficulty in Lancashire. Or it may be, improbable as that solution now seems, that the manufacture of food may once more become one of the gainful trades, and attract as market-gardening does, wherever the market is sufficient. Whatever the change, we may be sure that it will begin precisely when the old system has broken down; that it will involve a readjustment between agricultural labour and capital which we shall hardly perceive, but which will be as effectual as the introduction of wages was in extinguishing payment in kind; and that it will be effected by those concerned rather slowly, and quite in silence, and not by an panacea or far-reaching plan which newspapers or their "Commissioners" can discuss in advance. The great transfers of industry are never effected by conscious volition from above. Just remember the history of our own Lancashire and Yorkshire. Not two centuries ago they were empty provinces, hardly recovered from the centuries of comparative desolation which followed the great devastation after the Conquest. To-day they are not only teeming with life, but present this nearly inexplicable phenomenon, that although they, more especially Yorkshire, must have been filled by immigrants from all England, must, in fact, have been "colonised" almost as completely as any division of Australia, they present characters as definite and as separate as that of any nation. In the case of those two counties, everything, even character and aspirations, adjusted itself, unnoticed at first, to the new circumstances and the new needs; and so it will be with the great problem of country life. It will be settled, but not by plans or by anything which can result from the most careful or impartial newspaper analysis.

The series of articles in *The Daily News* is another most important sign of the times. We again cordially congratulate our contemporary on securing the services of a correspondent so able. The force of the drear and telling picture which this correspondent has drawn has been augmented, not limited, by the evident conscientiousness and the palpable impartiality of the writer. It is a welcome proof of this that even the acridly Unionist *Spectator* has been forced to bear testimony to the ability, truthfulness, and convincingness of the letters.

Tuesday, September 8, 1891

(FROM OUR SPECIAL COMMISSIONER.)

The Allotments Act, I suppose we are all pretty well agreed, has proved a wretched failure so far as any direct action has gone; but the attempts that have been made to put it into force and the discussion it has called forth, and the attention it has been the means of directing to the subject of allotments have not been without their effect, and if small holdings could solve the agricultural problem it would, I think, be in a fair way of solution. Public opinion has done much, and in moving about the country I am struck by the extent to which allotments are being provided. Dr. Wallace suggested in a letter to *The Daily News* the other day (page 51) that I should make a point of inquiry of every labourer I talked with whether, if he could get land of a good quality, at a fair rent and on a practically permanent tenure, he could not make a good living out of it. I have not acted on Dr. Wallace's suggestion for it has seemed to me unnecessary to do so. Without any exception, so far as I can call to mind, allotments not of the best quality let at anything but a fair rent and on a tenure terminable at the caprice of the landowner or his agent, have been taken with an avidity which renders it quite needless to inquire whether labourers would be glad to have land on the terms suggested.

I have seen a great many allotment grounds, but I do not remember coming across any instance of a plot unable to find a tenant. I have seen some to-day on the Duke of Marlborough's estate near Woodstock, not by

142

any means the best of land, let in plots up to two acres at a rental of thirty-five shillings an acre. As allotment rents go that is moderate; yet an overseer informed me that· the farm out of which the plots had been taken was let at either thirteen and six or fourteen and six, he was not quite sure which - certainly not more than fourteen and six. They were all readily taken at this, and the general opinion was that they would pay very well, though none of the men I talked with seemed very enthusiastic over them. "It's better nor nothing'," said one man. "It'll put a few taters in yer pot." Very grim and sarcastic was the smile that puckered the old fellow's face as he told me the rents the poor labourers had to pay for their bits of plots as compared with the farm rents around. He didn't know exactly what the farmers paid, but he knew the allotment rent was some't over twice as much. "They does a little charity and they doubles their income," said he, with a sardonic grin. I talked with many persons in this village on the subject of allotments, and I found pretty much the same feeling everywhere. These bits of ground were a very good thing, some assistance, but nothing at all calculated to keep young men in the village. "They ha' been goin'," said an intelligent thatcher, "and they 'ool go." The state of things in that village he thought was scandalous. There waun't nigh cottages enough. People were bound to stay where they were. There was nowhere for 'em to move to, and they had to "pig in" just as they could. "There's quite big families in the village," said one woman, "and they on'y got one sleepin' room. It's no business to be."

"It's pretty nigh time somebody came round and spoke a bit for poor people," said one young married woman as she stitched away with unflagging energy at a white glove she was making. She was in one of a row of cottages with their backs towards the public highway and their fronts looking out over long strips of garden, beyond which were the new allotments that had been taken possession of last September, and were now full of a good crop of potatoes and beans and wheat and barley. The little places looked extremely pretty and pleasant with their vine-clad fronts and clean-looking rough-stone paving and picturesque old well and smother of flowers, and chubby, rosy-cheeked children playing about, the pictures of health and bucolic content. "He don't look bad on bread and lard and fat bacon, do 'e?" said a proud mother of a two-year-old cherub, who had come up towards us gnawing a green kidney bean by way of varying his somewhat monotonous diet. "No, he really doesn't. Is that all he gets?" "Yes, sir; that's about all." "Well, he won't starve while he can get plenty of bread and lard and fat bacon." "No, sir, that's true enough, if us could on'y be sure o' getting enough on't." The little places looked the very picture of peace, cleanliness, and comfort, and yet the impression one brought away after ten minutes' chat with the people was that they were constantly engaged in a hard struggle for existence, and were worried by a sense of the precariousness of their living. Just now there was work for all, but it was the winter that was the great dread, when the women very often had to keep the men. Yes, there was a bit o' glovin' round about there, and that helped 'em wonderful, and it was work as they could do at home and look after the children. But that ain't so good as it was. Prices had gone down a penny and twopence a pair, and the Duchess of Marlborough had set up a factory in Woodstock for makin' gloves by machinery. No doubt she meant it kind, but it had done 'em a lot o' harm. They found a'ready as there ain't so much work to be got, and prices was lower. They didn't know what'd come of it. The summer wages were twelve shillings, and some o' the men were very often out for three months and goodness knows 'ow they lived. Twelve shillings a week wasn't none too much.

I tried to get these women to give me some statement of the way in which they spent their twelve shillings. "Now just tell me," I said, "how people manage to live on twelve shillings a week." "Oh, Lord ha' mussy! I can't tell 'ow they does it." said one of them. "I dunno' myself 'ow the money goes. There's seven of us - me and my husband and five children, all too young to do anything but eat 'earty and kick out shoe leather." "Well, now, what do you manage to do with twelve shillings?" "Well, there's two goes for rent to begin with, and five and threepence a quarter for club money." "That is in case of sickness?" "Yes, sir; if my 'usband was sick he'd get ten shilling a week and the doctor." "Well, that is about fivepence a week, so that you have nine and sevenpence for feeding and clothing the seven of you?" "Yes, I s'pose that's it." "And how does that go?" "Blessed if I knows, sir. You goes to shop with five shillins, and it don't seem to go nowhere." "No, that it don't," chimes in another. "I often says to myself 'I dunno' 'ow the money goes.'" "Oh, drat the money!" exclaims another in the innermost corner of the room. "I wish there wa'n't none." It is a pleasant little scene of rural life this. There is no pressing anxiety as to the immediate future. The women now and then sigh, it is true, but they jest and laugh at their troubles, as we are all apt to do when our troubles are at a distance. It is the high tide of the year's prosperity, or it would be if the skies would only clear. And these villagers are among the most fortunate of their class. Some of them have a little supplementary industry to rely upon, and the summer pay of the men is twelve shillings. I have just left an Oxfordshire village where the normal summer pay till two or three weeks ago was ten shillings, and I have had indicated to me villages in this part of the country where wretched families have to subsist as best they can on nine shillings a week all through the winter. What wonder if now and again people die outright of cold and starvation.

Since beginning to write this my attention has been directed to a case that came before an Essex Coroner just after the last bitter winter. A woman died, and her husband was charged with "culpable neglect." Oh, the ghastliness of some of our judicial jokes! The poor fellow had struggled and striven through the cruel winter, he and his wife and family, on nine shillings a week with stoppages for wet days and snowy days, and days when the ground was frozen hard as the heart of the world around. It was proved that when in full work he had but nine shillings, and sometimes he had but two or three days work a week. A short time before the inquest he had been out of work for a month at a stretch. The coroner said the man couldn't be charged with culpable neglect. No; clearly not. Poor fellow! He had battled with hunger and despair and misery, and had come bravely through till towards the spring when times would be better. But the wife had grown thin and feeble. She had pined and starved, and presently came what the doctor called "accidental haemorrhage," syncope, and the children were motherless. There must be an appalling amount of this kind of thing coming within only a very short step of the final catastrophe in some of these remote villages especially, even where, in harvest time, all looks so peaceful and pleasant and prosperous. As I have said I have just left a village where till recently ten shillings was the weekly wage. The agricultural unionists have been round there, however, and two or three weeks before the ordinary time of harvest the masters consented to give twelve. "Do you think that will stand good after harvest?" I asked a man likely to know a good deal of the masters as well as the men. "No," he said, "I reckon it won't. As soon as harvest is over the farmers will get rid of all they can anyhow do without." "Are all the men kept on here during the winter?" I asked a labourer in one of the villages. "No; not all on 'em in the winter," he replied. "How many should you think are out in the winter?" The fellow took a puff or two at his pipe and looked out across the garden. "I should say there was a dozen or fifteen." "Married men?" "Most on 'em." "And what do they do?" "God knows. Starves I s'pose."

When a man has got a piece of ground it seems pretty clear he need not starve, even when he gets out of work in the winter. "Thank God I be independent o' the farmer this winter," said a labourer to an intelligent artisan with whom I was talking yesterday, "I get half an acre o' wheat, half an acre o' barley, and a quarter of acre of potatoes." There was wheat for his bread and barley meal for his pig. "With bread and bacon and potatoes I shan't starve, and it'll go 'ard wi' me if I can't find a job or two as'll pay the rent and a bit o' firin'." That looks like a solid, unquestionable advance in comfort and independence; but it is the special perplexity of a task such as mine - the task of moving about the country and talking with everybody, that one no sooner gets hold of a bit of firm and solid footing than he is sure to meet somebody who pushes him off of it. "My dear sir," exclaims a leading Liberal of lifelong standing in this constituency of Mid-Oxford, "this talk about affairs in the villages being put right by allotments is the sheerest humbug." His contention is that the advantage derived from the allotment, though real and substantial enough, will prove only temporary, and that the man who can make a little in this way will be able to work for rather lower wages, and that sooner or later he will be bound to do so. John Stuart Mill argued in the same way, as one of the correspondents of *The Daily News* pointed out the other day. The force of this argument may, however, be somewhat modified by the fact that the population of the villages is going down and labour becoming scarcer. On the other hand, the demand for labour is growing less. Machinery is still displacing men, and grass lands are extending. There is a balance of arguments for and against, and I must leave the readers of *The Daily News* to say which side has the preponderance.

I may have further opinions to quote on the subject of allotments in another article. Meanwhile I may say that I was very much struck by what I found in an Oxfordshire village to which I had been directed as one of the poorest and most ramshackle places in the county. I strolled through the place and felt at first that I had been misdirected. I leaned over a garden wall and talked with an old man who had just been digging up half a barrow load of splendid potatoes. They were "magnum boneys," said the old fellow, and very nice taters, and he proudly held up one or two for my inspection. I suppose the fine turn-out of potatoes put the old man for the moment in an optimistic frame of mind, for everything about that place seemed highly satisfactory. The cottages weren't so bad and rents were very reasonable, and they all had gardens and there were plenty of allotments and work for those who could do it and hardly anybody on the rates and nobody had left the place so far as he knew. Sons? Yes, he had sons, but no, they weren't in the village. One was in "Birmingham" and one was gone to America and another to Australia, and I rather think he said another had gone to Yorkshire. Why hadn't they settled in the village? Why, 'cause they could do better. The old man's wife now came out to call him to dinner, and they both agreed that it was a poor, beggarly place, and no good for nobody. They didn't want their boys to settle there. "I don't want my children to settle too close round me," said the little old woman, whom I put down to be over 70 years of age, with a healthily bronzed face, wrinkled all over, but full of vivacity. "I don't want 'em too close round me. I'd like 'em to be in Banbury or Oxford, where I could go and see 'em sometimes; but drat 'em if they be close round 'e, they al'ays runs to the granny, whatever's the matter. I like 'em best a little way off, and it is a poor beggarly place this. But there, the Lord al'ays makes a way for them as wants to do," and the dame chattered on, all the time seeming to hurry her spouse away to his dinner. She had been up that morning at six o'clock, had had a turn in the garden, and swept round her house and run round the village with her papers. Yes, she sold papers. She had got fourteen customers, and she got a halfpenny a piece out of 'em, only she had to pay twopence for carriage. Bless the Lord, very few people could do as she could at her age. I don't know how many yards o' lace she hadn't made since the New Year, and there were "arrands" to run, and one thing and another. I was told afterwards that she was considerably over seventy, and if anybody would offer her sixpence she would think nothing of trudging away to Bicester, four miles off and four miles back again, to execute any little commission, and it is, I am told, no unusual thing to see her come in with a basket on each arm and another tied round her waist.

Now these were the first people I spoke to in the village, and I found that when the old people united in pronouncing it a beggarly place they were quite correct in some respects at least. This was the village I have already alluded to as the place in which ten shillings a week had been the rate of wages up till just before harvest - a shilling a week lower than in any village I had found in Essex or Suffolk as the summer pay. Yet in this village allotments are to be had in abundance, and I am assured that the number of people who are doing well with them and who have pigs in their styes is quite exceptional. I ought to add, however, that the cottages, bright and pretty as they looked outside, were, some of them, of the most beggarly description, and are actually letting at three-pence a week, or with a bit of garden and a chain-and-a-half of allotment ground at fourpence-ha'penny. These, it must be understood, are not the rents to the labourers alone - the old man with the magnum boneys had not worked for a farmer for five years, and paid fourpence-ha'penny - so that low rents are not to be regarded as equivalent to pay for labour. This village struck me as affording a remarkable illustration of the tendency referred to by the leading Liberal whom I have quoted - the tendency for wages to keep down to bare subsistence. Here are the cheapest cottages, and the most thriving allotments, and the lowest wages I have found anywhere yet. In 1881 the population of this village was about 360 souls; now it is 325, and still dwindling. These are facts, whatever may be the inferences from them.

TO THE EDITOR OF THE DAILY NEWS.

SIR, - Life in the Villages, appearing in your paper daily, is interesting, and will, I hope, do much good. The anecdote about the Duke of Grafton and the Methodists (page 93) reminds me of a similar one concerning another large estate owner in distant part of the country, perhaps equally to the purpose, which ran as follows: The Methodists applied to the agent of the estate for a piece of land on which to build a chapel. He was secretly in sympathy with the movement, and brought the matter before the "Earl," in the most favourable light possible, but was refused with a warning to have nothing to do with these people. Upon the answer being made known to the leaders it was decided that a series of open-air prayer meetings should be held in the village. At this, the "Earl" was much annoyed, but so far curious that he told his agent of an intention to attend one evening in disguise and hear for himself what they really had to say. The agent at once gave the information in the right quarter, and to suit the occasion a "brother" specially powerful in prayer was selected to lead at that particular gathering. The weather chanced to be very unfavourable, and in the course of his appeal he shouted, "Lord, your servants want a chapel very bad, but there is one who refuses. You be a greater Lord than he, remove him out of the way, we beseech Thee." To this request the other people, in true Methodist fashion, called out, "Amen, amen." The following morning saw the agent before his master and told he must by some means stop the meetings; but he replied that he knew of no way to stop them, and was afraid to appear too much in opposition, having heard of several instances of direct answer to special prayers. Later in the same day the agent was sent for, and asked if there was any fresh news of the Methodists, he replied, "No," only that they were again praying, and made him quite ill. "Well," said the Earl, "I am feeling d----- queer myself too, go quick and give them the ground and bricks also."

T.M.

SIR, - Mr. T.H. Phelps (page 139) complains of the absence of practical suggestions in the correspondence under the above heading. Allow me to make one. The labourers are running away from village work, we are told, and crowding into the towns. Then let townspeople take to farm life. It is one of the most striking of our Colonial experiences that town-bred people often make the most successful farmers. One of my neighbours in New Zealand, who recently died leaving behind him a splendid farm of some 2,500 acres, worth at least 12,000l., was a Northampton shoemaker. Another successful farmer of my acquaintance was a Berkshire ironmonger. As I have watched these energetic men and their finely-developed sons at their field work I have often thought what a revolution would be effected in English rural life if the stupid notion could be got rid of there, as it is in the colonies, that there is something undignified in manual labour. We have so long pitied the agricultural labourers as a sort of social pariahs that we have overlooked their compensations. I have never met a New Zealand farmer - which is only another name for a New Zealand agricultural labourer - who was not in love with his work, unless it was some ex-English labourer who had brought with him his love of beer, and so kept at the bottom of the social ladder. The bulk of our young farmers are gentlemen event the plough-tail, and when work is done they enter readily into all the social amenities of life with a zest which I very much query whether the thousands of young clerks whom I meet on their way to the city could feel.

Farm life is now quite a different thing from what it was fifty years ago. Most of the drudgery is gone. Labour-saving machinery has revolutionised the whole thing. Just before I left New Zealand last year I saw a ten-acre field of oats disposed of by a Hornsby's self-acting reaper. Half a dozen young farmers were in the field, and in eight hours' time the whole crop was cut, tied up in sheaves, and stacked ready for carting. In the evening those more or less cultured youngsters would be at the farm house enjoying a game on one of Bennett's full-sized billiard tables. They would smile at the thought of their life being monotonous or in any sense degrading. Here then is at least one way out of the village-life difficulty. Let the whole tone of the thing be elevated by a better class of workers. The question of physique need not be a difficulty. I have seen a delicate youngster, who was little better than a spoilt lap-dog in his luxurious English home, transformed by out-door work on a colonial farm into a perfect athlete. It is the conventionalism of English society which is responsible for half our social distress.- I am, &c.,

ARTHUR CLAYDEN.

SIR, - Any effort to mend life in our villages must be based upon an actual knowledge of village life as it is. Nothing is more striking than the wide and often wild views of your correspondents, heartfelt in the generous wish to help on improvement, but the force for good stultified by want of "touch" with working farm folk. Take one point: It is accepted, with very little actual proof, that there are not labourers enough to till the farms. Well, no; but enough at the old wages, hopeless enough to endure the old serf-like conditions, not a lot of half-grown lads and great maids hanging about the villages, hungry and ready to take any pittance a farmer's conscience permitted him to offer them (which included doing five shillings' worth of work for three and sixpence), not enough of that class of labourers so common before Free Trade and railways sent bread and movement to bless our land, to set the idlers to work, and to reduce the numbers in our gaols and workhouses. Nor is it sufficient to offer high wages when work is pressing and expect skilled farm workers to turn up like dock hands at the East-end directly they are "wanted." But I contend that the assertions in my former letters are uncontradicted by the evidence of the life-like pictures of your Commissioner or the earnest letters of your correspondents. Give independent homes at fair rents, foster freedom and simplicity in the sale of land, and the men who understand and love country life will cluster on the good soils, and work on the improvable ones with a vigour and zest, startling to those who ignorantly call farm folk dull and spiritless. Let me say a word for the class of men among whom I have lived in close sympathy for so many years. There is no trade in which a year's work requires so many distinct forms of handicraft as that of farm workmen. Set a man, not a farmhand, to harness a plough team, to build a rick and trim it, to cut fodder and feed a herd of cattle, to handle a field of cut grass or corn, to cut a fence, dig a bit of ditch, or stop a broken hedge - to say nothing of the breeding and handling of stock, and you will understand that a long and intelligent apprenticeship is not too much to make a decent farm-worker. I hate to hear him called "Hodge" and branded as dull and heavy because his work, being solitary, and wanting more judgment than words, does not fit him to cope with the brisk chatter of the townsman. The result of the stroke of work which he does to-day cannot be seen till at least a year has passed, and its value and quality can only be grasped by experts. Dull and spiritless! Why directly he could bolt from his squalid home and eighteenpence a day he was off! But do not be alarmed, the children are swarming, and although this afternoon I saw ten in our school who could hardly speak, but who were learning to draw and sing. Let them see the bright, clean cottages (without the fear of eviction), the plots for sale, that father can rent and have a run for his pigs, or even for a cow, and in less time than it takes to grow and finish a crop of University B.A.'s there will be sturdy, independent farm workers enough who will not demand absurd wages or expect impossibilities from either farmer or Government.- Yours faithfully,

JOHN HIGGINS, Pylle, Somerset.

"Cantab." suggests that in the village schools agriculture should be taught, and he has no doubt allotment tenants would be glad of the boys' help on their plots. He is an advocate for cottage gardens.

Mr. George Webb, Plumstead, says: There is no doubt landlord, farmer, and labourer have all suffered through bad seasons, and necessary changes, brought bout through a variety of circumstances; but go where I will, the farmer, in a majority of cases, seeks to keep himself right, "by keeping his labour account as low as possible." There is about as much sense in it as killing the goose which lays the golden egg. Let us face it boldly. Instead of starving the land and grinding the labourer, why not go in at once for the three F's - fair rent, fixity of tenure, and free sale. Is it necessary that we should devote the tithe as now, seeing the Nonconformists are quite half of the religious people of England, and they keep their own ministers. The tithe would pay a lot of expenses the farmer has to meet now, and would, I venture to assert, benefit all three parties - landlord, farmer, and labourer.

"An Oxfordshire Tenant Farmer," defending "Oxfordshire Landlord" from the doubting remarks of Mr. F.C. Rivers, (page 87 and page 116) maintains that there is not a village in Oxfordshire where the agricultural labourer in regular work does not have more than 13s. 4d. a week on an average. The wages of 9s. and 10s. a week quoted by Mr. Rivers have not, he says, been paid of late. He admits that there are a few villages where the cottages are old and not good, but thinks that in the county of Oxford as a whole they will pass muster. He thinks the farmer worse off than the labourer. It is, in his opinion, the amusements and excitements of the town rather than the better wages which attract the young men. Those that are not "up to much" in town remain, and so he thinks the farmers get "the worst end of the stick." He advocates as much innocent amusement in the country villages as possible, with the view of retaining the young people. Our correspondent is severe upon allotments, and thinks the labourer must be taken for a natural fool by those who suppose that in a village far away from markets he will invest his savings in an allotment to which he will be a slave of every spare moment after doing his day's work elsewhere; but the writer refers to large allotments, and says "most farmers let their men have as much land as they require for vegetables" in his county.

"Western Counties" says, in reply to Mr. James Rayner (page 107) :- I advocate a fair rent and fixity of tenure because only by these means can you give that feeling of independence which it is for the best interest of the country to establish amongst its rural dwellers. To talk of robbing the landholders is the foolish talk which we always hear when the English land laws, carefully made by English landowners in their own interest, are attacked. The landowner who objects to a fair rent argues that he wants something unfair. To give what I advocate is an easy matter; it would create little difficulty and only be a development of the present system. Till something of the kind is tried, and it does not mean "coddling," it is ridiculous to recommend that men should seek a colonial home when England wants such sons. Mr. James Rayner means by municipalisation of land I do not pretend to know; but on one thing your correspondents are all agreed - the present plan does not give satisfactory results.

Mr. Charles Fox, Gloucester, writes: Your Correspondent should if possible visit the northern borders of Salisbury Plain, where wages (9s. a week) are at their lowest, where large unlet farms are miles in extent, and where spade-culture on the light sandy belt is carried on by scores of small tenant farmers, where the little man pays 4*l.* an acre for ten acres, and his neighbour 1*l.* an acre for five hundred of exactly the same quality the other side of the hedge. There he has paid these rents for many, many hard grinding years, raised wheat to pay a profit, raised a family to drift away to a less toilsome life in town. Let him calculate how much that 30*l.* a year extra rental would amount to as a resource in old age. Rent among this class of holding is the great hardship; they cannot get small holdings at small rents there, at all events. A practical suggestion of one grey-haired ex-chartist might be mentioned as typical of the decided views of the Wiltshire labourer - "That all unused farms should be put up to public auction without reserve annually, and that the people might club together to buy it for themselves." Some weed-choked farms on Salisbury Plain might be bought for very little more per acre than these labourers and market gardeners pay yearly in rent for similar land. They used also to consider it unfair that land laid down in parks or preserves should pay less in rates than the adjoining cultivated fields. This even to an unagricultural mind seems an anomaly.

"West Somerset" agrees with one of our correspondents who says it is the farmers' interest to make common cause with the labourers instead of hanging on to the landowning and (mainly) Conservative interest. A few small holdings of a few acres each may be made to pay; but I think (says West Somerset) you would find that in purely rural districts there would be much difficulty to make a living out of them, owing to a lack of good markets for their produce. Wages are not so low, compared with town wages, as your Commissioner seems to infer. In this district most of the men get from 13s. to 15s. per week, and with the purchasing power of money so vastly increased from what it was twenty-five years ago, the men are in much more comfortable circumstances than they were then. The greatest curse the labourers have is the drink shop, and I feel certain that at least one quarter of the wages paid in our village finds its way into the publican's till. The only thing to be done is to give the labourers cottages near their work and as much land as they can cultivate in their spare time, and in the larger villages some sort of recreation rooms and coffee house where the young fellows can spend a social hour without the debasing company of the taproom.

Mr. Henry Norton Palmer, M.A. Cantab., maintains that in the majority of cases a man is better off as a tenant than a small freeholder. The rent paid never exceeds 3 per cent. of the money he would have to invest in the purchase of the farm, and it is far better to pay a fixed rental, be relieved of all repairs, and to invest one's capital in the business of the farm. The larger landlords have been the salvation of the farmer and the labourer during these years of agricultural depression. He hardly knows a parish in England where land cannot be purchased by those who have the money, and where land is not constantly changing hands. It must not be forgotten that a labouring man gets some 50*l.* a year as wages, and in order to get this equivalent from cultivating his own holding the labourer must have not only capital but skill. Mr. Palmer is a great believer in co-operation, and would only be too glad to see co-operative farms and co-operative shops in our villages, and more co-operation amongst the labourers themselves, and the different classes for the general well-doing and the rational enjoyment of the whole community. Relatively, in Mr. Palmer's opinion, a villager is better off than a town-worker, so far as his work and his wage go, but there is no doubt he is monstrously dull, and anything that gives him occupation and rational amusement would be the greatest boon he requires.

Mr. W.M. Hawkins, Hundon, Suffolk, says:- I do not think that any of your correspondents have touched on one point that I have for a long time believed to be very important, viz., the bringing of wealth to the country places. There are many people who live in and about large towns who would prefer to live in the country if they could get houses with a few acres of land. They do not want the land to get profit from it, so much as for its convenience and healthiness. It matters not to their incomes whether they live in towns or in villages, but very many prefer the country. I know villages in Suffolk and in Essex to which it would be an unspeakable blessing if the landowners would build houses with land, suitable for people who have means to retire on. But if they will not do that and thus bring wealth into the starving villages, why do they not sell land ·for others to build on? I can name villages and small towns that would soon grow if land could be got to build on.

E.C.H. writes: In most agricultural neighbourhoods the wages are totally inadequate to supply the necessaries of life, and as a result, charities, so-called, exist in abundance in the form of clothing and other clubs. One of these clubs, known to E.C.H., was called a National School Clothing Club, into which the children of the school, or their parents through them, paid their weekly pence, receiving at the year's end certain additions from 6d. or 1s. to 2s. 6d., according to the amount deposited, but no money exchanged hands. With these cards duly filed, they were then to go to some draper of the vicar's choice and procure goods to the amount represented, leaving the tradesman and the vicar to settle accounts. Finding that several of the people were anxious to obtain their clothing elsewhere, the vicar was expostulated with, and replied that he had a perfect right to do what he would with his own. He was asked by what means money became his which had been deposited week by week by the members of the club, upon which he curtly declined to enter into any further correspondence on the matter. The same correspondent mentions another village where existed a clothing club, whose members were adults, under the supervision of a clergyman's widow. When the goods required were to be bought, all had to accompany her upon a day of her own fixing, to her favourite drapers, while she literally examine every article purchased and allowed nothing whatsoever to be chosen which did not meet with her approval, or she

155

thought unfitted to their station in life. Can it be wondered at, says E.C.H., that such a state of things should have disastrous results?

Mr. A. Martin, 122, Lancaster-road, W., criticises the panaceas prescribed by "A Villager" from Yorkshire (page 125), and concludes that the amendment of the poor laws, sanitary laws, and provision for old age are far more useful measures to the majority of the poor in the country than the points urged by that correspondent: and in these matters he says the poor must learn to help themselves.

Mr. Stuart Erskine, 4, Buckingham Palace Mansions, says:- The case against the landlords - grave and desperate though it may be - must necessarily admit of numerous qualifying and extenuating circumstances. He refers to a certain village in Northamptonshire, in which he had seen streets in a notoriously unhealthy and insanitary condition, in spite of the landlord, who had even compounded with his tenants by offering to build habitable and presentable dwellings in the room of the stinking hovels which it was their perverse pleasure to occupy. In spite, however, of his utmost and repeated endeavour, which only fell short of actually expelling the people from his property, the people continued to occupy their unwholesome houses.

"Dorset" writes: I have read with great interest the articles by your Special Commissioner describing the state of agriculture in the villages of the Eastern Counties and the letters of the many correspondents who have favoured us with their views on the same subject, and a very dark picture they have between them managed to draw of the state of the agricultural interest and village life in general. Thousands of acres of splendid land are said to be unlet and uncultivated, bearing such abundant crops of thistles, sufficient to stock the whole country, and all because farming doesn't pay, and tenants cannot be found for land at any price. But that seems a strange statement to us who live in this part of the country. Somerset, Dorset, and Wilts (especially South Wilts) have generally been looked upon as the poorest and most poverty stricken counties in England. I live on the borders of the three counties, so that I know something about each of them, but I know of no land out of cultivation, or any for which tenants cannot be found, unless it is a very large farm or land for which an unreasonable rent is asked. I know a man who a few years ago went into a poor dearly rented dairy farm, with a very insufficient capital, even for that small farm, and part of that capital was borrowed. (He milks something like a dozen cows.) He has now paid off the borrowed capital, well stocked his little farm, and just bought, and nearly paid for, seven or eight acres of corn land at a good price to add to his dairy land; and this he has saved out of his poor but dearly rented farm. I know another tenant farmer who milks upwards of 60 cows, and has some corn land, and I have no hesitation in saying he has saved upwards of 200*l*. per year for the last twelve or fourteen years, and this in a purely agricultural village in Wilts. But, remember, the persons referred to work themselves. Their wives, sons, and daughters all work. In the parts of the counties mentioned that I am acquainted with - and if there were ten times as many small holdings they would immediately find tenants - I have no hesitation in saying that farming does pay now if carried on upon the right lines, not I grant, quite as well as it did when bread was 1s. or 1s. 3d. per loaf, and the poor downtrodden labourers' pay seven or eight shillings per week, nor is it right it should. If farmers wish to make both ends meet, as their forefathers did, let them do as they did. Since I can remember, the generality of the farmers walked to market if it were a reasonable distance, or drove Dobbin in a very plain trap (some had nothing better than a cart), and put up at the most inexpensive inn in the town. Now they drive Mrs. and the young ladies with a slashing horse and a stylish waggonette, and put up at the head hotel in the town. In fact, they are not satisfied unless their turn-out beats the squire's. As for the parson's pony chaise, that is altogether beneath them; and then the father and sons must be seen in the hunting field booted and spurred and splendidly mounted like other people, and the style of living at home and abroad must correspond with all this. And because the profits of farming will not enable them to maintain this they declare farming does not pay.

"North Herefordshire" writes: Your correspondents have, so far as I have seen, curiously omitted to point out the grossly unfair manner in which mansions, with their parks, and woods, &c., are rated for public purposes, and the almost impossible task of righting this, as guardians are at present elected, and so long as petty sessions or quarter sessions are the sole courts of appeal for assessments. We, in the country, want our local authorities elected on a popular - one man one vote - basis, with an appeal court quite free of any "county families" influence. Another matter of vital important to rural prosperity is the question of railway rates; these at present are simply

157

prohibitive of any. progress being made with an extended mode of agricultural or horticultural development, or, indeed, any introduction of new industries being started with any hope of success in our small country towns or villages.

Wednesday, September 9, 1891

SIR, - I can confirm the statements of your correspondent, Mr. Charles Fox (page 153), as to the condition of agriculture on the northern borders of Salisbury Plain, and I desire earnestly to supplement his invitation to your Special Commissioner to visit that district. Land in that locality is now let to large farmers at 5s. per acre, only one man is employed on 600 acres, whereas we know by abundant experience that five acres would enable a family to earn a net profit equal to one pound per week. Thus one hundred men might be earning each twenty shillings per week instead of one man receiving 10s. Landlords refuse to let more land to small working farmers in order to keep down wages. In the meantime landlords import fox cubs by the score into the adjoining woods, and rush about after them over the cultivated land of small farmers, thus destroying their crops and making it impossible to keep poultry. In fact, the landlords are taking the country back to barbarism as fast and as far as it is in their power to do so. So strongly have the evils of the present system impressed themselves upon the minds of some of our friends that I am authorised to state that three gentlemen are prepared to subscribe one thousand pounds each, provided two others will do the same, in order to maintain five perambulating vans in our agricultural districts during the next five years. The educational work done during the present summer by the van of the Land Restoration League has been most successful. The experience gained shows that two hundred pounds will maintain a van throughout the greater portion of the year, and five vans will cover a large portion of the country, each van visiting a new village every evening. The villagers, when effectively addressed, willingly enrol themselves in the ranks of local unions and subscribe from their small wages 1d. per week towards the support of local organizations. Thousands have thus been enrolled during the present summer. The great success of the movement has created a desire for its extension. I trust that some of your correspondents will enable me shortly to announce the completion of the required subscription.

I am, yours truly,

WILLIAM SAUNDERS, Treasurer of the English Land Restoration League.

9, Duke-street, Adelphi, London, W.C.,   Sept. 8.

SIR, - Your correspondent, "A Country Parson," is, like a good many of his cloth - a stickler for words. It appears to me that the statement put into the Vicar's mouth was substantially correct, but then I only possess an ordinary lay mind. I have endeavoured, however, to find "a very different meaning" in the two phrases as quoted by your correspondent. Is it this? That a man is to do his duty in that state of life unto which it shall please God to call him - that is the future; and not to do it in that state of life unto which it hath pleased God to call him - that is the present.- I am, sir, yours faithfully,

W.W. London,   Sept. 8.

SIR,- I believe it can only be in rare cases that allotments have the result of reducing the rate of wages. Ordinarily they have the opposite effect, and it is easy to see the economic causes of this. First, by giving the labourer a reserve fund to fall back upon, they put him in a position to make a better bargain with his employer. Secondly, they fix a fairly high minimum standard of wages. No man will work for a farmer for less than he could make for himself on his allotment. He even expects more when working for a master than when working for himself. Thirdly, allotments absorb a considerable amount of labour, and to that extent lessen the supply in the labour market. All this is not theory alone. It would be easy to show how in many parts the introduction or extension of allotments has led to a rise of wage.- Yours, &c.,

B.K.

SIR, - Everybody seems to take it for granted that the farmer is in a bad way, that he cannot afford to pay his labourers better, in fact, that he is almost on the brink of starvation himself. Why, Sir, he always has been. Fifty or sixty years ago, when wheat made 60s. to 70s. per quarter, and labourers' pay was six or seven shillings per week, it was the same old tale, and yet when he died he somehow managed to leave two or three thousand each to his children. And look at him now. Cricket and lawn tennis all summer; shooting, hunting, concerts, and balls all winter; living far better now than his landlord did then. Yet still we hear the same old cry. He is losing money, going to the workhouse, &c. Ah, Sir, it's all very well to tell that tale to City men, but we who are obliged to live amongst them know better. What is wanted is a system of small farms, say of 80 to 150 acres, and a class of occupiers like "A Leicestershire Farmer," (page 85) and the problem we are all so anxiously discussing is solved. We want some hardworking, human farmers, not gentlemen tyrants, from whose clutches all the high-spirited youth of our villages make haste to escape, while we who know and live amongst them do not wonder at it.

Yours truly,

"SOUTH BEDS."

SIR - I, in common with thousands of others, am extremely glad at the prominence you are giving to "Life in our Villages" in your valuable columns. The district where this is written is a model for the system of small holdings and allotments, having several hundred acres unenclosed and in plots varying from one rood to two acres, each plot a separate freehold or copyhold property, the plough furrow being the boundary in each case, which gives great facilities for a poor man to acquire small lots either as owner or tenant. Many of our farm labourers occupy one to three acres, and keep one cow and feed two or three pigs, they and their families doing the necessary hand labour at times when it does not interfere with their ordinary employment, except an occasional day in harvest. I don't know one man in ten in this and the adjoining parish of Belton that is now farming from thirty to one hundred acres that either they or their fathers have not been farm servants or farm labourers in their early life, and all, or nearly all, rising step by step through this system of small holdings commencing with one, or at most a few acres, and gradually adding to or exchanging their holdings as their means increased. There are in the district a number of men holding from ten to twenty acres who, in addition to cow and pig, keep one horse, and for the heavy part of the work on their land two will yoke together, which effectually gets over the difficulty of one-horse farming. This parish contains near 6,000 acres, occupied as follows:- Only two occupying over 200 acres; from 100 to 200, twelve; from 50 acres to 100, fourteen; from 20 acres to 50, thirty-one; from 10 acres to 20, forty; from 2 acres to 10, 115; and from 2 roods to 2 acres there are eighty occupiers. A fair question to ask would be: Under such a system of small holdings would as large an amount of food be raised as on an equal quantity of land in large farms? I have no hesitation in saying that there is a larger amount of grain, at least an equal amount of beef, a much larger quantity of pork or bacon and vegetables, but a smaller quantity of mutton, very small holdings not being adapted to sheep-walks. Some two years ago I was summoned to give evidence before a Committee of the House of Commons, under the chairmanship of Mr. J. Chamberlain, sitting to inquire into this question of small holdings, and to ascertain whether there was any general desire for its extension. From the cross-questioning by Mr. Chaplin and some others I concluded that the Tory members of the Committee were dead against any compulsory clause, whilst such men as Mr. Halley Stuart and Sir Walter Foster were the men who were anxious for powers to place the land in a great many more hands than any voluntary system is likely to accomplish. Before leaving home to attend the Committee I called together at least a dozen men that I knew had been in possession of from one to two acres each for a few years only, and after some conversation with them, I suggested that they should strengthen my hands by signing a paper expressing their experience, as given me then, to which they gave a ready consent. It was to this effect, that before having their allotments they had a great dread of a long frost in each winter as they came round, feeling that a few weeks out of work would mean either being thrown on the parish for support, or they and their families would be on the verge of starvation. But since they had had the land they had grown half-acre each of wheat, barley, and potatoes for the winter, and in some cases for the great part of the year, at but little cost, they having done the work required when not otherwise employed. And now, they said with one voice, we can face the

severest winter without any fear of either hunger or of being pauperised.-
Yours, &c.,

J. STANDRING, Epworth, Doncaster.

Mr. W.H. Cooper (Cheltenham) gives the following illustration of the tardiness
of landowners in making necessary reductions in rent. A farm in
Gloucestershire was let on lease at a rental of 237*l*., and about 35*l*. tithe. The
tenant managed to pay fairly well till the disastrous summer of 1879, when he
fell a little into arrears. The landlord returned 10 per cent. and thought he had
done a great deal, making this 10 per cent. reduction a reason for not draining
the land or doing the necessary repairs. Time went on. The tenant got poorer,
prices did not improve, but tended downward ever since. When the tenant was
quite impoverished, and had sold off most of his stock, the landlord consented
to call in a valuer, who reduced the rental to 160*l*., the landlord to pay the tithe.
By this time, however, the tenant was too impoverished. The reduction came
too late, and the farm is now in the market.

Mr. W. Pearson, Stapleford, Cambs., says: At the market dinner
table the general flow of conversation is strictly connected with the farming
interest. There your Correspondent would hear the results of various kinds of
farming operations, the value of steam machinery, the importance of good
drainage, the relative properties of artificial manures, the rearing of stock of
various kinds, &c., &c.; but directly the labour question is approached the men
are denounced as not taking any interest in the welfare of their employers. It is
maintained that as much work per day is not done at the present as formerly,
that allotments are only introduced by paid agitators to make the men
dissatisfied, and that education unfits the rising race for the work that needs to
be done on the land. Till this spirit on the part of the masters can be removed,
the most serious obstacle to the improvement of the labourer's position will
remain. The vote of the labourer is another source of grievance, and I fear
(says Mr. Pearson) that the breach between employers and employed widens
rather than otherwise. The men are not valued as men ought to be, and until
those who suffer can find some more direct expression either in parish council
or something of a similar character, their lot will remain as it is. To bring this

162

about will not be an easy task, but if village life is to be improved and labourer's prospects brightened in the future, some important change must be introduced to help to bring it about.

R.C.R., Hampstead, says T.M.'s story (page 148) of the conduct of a certain earl in relation to the Methodists on his estate reminds him of an anecdote of the late learned and liberal-minded Connop Thirlwall, Bishop of St. David's. An old widow of the name of Blank, who lived in a parish in the Bishop's diocese, and who had always had her share of the winter gifts of blankets and coals, was visited by a new incumbent, or curate, who had only been a few months in the parish. The distribution of good gifts was about to take place, and with that fact no doubt in the zealous parson's mind, he thus addressed her - "Mrs. Blank, my memory is generally pretty good, and I do not remember seeing you in church for a long time." Now Mrs. Blank was a Dissenter, as it is not uncharitable to suppose the parson in a small village very well knew, and having, like John Gilpin, "a pleasant wit," she replied, "And my memory, sir, is wonderfully good, considering my age, and I don't remember ever seeing you in chapel!" "Ah, luckless speech!" Next week came a shower of blankets, one to each of her neighbours right and left, but none for the old body - a barrow of coals, too, for each of the deserving, but none for old Mrs. Blank. But the old woman's punishment was of short duration. The story got wind; it reached the Bishop, who was amused, it was supposed, at Mrs. Blank's blunt independence, and at once ordered a pair of blankets and a double allowance of coals to be sent to her from the Palace.

The Rev. J. Denny Gedge, Methwold Vicarage, Norfolk, observes: The explanations of the exodus of the labourer with which your Commissioner has been plied are most of them but subsidiary causes; and, Liberal though I am, I am constrained to own that the Tory Vicar held up to ridicule in your Saturday's issue has, instinctively, if unphilosophically, come nearest to the right explanation, unpleasant as it may be to some of us who have to confess this. Increased information is the main cause of the trouble. For the chief trial of country life is its monotony. The Vicar is right - they have lost that blessed ignorance which enabled them to be happy in their condition, and much that was available and satisfied their forefathers is too coarse and rude for them. There are not wanting in every village those of a nobler and sweeter disposition who have turned their increased information to the account of personal culture and considerable refinement; but such tempers are equally rare in all classes, and the greater number, especially of the young, have, as a knowledge of human nature should have led us to expect, simply become unsettled, and crave after a variety of experience and interest such as the country can never afford. For those whom necessity or prudent acquiescence retains in the country charity should teach us to provide all the recreation possible. It is simply terrible, when, as in my own place, ground cannot be had even for cricket and other suitable sports. Every village should have its cricket ground, its fives-court, and its apparatus for athletics; every village schoolmaster should be capable to train for a cantata; and no better gifts than that of a piano for the village platform, or of instruments for a village band, can be made to a village by its wealthier neighbours. It is sad indeed when almost the only excitement, even for the young, is to be found in the society of the village alehouse. Dancing should be encouraged and, if possible, taught, in every schoolroom. Nothing refines more the relations of the sexes under proper management. One will always welcome the political meetings of either party, which are always largely attended, and find most considerate and patient bearers in our labourers, unless the speakers insult them by turning firm, conscientious, and reasonable argument to rude invective, which, I am glad to say, is largely condemned from whatever side it comes. Everything in the way of wholesome sport and interest is to be encouraged. In Imperial days Rome had to work her farms by slave colonies, and the working of our farms has become difficult because we no longer have either ignorance or serfdom. Enormous is the difficulty that lies on the country landlord, still more on the impoverished clergyman, who can rarely escape his surroundings, to find variety sufficient to satisfy the craving interests of to-day, especially in the case of the young. For the elder man many of us hope that some relief will be found when, through village councils and suchlike, he has to do the work that his hitherto been done for him; in which case, after a little period of disturbance, I, for one, do not fear but that the labourer, once settled in his harness, and face to face with realities, will show the same good business sense and moderation in office as other Englishmen, and take a pride in being sensible.

"A Devonshire Squire's" tentative suggestion (page 103) for solving the agricultural problem by bringing farm work under the operation of a limited liability company, having met with some approval, he writes to us

again on the subject a long letter, from which we make the following extract:-
There is no keeping the young men at home by artificial means. The only real
cure for the evil - if evil it be - is to accept the situation and make the best of it.
My suggestion is not put forth by way of remedy, for in some ways it would
tend rather to increase the depopulation of the country rather than lessen it; but
only as a possible method to make farming pay better than it does now, and to
render those actually engaged in it more prosperous and contented. My
contention is that in farming on a large scale better wages can be paid, and yet
the same or even improved profits be attained, by reason of the greater
economy in working. Where it is possible to farm after this manner, by one
and same person finding the capital and the capacity for farming, the best
results may be looked for, but as such cases are the exceptions, the next best
possible would be to provide the capital of a company, and do the farming by
properly directed managements. If the company could purchase its own land,
so much the better; otherwise it must rent it on long repairing leases, and be
placed, as nearly as may be, in the position of landowners. What then, would
be the probable result? First, the tenant farmers of small acreage would be
improved off the face of creation; but if the signs of the times point to his early
extinction, it would be no great harm to antedate his departure. The landlord
would benefit, rather than otherwise, by having a company for his tenant or by
having his land taken off his hands altogether, a blessing which many an
impoverished landowner longs for. While the labourer, the foster child for
whose welfare the present generation, judging from the letters on the subject, is
so interested, would benefit most of all. His wages would certainly go up, his
home would be improved, he would be placed in a position where he could sell
his labour to the best advantage, and would have enough to lay by for the
future. The suggestion of one of your correspondents, that the labourer should
share in the profits of the concern, is a good one, and one that I had not
overlooked. It would be well also, if the manager labourer, and everyone
employed should be shareholders as well, and that the scheme should be so
worked, that after a certain final percentage had been paid to the shareholders,
the remainder of the net profits should be divided between the shareholders,
and workers, after some previously arranged scale.

LETTERS TO THE EDITOR .

SIR, - In your to-day's issue, an Oxfordshire Tenant Farmer (page 152) rushes to the defence of an Oxfordshire landlord (page 87), and out-Herods Herod by asserting that the average wage of the Oxfordshire labourer is more than 13s. 4d. weekly. May I invite him to peruse the preceding column, and there, parallel with his letter, are some words penned by your able Commissioner, who I fear is in danger of the woe pronounced upon those of whom all men speak well, for even the Unionist *Spectator* lauds him. Says he:- "I have just left an Oxfordshire village where the normal summer pay till two or three weeks ago was 10s., and I have had indicated to me villages in this part of the country where wretched families have to subsist as best they can on 9s. a week all through the winter." (page 139). Now, sir, lest there be still in "Tenant Farmer" and "Landlord," "an evil heart of unbelief," if they will kindly call upon me I will undertake to introduce them to Oxfordshire villages where they may speedily ascertain that they have drawn upon their imagination for their facts. At one village, within six miles of Oxford, the men were last winter receiving 12s. weekly; but a little inquiry elicits the fact that all wet time was stopped, and some weeks the sum total earned, or rather received, was six shillings, and this in a place where the houses are let at an exceptionally high rate. In another village the wages are now 11s weekly, the rents being 1s. to 1s. 6d. I dislike the occupation of flogging a dead horse, or I would give many more instances. Surely it must now be admitted that 'tis true, tho' pity 'tis, 'tis true, that there is· "something rotten in our state of Denmark." The question that I should like to see some of your able correspondents deal with is, what is the remedy and how to apply it? I do hope that something practical will be the outcome or, like the boy and the famous battle of Blenheim, we shall have to inquire "But what good came of it after all?"- Yours, &c.,

FREDERIC C. RIVERS, Oxford,   Sept. 8.

SIR, - Will you allow an ignorant man, a man from the dunghill, to make a few remarks upon the great question which your correspondent has so ably put before the public during the last few days? I know something about the cultivation of the land; for years I worked at the roughest work done on the land, cleaning out pig-sties, turning manure, digging; and to-day, after twenty years of laborious work, I occupy the land I worked on and employ fifty hands. And, Sir, if I had to start life again, as poor as I was twenty years ago, with only 5s. in my pocket, I would choose the land. If I had to start afresh to-morrow, with a balance of 1,000*l*. at my banker's, I would choose the land. Nothing is so grateful for care and intelligent management as the land. Look upon the cultivation of the land as men look upon any other business or profession, put into it the same intelligence and determination, and I have not the least doubt the same favourable results will follow. Many of the present occupiers of the land are ignorant of their work; they do not grow the right thing, and if they discovered the right thing they do not know how to grow it. Farmers (if they hoe), and also market gardeners, hoe to kill the weeds, and if there is no weeds they do not hoe. They are ignorant of the need of hoeing and why they should hoe. They are too slovenly, untidy, wanting in trimness, thoroughness; and yet, Sir, they are not altogether to blame. They are the product of a bad and vicious system. If the land is to be cultivated profitably and the villagers are to be prosperous and contented, the present occupiers of the land must be got rid of; there is no other remedy. The intelligent and enterprising men' avoid the land, and it has been handed over to the incompetent.

How could any industry compete with the foreigner if all the best men were driven out of it? If a man takes land to cultivate he wants security. When I asked an agent to give me a lease and compensation for necessary bulkings and improvements, he simply laughed at me and said: "We do not want such tenants as you are; we should never get rid of you; you would spend so much on the land we could never buy you out." Just so, Sir, and that is why the land is a failure, they do not want intelligent and independent tenants. An Act of Parliament is wanted that will enable a man to buy land as simply as he would buy anything else; he should not have to run the risk of a heavy lawyer's bill, and perhaps a long delay, before he takes possession, they only cost should be the cost of a stamp for the benefit of the revenue, this would bring about a

167

revolution in our land, and the revolution would be gradual. Thriftless landowners would soon be rid of their land, and other landowners would soon find it an advantage to part with their land, and thrifty labourers and small occupiers would soon become owners, and the revolution would be complete. Men of intelligence, men of will, would soon discover that the cultivation of land was profitable, it is profitable now, where the men are the right men. A remark was made to me the other day that Mr. Smith was a good and successful farmer. I replied, "Yes; he was a clock-maker till he was 30 years of age." "So-and-so is a good farmer." "Yes; he was a draper up to 35." These two men brought business ability into their work. They had not the prejudice of the farmer, and what they did they did with all their might. If, Sir, it pays men living in Russia and America to grow food to send into our markets surely it will pay men at home to grow the same thing. We have become so used to foreign produce that we think there is nothing strange in having it; but, Sir, it shows on our part incompetency and ignorance. Why buy eggs from abroad? Why buy apples? No country is better suited to growing them than ours.

Allow me to give one illustration to show the stupidity of many English growers. A London herb dealer wanted 20 to 30 tons of marjoram to dry, also other herbs. He says to the English grower: "Will you cut these herbs off close to the ground, and not pull them up by the roots, and dry the herbs for me." The grower says: "No; our way is to bunch them up for the London market with the roots; if that does not suit, you can go without." Our London man is a man of business, and will not be played with, so he goes to Germany, and the German gives him what he wants, and the bottled herbs and packet herbs the grocer and greengrocer supply mainly come from Germany. I could give endless illustrations of the ignorance and stupidity of the English grower, also his prejudice against properly packing fruit; but I have done. Allow me to thank you for bringing public attention to so important a matter. There are men in England with brains and energy to restore to England that prosperity in her agricultural districts which she so much needs if our Parliament has only the wisdom to spend a little time in framing an Act that will give security to the occupier.- I am, Sir, yours respectfully,

HODGE.

SIR, - Now that you have got the ear of the country through the reports of your Special Commissioner on the agricultural question, I hope you will be pleased to have these reports continued until late in the year. The question has never been put before Londoners so clearly before, and it seems to me that a very important feature of the Liberal programme at the next election should be immediate legislation for the amelioration of the position of the agricultural classes, which is at present deplorable.- I am, Sir, your obedient servant,

E. HEYS-JONES, Addison-gardens, Kensington,   Sept.9.

The President of the Primitive Methodist Conference (the Rev. Joseph Ferguson), writing to *The British Weekly*, gives among the reasons for the depopulation of the rural districts one which gives him pain to record. He says: Occasionally the most intelligent and the most earnest members of our churches, not being in favour in special quarters on account of their Nonconformity, have to leave their farms or cottages and seek employment and freedom in the cities. In other cases, if their sons or daughters aspire to the tutorial office, in some parishes they cannot enter without sacrificing their religious connections or practising dissimulation. To save their children and to find positions for them according to their taste and trend, they are compelled to leave the villages. The greatest cause, however, says Mr. Ferguson, lies in the condition of agriculture. The farmers, with whom we have much sympathy, are in fierce competition with those of other lands, where rents are lower, rains less, and where, in millions of cases, the farmers are the proprietors ... In thousands of instances the farmers are over-rented and too heavily rated. They need greater security and a wider freedom to farm according to the improved methods ... The Parliament should abrogate the sale of land by lease, or else ordain that the lessor at the expiration of the lease shall pay to the lessee the value of the necessary improvements made in both buildings and land; the abolition of the law of lease would be more just and satisfactory. The "Law of Entail" should be annulled ... The Legislature should make the sale and conveyance of land easier and cheaper. The one thing needful is that bodies elected by the people should be invested with power to borrow money to buy land on proper conditions, and to sell it to industrious labourers with the privilege of repayment of capital and interest by yearly instalments. Our landowners are too few. At present thirty-six people in the United Kingdom possess 6,696,493 acres of land. If our villages are to be populated according to their capacity, and our towns saved from the dangerous influx of farm labourers, the land of the country must be owned by the millions of the people, who would personally cultivate the soil to the national well-being.

The President of the Methodist Free Church Assembly (the Rev. M.T. Myers), writing also to *The British Weekly*, says of one of the villages of Lincolnshire that some of the people live in houses worse than dog kennels and stables for the horses of the landlords. "The landlords spend their money in gambling, time in hunting and horse-racing, and care nothing for the physical, mental, or spiritual welfare of the people, only as they will serve their interests. They have to work nearly sixteen hours a day summer and winter for a bare existence, and to be known to go to a chapel is to be tabooed by parson and squire. The clergymen manifest no sympathy with them in their struggle, but preach up submission and obedience. Their children grow up, get a little more education than their fathers had, see the difficulties they have to contend with, determine they will not submit to the treatment, and escape to the large towns. I have met with scores in London I have known in Lincolnshire and other farming districts, who have just corroborated what I have now said. Disestablish the English Church and throw the minister upon the support of the people, and in twelve months he will know where he is, and so will the people. After the land laws so as to connect the people with the soil, and give them some interest in it. That is nature's law; carry it out, and you will soon effect your purpose.

Friday, September 11, 1891

(FROM OUR SPECIAL COMMISSIONER.)

It has been difficult to move through our English villages during the past two or three weeks and then to sit down and write about them without gushing a little. Even the stormy weather of this memorable summer, trying as it has been for all who are concerned in harvesting, has in many respects enhanced the loveliness of the village and its surroundings. The drenching rains have kept the grass in the fields and the mosses and lichens on the cottage roofs exceptionally brilliant, the roadways white and clean, the orchards and woodlands fresh and verdant. Never can rosy apples have looked rosier, or apricots sunnier, or plums juicier, or flowers gayer than they do this year in their setting of lustrous foliage, quite free from dust, and as yet scarcely touched by any indication that

> Winter comes to rule the varied year
> Sullen and sad.

Even the lowering rain clouds, that to the farmer have kept rolling up behind the hills like demons of destruction, do but add sublimity to the peaceful and pastoral scene, and, combined with sudden bursts of sunshine, often lend a breadth of effect and vividness of colour surpassingly beautiful. Step for a moment into this little ancient church, with its ivy-mantled tower and hoarse-ticking clock, its open doorways overspread with nets to keep out the birds, its massive stone walls with their queer little nooks and niches telling of holy water and images of saints, its venerable font and antiquated wrought-iron work and worm-eaten old seats. An appropriate place to wait out of a thunder shower for a few minutes - to wait and muse how

> Out of the old fieldes, as men saithe,
> Cometh al this new corne fro yere to yere.

And now while the last big drops of storm are streaming down slantwise through a dazzling flood of sunshine, step out again under the roof of the liche gate, with the rain-bespangled grass and the mossy gravestones at your back, and before you on the other side of the way an orchard with its ten thousand ruddy apples blazing like gems under the pattering raindrops. Over the top of the broken wall you can see through beneath the tangled boughs of the shady orchard into the sun-flooded meadow, where brown and white cattle are grazing in groups of indescribable charm. Away to the left the pretty cottages with their thatchéd roofs, their steps of unhewn rock, their windows full of geraniums and fuchsias, and their porches overgrown with autumn roses and canariensis, are hobbling down the broken pathway in a picturesque, irregular line, their red chimney-stacks gently streaming out into the trees above the soft, blue smoke of the wood fires, on which busy matrons are beginning to prepare the evening meal for father, whose work has been stopped by the drenching downpour, and who will presently be home. The rain is over now; stroll down the village and gossip with the people. There is nothing very startling or sentimental to be gleaned, but you get some valuable side-lights on village life, and most of them have something worth listening to. Here is a venerable patriarch with a marvellous memory for what "I says to he" and "he says to me says he," fifty years ago. His father met with an accident when he was a young man, and died in a day or two, leaving his wife to the care of the parish. And the grey-headed old man tells you - as no doubt he has been telling for many a year - how that the next day was relieving day, and the guardians made an order that he was to keep his mother as well as his own family on his eight shillings a week. Indignation still sparkles in the old man's eyes as he tells how he met Muster Sumkins, and Muster Sumkins said as he was to keep his mother. "I says to'n, I says I oon't keep my mother. He says, 'You oon't?' and I says 'No, I oon't, for any on 'em,' I says, and I oon't, neither. I'd ha' sell'd my sticks, and gone to Ameriky." Here is another villager, who has withstood the powers that be, and as he says, was "bunked out o' the place" neck and crop, with seven young children at his heels. Physically, the man is a splendid specimen of the agricultural labourer, and tells his story with evident satisfaction, though it doesn't seem to be entirely to his credit. He had just lost his wife, and the lady of the village wanted him to send some of his children to school, but he wouldn't. "Why wouldn't you send your children to school?" I inquired. "Cause I codn't," said the man, with a smile of dogged obstinacy. "I'd a mind to do as I liked." Seemingly the lady was right in her wish, and the man was wrong in his refusal. But to evict him from home and work and village in this fashion was just one of those high-handed exercises of absolute power that do so much to widen and deepen the chasm between the two classes of the village.

At another place in the same neighbourhood I hear a droll story and yet another display of insubordination on the part of a labourer. A fine stalwart fellow, with a shrewd, intelligent face, stands at his cottage door in his shirt sleeves, with his hands tucked down deep into the pocket of his fustian trousers, and tells me of somebody or other who'll have to go up to the hall to-

172

morrow over some charity bread. In a certain parish, bread is given away to the cottagers every Sunday after church. So many residents in the parish take it in turns, and, till recently, the wife or children of the men entitled to it could receive it. The church-wardens, however, lately resolved that this should not longer be permitted, and that the man who didn't personally come and take his sermon should have no bread. The truant villagers resented this, and one of them, who had lost his turn at the loaves, went the following Sunday and helped himself, at the same time dealing out to the good people at the church some of his private opinions about them. My informant, a Radical politician, was evidently in sympathy with the insurrectionary villager, but he shrewdly suspected that he would have to pay for his audacity. He'd just like to see one o' the newspapers get hold o' that story. They'd make sommit on't, he'd bet. The man would certainly have to pay, for they would make it out that he had been brawling in church, and he would have nobody to defend him. "What 'e wants," said the man, "is a good sharp lawyer to tackle 'em for 'im. If'e could only get Sir Charles Russell to tak't up for'n he'd let 'em know. They'd soon put their tail atween their legs when they sin 'e." I am afraid the occasion is gone now, and that Sir Charles has lost a fine opportunity of acquiring undying fame. Before the day was out I was destined to hear a little more of this case. I stopped at a village inn and called for a cup of tea. The landlord refused it point blank, and I was immediately invited by the company in the tap-room to "have a pull" at their quart pots. As graciously as I could I declined the beer, and insisted on the tea, and after some little wrangling I got my way. While the tea was brewing I studied village life in the tap-room, and out of curiosity I brought forward the charity bread. Oh for a phonograph that would reproduce for me just now the little tit-bits of dialogue that ensued as the wizened little old man in the smock frock and the wideawake told how as they did say that Joe Stuggins, or whatever his name was, had in the height of argument bobbed his nose again the church-warden's. It was inexpressibly droll. In the course of the discussion it was asserted and evidently believed by the men that in the village in which they sat a hundred pounds had been left for charity and had entirely vanished, and there were dark allusions to money that had been paid to hush up somebody's theft of brasses from the church.

The scene was amusing enough while one could shut one's eyes to all but the humour of it; but it had its painful and unpleasant aspect from

173

another point of view. It is of no use crying down public houses. We must have houses of entertainment, and before I close this series of articles I hope to be able to say something on the subject of what they ought to be in the villages. This place I chanced to go into affords a fair illustration of what they ought not to be. I got my cup of tea; but suppose one of those labouring men had preferred a cup of tea to a pot of beer, what would have been his chance of getting it? One of the party when I went in was quite evidently drunk, but he called for another quart, and the landlord brought it to him without the least hesitation. What hope is there of rendering our peasantry sober, and thrifty, and self-respecting, with dens of this sort in their midst? Where is the parson of that old ivy-mantled church? Why doesn't he put his foot down and say this shall not be, and that a landlord who turns a drunken man out into the village shall have the rector of the parish to deal with before the magistrates next licensing day? What is the good of having a "Christian gentleman" in every village if that gentleman can't tackle a flagrant iniquity of this kind and by hook or crook put an end to it? I don't like to attack the clergy indiscriminately. I can see, and I am sure that many of the country clergy are even entitled to every respect, and are doing an invaluable work in the dark corners of the land. But as I move about and talk with the people I cannot shut my eyes to the fact that half the evils of village life could be remedied if the parsons were worth their salt. Half of them seem to me to be mere nonentities, with no understanding of the people, no sympathy with them in their hopes and fears, their struggles and sufferings, no sort of fellow feeling with them whatever. "Haven't you got a clergyman here?" I enquired of one woman in reply to her plaintive and spiritless wish that somebody could look after its poor a bit. "Yes, sir," was the reply, "we got one but we don't see much on 'em. I been here ten years and I don't know as he ever been near my house." "He aint much good to us," said a bystander. "Oh, I dunno," said another anxious apparently to say what she could, "I never 'eard as he done nobody no harm." Damning with faint praise, this, with a vengeance. Few of the villages I have been through have any place where men may go and talk over the news together, and smoke their pipe and sing a song without the necessity for beer drinking. I passed through one village and talked with a Nonconformist local preacher, who told me that an effort had been made to set up something of the kind in that place, by the joint action of three or four of the dissenting bodies.

174

They had built a hall, and it was to have been a place for healthy recreation and entertainment. But none of the good people seemed to understand the necessity for anything but religious service, and as it was not specially identified with the "cause" of either sect, the scheme fell through. One of them has now monopolised the use of the place, in which services are occasionally held, but ordinarily it is shut up, while five or six public-houses are in full blast - two of them I noticed actually standing back to back.

TO THE EDITOR OF THE DAILY NEWS.

SIR,- Now that your Special Commissioner has described life in our villages under its most unfavourable aspects, he would, I am sure, greatly interest your readers by perambulating those villages on the estates of such progressive landlords as the late Lord Tollemache and describing life as he finds it there. Not only should we have the best phase contrasted with the worst, but the best may suggest some practical solution of the many difficulties which beset the whole subject. If I remember rightly, from a description given some time ago in *The Daily News*, the arrangements on the estate referred to above secured to all the parties interested in it most of the advantages aimed at by the co-operative system, while they were free from at least some of the drawbacks which attend that system in its infancy. I venture to hope that others beside Lord Tollemache have been benevolent and wise enough to do for themselves and theirs what, it is to be feared, can only be brought about in respect to some estates by Acts of Parliament.- Yours faithfully,

.A CONSTANT READER, Oxford,   Sept.8.

SIR, - It may interest your readers to know that labourers' wages in this part of the world (Lincolnshire) are now 15s. a week, exclusive of hay and harvest wages. All labourers, who are tenants of mine in this place, have allotments, in most cases quite close to their houses, and none of them pay more than 1*l*. an acre for the arable land. The allotments vary in size from half an acre to four acres, and some of the labourers have grass land and a cow as well; for the

175

grass the charge is 30s. an acre. The cottage rents described or suggested by some of your correspondents seem to me too high. I do not charge more than 4*l*. 4s. a year for a new cottage with three bedrooms and a rood of garden. I have never regarded it as any business of mine whether any of my tenants, labouring or otherwise, attended church, chapel, or neither, though being a Churchman myself of course I am glad when they come to church; neither do I concern myself with my tenants' politics. It is not my experience that labourers who live on my property seem very anxious to "flock into the town," and I do not see why my experience should not be that of most landlords if they treat the labourers round them as friends, and "arrange for" and patronise them as little as possible. I may add that with a population of rather more than 300 we have a flourishing co-operative society turning over an average of 20*l*. a week, where the women spend their clothing club money or not, and as they please.- I am, your obedient servant,

"A LINCOLNSHIRE LANDLORD".

SIR, - Small holdings were declared by the late Parliamentary Committee on the subject, to be a "national necessity," and the Government proposes to introduce a measure with the object of enlarging their number. But, to be effective, it must be compulsory. Mr. John Morley most truly said at Stoneleigh that "A Small Holdings Bill, without compulsion, would not be worth the paper it is written on." No readers of your paper will dissent from that statement. It is a recognition by a front-bench statesman of the fact, long seen by others, that individual landlords cannot be relied on to provide that access to land which is necessary in order to make the labourer an independent man with a reasonable prospect of rising in the world according to his ability and worth. That even with the best system of land tenure, which I hold to be state or municipal tenancy, there will be some flowing of the population to the towns, one can hardly doubt. But it is reasonable to suppose that the drift to the towns of the young who love excitement will be counterbalanced by the drift from the towns to the country of those, and there are many, who prefer the quiet of a rural life. For village life is at present unattractive, because the villager has been neglected, not so much in the dispensing of alms as in the according of justice. Dullness is by no means an essential of a life among the fields and flowers. Repeople the villages by improving the men's prospects, and the diffusion of education will yet make possible a high state of social life there. The library and the concert room need not be the peculiar possessions of towns. In conclusion I would repeat what Mr. Burt said yesterday as president of the Trades Union Congress. "The land question touches us at every point - the question of food, of health, of recreation, of life." To seek its true solution is the bounden duty of all who desire the removal of the grievances which your Special Commissioner has so ably pointed out.- Yours truly,

JOSEPH HYDER, Land Nationalization Society, 14 Southampton-street, Strand, London,   Sept. 10.

SIR,- I know something of the management of estates and the land question, and do not hesitate to say that Hodge's letter (page 167) is by far the best you have published. It means that matters will right themselves if we dissociate political power from the ownership of land, and not otherwise. To do this it is necessary: 1. To disestablish the Church. 2. To largely alter the land laws so as to prevent the tying up of land, and make it easily transferable. 3. To give a thorough system of Local Government. All that is necessary will follow naturally when these three things are done, and until they are done the present evils will continue.

H.

SIR, - The interest in the question of "Life in our Villages" seems to increase daily. The letter signed "Hodge" (*ibid*) in *The Daily News* of to-day is a solid help to the discussion, and deserves that the writer's name should appear. I, too, have had an experience, over more than half a century, of working in the fields with labourers at all kinds of work, two-thirds of the time as an employer as well as a sharer of their labour, and I claim to have some knowledge of their ways and their wants. The first of their wants is increased wages. The Legislative has the power to give better security to capital invested in the land,

and this would lead by the most direct and natural road to increased demand for labour and increased wages. Although a life-long Liberal, I am not a bigoted partisan, and would gladly entrust a Conservative, like Mr. Clare Sewell Read, to produce a good Holdings Act, which should make the tenants' capital as secure as if he was the owner. The one thing to avoid would be the advice of stewards, agents, and valuers, whose dearest interests lie in the direction of frequent changes of tenancy. I am quite opposed to the assumption that only large farms can be made to pay. In the course of my long experience, I have seen many instances of labourers who, after serving a twelve years' apprenticeship in a farmhouse, have by a little extra thrift and industry been able to purchase one cow and rent a small field, and have gone on by degrees to a considerable farm, in the way described by your correspondent. Capital and thrift, in proportion to the size of the holding, are all that is required. I have no doubt that with real security for capital, we should soon see a decrease in the disproportion between the few successful labourers and the many who end their days in the workhouse.- Yours truly,

H.H WATSON, 14, Loudoun-road, St. John's-wood,   Sept. 10.

SIR, - I know something of life in our villages, and thank you for bringing the conditions of rural life so vividly before the public. I am over fifty years old, was born and reared on a farm. I have lived in mining districts, and for twenty years in the West Riding, in the midst of a busy manufacturing people, and am now living in a small, old, and decaying rural town. I have lived and laboured here as a Nonconformist minister for six years. When I came here I was painfully impressed with the number of old, sick, and very poor and pauperised people in the place. So large a proportion of the people are broken down by age, by disease, by mental weakness, by drink, and by helpless and hopeless poverty. With the invaluable help of Mr. Winterbotham, M.P., and of others, I have tried to do something to improve the conditions of life for the labourers in our parish. Things are not as bad as they were, for nearly all the labourers now occupy plots of land varying from a quarter of an acre to three or four acres. In this district there is still deep-rooted discontent. The owners, the occupiers, and tillers of the soil complain. Probably all have some just ground of complaint. The owners and occupiers are well able to give voice to their grievances and needs. The labourers suffer most, and are the most silent. Why is the condition of their life so bad, and why are they discontented? The question is easily asked, but most difficult adequately to answer. Some of the blame must rest on the labourers themselves. Are others to blame? A neighbour of mine, who is a Tory, and an owner and occupier of land, shall in part answer. Some few months ago this gentleman farmer read a paper on "The Future of Agricultural Labour" to an influential meeting of farmers and landlords and clergymen, a Canon presiding. In this paper, after speaking of the general complaints made by employers, he admitted that the farmers and others in positions of influence had been opposed to the labourers being educated, opposed to their having votes, opposed to their having any direct interest in the land by having allotments; that they had treated men as goods and chattels, valuing them as they would a one-pound note; that all this had been done deliberately to keep them men down in the supposed interest of the farmers, &c.; that this old spirit still exists and is as difficult to root out "as spavins are to breed out of horses." Though the meeting was open for discussion, no one questioned one of these frank statements.

Now add to these things the low wages paid, the irregular employment, the wretched houses in which many of these labourers live, their almost absolute dependence upon the farmers as described by one of the themselves for home and work, and the dullness of rural life, and we cannot wonder that men and women are discontented, and that so many of the young and more enterprising leave the country. Who are the girls that remain in our villages to be the future mothers and trainers of the men and women that are to be? Too largely the lazy, the incompetent, or the fallen. Our parish has been decreasing certainly for over twenty years. We need more trust in one another, a more brotherly feeling. But this must spring from and rest upon righteousness. There must be a door of hope opened to men in the country. It must be made easier for the men who wish it to get a secure footing on the land. The temptations to excessive drinking must be as far as possible removed, the inducements to thrift and self-improvement multiplied, their homes made more secure and comfortable, the State must do all it can to secure fair play for the weakest. In a word it must become more Christian in its spirit and aims and acts.- I am, sir, yours faithfully,

PHILIP LEWIS, Chipping Campden, Gloucestershire.

The Rev. Henry Brandreth, Dickleburgh Rectory, Norfolk, agrees with many of our correspondents that every facility should be given to every labourer wishing to own or occupy small portions of land. He says:- "Sixty years ago this purely agricultural union contained 24,768 inhabitants; in 1881 it had 23,583, not a great difference considering how much work is now done by machines. The difficulty is not that there is any want of labourers, but that such as remain are often without work. Rightly to appreciate the condition of the agricultural labourers, we should contrast their present condition with actual facts at other times and places; with the French peasants, who, as Lord Rosebery said, can maintain themselves, because they know how to live on an old shoe; or with Switzerland and Germany, where their comforts are less, though the women do heavy field work for long hours; or with our English labourer of fifty years ago. There is no class in the country that has made more substantial progress. They do less work, the wife rarely goes out in the fields, the children are much less employed, and the men do not work so hard. Altogether, the labourer and his family do not do more than half the work of fifty years ago, and yet with half the labour they enjoy twice the comforts of life. All this is real, quiet progress and improvement. Another circumstance of their condition is that all their work is in fresh air, and green fields and clear skies, such as the town artisan looks forward to as the delight of an occasional holiday. And their work is of an interesting and varied character. The factory hand amidst unhealthy and depressing surroundings, gives his life to the wearisome monotony of constantly repeating one of the minute parts into which manufacturing work is divided; he may watch the same spindles for thirty years, or put heads to millions of pins, merely constantly repeating the same mechanical drudgery. But country work is constantly varied and interesting; each man takes his turn at ploughing, mowing, care of animals, ditching, draining, and all the different works by which man subdues animals to his service, or increases the produce of the soil or adorns the face of nature. I heartily wish you God speed in your endeavour to enable any man who desires to work a little land for himself. The object of all government should be not to make our fields grow more produce, but to make them support more men; not, however, because the agricultural population are pitiable objects, but because their lives have many advantages, and on the whole contrast most favourably with the lot of their town brethren.

"A Woman" writes from Shrewsbury:- I have read with interest the articles and correspondence on this subject in *The Daily News*. I have watched with interest for many years past the perfectly rural scenes round my home. I would strongly advise each Londoner to refrain from hasty conclusions. As the vast changes attending the introduction of machinery work themselves out, the order of things must dissolve and reform the system of agricultural pursuits altogether. I have seen much capital spent in turning small holdings into fewer large ones, and after an agony of suspense, during which it has been proved that loss not gain has followed, I have seen the holdings again divide and the cottages built for the labourers on them remain empty and fall to pieces, save the one or two that have become shelters for the reappearing small holders. Each case must be met on its surroundings. The less done the better till a man is sure what is best to be done. In the meantime, let him cherish every tolerable tenant, and make him as comfortable as he can by judicious building of economical little buildings suited to modern feeding, &c. Also let him promote the keeping of good machines for hire. Small holders make out a living by letting machines and tending them, and the use of them enables a number of such holders to do with very few horses. Then a wise landlord would watch the families of such holders and advise the fathers to let their children have a heifer and a few poultry, and by degrees get a little stock, with a promise of a few nice fields and cottage farm when they were old enough to take it. There is one place here, a common some time since enclosed, where a number of small holdings exist, and great satisfaction is expressed by the tenants. One is a carpenter, and often such holders have a trade, as butcher, or cattle dealer, and these make very secure good tenants. The scarcity of labourers is unfelt by them. Not only can they work their own fields, but they often lend a hand at busy times to the larger farmers.

Mr. Henry B. Soden, 5, Warwick-terrace North, Upper Clapton, N.E., asks: Would it not be greatly to their own advantage for the various trades unions to take up the interests of agricultural labour? Would it not be wise of them to give financial aid to their union? With their great power they could do much more towards the solution of this question than they have done.

"T.G.M." writes:- I am myself the son of a farmer, and the one thing impressed on my mind from infancy, and rightly impressed, was to escape from a condition in which incessant labour in the long run benefited the landlord only, and in which the inevitable reward for the exercise of skill and care was simply an increase of rent. Carlyle says somewhere that there is no man so mean in spirit but that he will rebel against injustice; and there are certainly few who will willingly remain where they must submit to it. The remedies I would suggest are perhaps of a somewhat radical character; but the subject-matter requires radical treatment. They are; (1) to give to every man who cultivates land fixity of tenure, at a fair rent fixed by an impartial court; (2) to give to every labourer for whom there is room a right to an allotment of a substantial size on the same terms; (3) to give to local authorities elected by popular vote power to grant such allotments, and to advance money for the purpose of working them; (4) to enforce the old land tax of 4s. in the pound upon the present annual value, the proceeds so far as necessary being devoted to local purpose; and (5) to tax at a higher and an increasing rate land devoted to non-productive use.

"A Constant Reader" says:- High rents make high rates and taxes, and it is these that prevent the farmer, struggling to keep his own head above water, from paying higher wages, if he would, to his regular and more trusted men. This and the cribbed and cabined hovels in which men and their families have to drag out a monotonous existence drive them more than anything else to seek better service. A great part of the instruction they receive at school should be technical as well as scholastic in the library sense, so as to give a practical knowledge of husbandry and other subjects which would fit the children as they grew up for the course of life they had to pursue. The labourers should have better dwellings, with land attached, from which they could not be turned out at the caprice of their employer; and there should be village assembly rooms, where concerts, readings, and lectures should be given gratuitously, or for a nominal sum, which would be the more appreciated as the people became more enlightened. They should be given the opportunity of taking excursions to the city often enough to incline them to turn more fondly to their native village, and find after all there is no place like home, if anything in that name is barely habitable.

Mr. J.P. Sheldon, Sheen, Ashbourne, Derby, writes: Certainly, in every case a labourer should have garden land enough to grow all the vegetables he requires for his family; more than this will be of dubious advantage, save in places where he may sell some of his garden stuff to advantage. As a matter of fact, the Allotments Acts require to be superseded by one which will freely and generously acknowledge the much reviled "three acres and a cow" as a principle on which legislation on the subject should be based. I have admitted that allotments for spade cultivation will be an advantage in many instances, but three acres and a cow will be a blessing in every instance. If you give a farm labourer a mere quarter or half-acre plot of land you saddle him with a lot of gratuitous toil which possesses no charm of novelty, and which is not required for health and exercise in his case as it is in that of an artisan; but if you give him land enough to winter and summer a cow and a calf you add little or nothing to his toil, you give his wife something to look after beside her cottage, and you supply his children with milk at first cost - a most beneficent thing!

"A Bucks Farmer" asks:- Why should farmers work for nothing, as some landlords seem to think they ought, and keep their family on the land, to live on beans and bacon, and see their children grow up dependent on the squire and parson for a subsistence? A great many people talk about agricultural depression who do not understand the question. If we want to keep the agricultural labourers in our villages, we must find them work and pay them better wages. I should begin at the top of the tree, and compel the landlord to let his land at a fair rental, and I should allow the tenant the privilege of having his holding valued by a competent, practical, and sound valuer, not by a man sent down by the landlord or his agent, who knows well if he puts the rent at too low a figure his services will not be required again. It is impossible for the tenant to employ labour if the landlord exacts an exorbitant rental for his land. The consequence is our villages are emptied of the best hands, and life is not worth living in agricultural districts.

"O.C." advocates cheap land transfer as a definite remedy for the evils discussed in this correspondence. He says: "Quite apart from the many village-born men in towns who would be glad to buy a bit of land with their savings, and settle down 'at home,' there are plenty of young labourers ready to buy land if it were possible. Many will hardly believe that a young labourer, 20 to 25 years of age, earning an average wage of 13s. per week, can be able to buy land, yet they almost all buy black coats and bicycles, and I will explain how it is done. A young man will pay his mother 7s. per week for board and lodging, he will spend 2s. per week on clothing and have 4s. per week to invest till he marries, when his poverty commences. If for the 4s. per week or 10l. 8s. per annum he could buy half an acre of land each Michaelmas, every young man might have three acres and a cow before marrying, and be trusted never to desert his native village. At 20l. 16s. per acre there would be many a willing seller, including myself; but the costs of transferring one or two roods of land preclude the idea even when there is no lord of the manor or mortgagee to deal with. A well-digested scheme of co-operative land purchase would be very useful."

"An Out-and-out Radical" says:- A great error, and a very common one is to suppose that a farmer (that is to say, a large farmer, one farming over 100 acres) would be benefited if he could purchase the freehold of his farm. No farmer could afford to have so much of his capital sunk in the freehold purchase; that money (which of course would be a large sum) is what should be his stock-in-trade, which he wants to turn over in the course of the year at a higher profit than that which he would get by the saving of rent-paying. On the other hand, I think, a small farmer should own his land, or hold it in such a manner that his holding shall not depend on the caprice, malignity, or greed of a landlord. The free selectors - i.e., the farming class - in New South Wales are virtually freeholders, but the Government never required them to sink their scanty capital in purchasing the land at the first onset. They have utilised their small capital in improving their selected farms, and have to pay their purchase money in the shape of a rent extending over twenty-one years. The large farms and the large farmers may be let alone for a while. What is first wanted is to assist the small man, and enable him to get a footing (a freehold), and this done, you will have made the first and most necessary step towards checking the serious depopulation of the country. Of course the fact that land, as a rule, is held in so few hands is the primary cause of this evil, and this is most noticeable in parishes where the land is richest. By a strange anomaly, the labourers and "small men" are best off in parishes where the land is poor; and for this reason - in the latter you will find the greater number of freeholders, their holdings being originally squattages or small enclosures made on commons and waste lands. One thing most noticeable in England is, as some of your correspondents have pointed out, the excessive rent that is exacted from the tenants of small holdings. The next thing noticeable is the tenacity of the landowners, and the desire to add acre to acre and to become the "big man in the parish."

From North Northumberland "A Daily Reader" writes: In this county of Northumberland, where the wages are higher and the surrounding conditions much better, still the rural population is decreasing to quite as great an extent as farther south. Here the average wage of the agricultural labourer is 15s. per week all the year round, cottage with garden ground attached and piggery rent free, lot of potatoes yielding on an average rather over two tons, coals had from nearest station or colliery free. The total may be taken at 20s. or 21s. a week. No broken time, no deduction for sickness, be it for a week or for a month. This wage will compare somewhat favourably with that of the labouring class in towns or even with mechanics when you take into account loss of time, house rent, and the greater expense of town life generally. Every farm steading is supplied with cottages for as many families as the farm requires; indeed, now they are in excess of requirements. The Public Health Acts are strictly enforced by the rural sanitary authority both as regards water supply and other sanitary surroundings. As things now are, the same number of agricultural labourers are not wanted ... The outlay required by the landlord is the great obstruction. If we are to retain the best of the agricultural population we must have a great many smaller farms - say, from 50 to 150 acres - where the thrifty labourer with a working family who can save a little, and there are many such, would have the chance of a small farm, and so have a living interest in the land. This, I think, would result in more and better labour, larger crops, extension of the smaller products of the farm, which are now to such an extent imported, and promote a healthier feeling of independence in the country.

Mr. William Jameson says:- If land reform in the interest of the agricultural labourers goes no further than the establishment of an extensive system of allotments, I for one can see no escape from the logic of John Stuart Mill - viz., that thereby wages will be generally lowered among farm labourers.

Far different results, however, may be looked for, if small holdings as well as allotments are placed within the reach of our rural population. To establish a system of small holdings - of cottage farms, in other words - means nothing less than the creation of an entirely new industry in the country, and an industry of a peculiar character in its economic effects; standing in marked contrast with all and every form of wage service, and destined, I venture to predict, to radically change the relations of employer and employed throughout the whole kingdom. For a cottage farm large enough (five acres?) to enable a man to produce the primaries of life for himself and family makes that man an independent factor in the labour world.

·

Saturday, September 12, 1891

LETTERS TO THE EDITOR.

SIR,- I have read with interest the correspondence in *The Daily News* referring to "Life in Our Villages." As an old agricultural labourer, will you allow me to add my testimony. I know that the chances for an agricultural labourer to improve his position are very remote indeed. I well remember when a young man how forcibly this was brought home to myself, and made me feel that my life was not worth living.

The only prospect I could see for me to improve my position was either to emigrate to a foreign country, or to move to one of the large towns or factory districts, or to take a wife and settle down, and as soon as we could get a turn take a small holding and farm it myself. I chose the latter, and sold my labour to a farmer for 12s. per week, with a cottage on the farm, at a rental of one shilling and fourpence per week. The rent was paid by my employer, but, alas! how soon I found I was to be disappointed with my small holding, for most of the small holdings were broken up to make large farms in consequence of the heavy agricultural implements brought out about that time. I continued with the same employer for over 21 years, when I found the vigour of youth had left me, and the infirmities of age were creeping on. My work began to go harder with me, and I knew that I should soon have to leave my work and my home to make room for a younger man, as my best days were gone. I saw no

186

prospect before me but to go to the union, there to be separated from the companion of my life; and that at a time when we most wanted each other's assistance, and there to die uncared for. I left my employment and my home in order that I might be at liberty to take to anything which might turn up, and after being tossed about from place to place for three years, a small holding of two acres of land with a four roomed cottage was offered to me at a rental of 17*l*. 10s. per year, which I took. I have cultivated it now with spade husbandry for over twenty years, and have found a good living from it. I have been able to pay every one their just dues, and have accumulated a fund from the profits which it has left me, the interest of which brings me in more money per year than I received for my wages when I sold my labour to another. I am now over 70 years of age, but am still able to work my small holding with a good profit.

What I have done others could do if the opportunity was given to them. It was a terrible mistake made by the landlords when they broke up the small holdings to make large farms. Very few of the large farmers employ sufficient labour on the land, and they do not pay the value for what they do employ. Hence the terrible state the land has been allowed to get in, which one sees in travelling through the country. Now they say the land will not pay for cultivation. The reason why it will not pay is because it has been allowed to grow sqitch, weeds and rubbish, so that it cannot, while in such a state, grow a crop of corn: but my experience proves to me that the land will pay very well if properly cultivated. Let the labourer have some of it in small holdings, so that he can have the benefit of his own labour, and he will soon find it will pay him a good profit.- I am yours faithfully,

"AGRICOLA".

SIR, - The writer of the articles alludes to opinions he has heard expressed adverse to small farming. I have had some experience of small farmers, and have found that there is generally a marked difference between the methods of successful and unsuccessful small cultivators. The unsuccessful man is generally one who starves his land, both as regards labour and manure. The successful small farmer invariably takes for his motto the axiom that land will always repay with interest the investment in it of labour and proper fertilisers,

and he lets a considerable part of the labour be that of his own hands. The very finest wheat I have seen this year is on the land of a cultivator of this sort, yet four years ago the land was in a very poor condition indeed. Adjoining his land is the farm of another small cultivator, managed on the starving system, and the system looks like carrying starvation to the cultivator. Men often stave land because the conditions of tenure on which they hold do not favour investment of labour and capital; sometimes because they begin with more land than they have the means to use properly; but, whatever may be the reasons for neglect, nature only responds liberally to liberal treatment. Landlords often prefer a large grazing tenant to a number of small farmers, because although a much larger number of people are kept from the land under the system of small farms, they - the landlords - can get a larger rent from the large grazier, and have less trouble in collecting, and landlords look to this as the great consideration. It seems to me that State ownership, with power delegated to local bodies, is required for dealing with this evil, and for the securing of proper terms of tenure, and for doing away with the monstrous tyranny exercised upon tenants on account of their political and religious opinions.- Yours respectfully,
W.M. REYNOLDS.

SIR, - It would be interesting to hear from your correspondent, the Rev. J. Denny Gedge, who advocates (page 163) the teaching of dancing to villagers, if he has tried what he recommends, and with what results? Last winter we started "happy evenings for the children." The co-operation of the schoolmaster was heartily given, and the children not only thoroughly enjoyed themselves, but were beginning to learn the rudiments of good manners and self-restraint. But our efforts were seriously impeded by the leading Nonconformists in the place, who denounced the ungodliness of teaching children to dance, withdrew their children from the "evenings," and, I believe, made special arrangements for our conversion. Allow me to give another instance of Nonconformist obstruction to village improvement. We allowed whist to be played in the reading room. Here again they opposed us. We opened the reading room on Sundays, hoping to attract some men from their Sunday drinking, and to encourage reading. This was too ungodly for anything, and subscriptions to provide papers, &c., for the room were refused on the ground of our teaching such wicked ways. But we hope to persevere in our wicked ways, and I am glad to say that during the last 17 months I have given out from the village library more than a thousand volumes of general literature for reading on Sundays. Your correspondent, the Rev. M.T. Myers, (page 170) will be glad to know that there are clergy who do not taboo chapel people, but who try to carry out true Liberalism irrespective of names. Indeed, I fancy that if Nonconformists would be at the trouble to inquire into the facts of so-called clerical intolerance they would find a great part of their occupation gone.- Yours faithfully,

A COUNTRY VICAR'S WIFE.

SIR, - An "Oxfordshire Tenant Farmer" (page 152) may not know of any village in the county where the average weekly wage of the labourer does not exceed 13s. 4d. I could tell him of more than one, but supposing that after deducting stoppages for loss of time through rain or sickness, and adding extra money earned at harvest (when wife and children help him), a man's wages average 15s., is there not some reason for complaint? I have made many inquiries among labourers, village shopkeepers, and others, in short have tried to get at the truth concerning this matter, and would ask "A Tenant Farmer" to look at the other side of the account, namely, the labourer's necessary expenses. Take the case of man with wife and four children, and this is something like the way in which his money will be spent: Rent, 2s.; coal, 1s.; bread, 4s.; grocery (the term includes tea, sugar, butter, milk, soap, oil or candles, kindling, &c.), 2s. 6d.; bacon, 2s. 6d.; club, 6d.; total, 12s. 6d. In other words, out of his income of 39*l.* per annum he will under the most favourable circumstances have a margin of 6*l.* 10s., with which to provide himself and family with clothing and to make provision for old age. Ought any man to be content with this?- Yours,

"A VILLAGE PARSON."

SIR,- Every Englishman who loves his country must be deeply interested in the series of letters from your Special Correspondent on "Life in our Villages." Your correspondent, "Hodge," (page 167) in your issue of this date, puts clearly one great cause of the evils that exist. Why, indeed, buy eggs from abroad? And not only eggs. The other day, in an old-fashioned inn in this city, I asked for Stilton cheese. The waiter replied, "We do not keep it; will you have Gorgonzola?" And in nine cases out of ten you will have foreign cheese and butter thrust upon you. English housewives, as well as hotel keepers, would do well to insist on English products - they are, as a rule, better than those from over the sea. Here, in the heart of East Anglia, Danish butter is everywhere advertised and pushed, and so with many other things. I believe in the utmost freedom of trade, and in open markets, but the weal of England would be vastly increased if English folk would buy English wares. As unions of all kinds exist, some for very petty fads, why not start a Home Trade League? This would do real good.- I beg to enclose my card, and am, Sir, yours faithfully,

HET VARKE, Norwich,   Sept. 10.

"Blankney Heath" remarks that though this correspondence is looked for with very lively interest every morning, and many opinions are advanced in it, he has not seen the suggestion that the Board of Agriculture should form schemes to redress the evils complained of. He is a voter in the constituency of the President of the Board, who at the general election had posted up all over the division "Vote for Chaplin, the Poor Man's Friend." What has he done for the poor man? asks "Blankney Heath." Is the Board of Agriculture of any use?

Mr. J. Crawford, Sherburn, Durham, says: In my part of the country the labourer gets 14s. per week. With the purchasing power of money and present price of necessaries - that is to say, tea, foreign meat, and cheese - this wage represents a considerable rise from that paid some years ago. That it is a satisfactory amount few will admit; but there is an old saying, that you cannot get blood from a gate-post, and if the farmer does not get his fair share, and that a remunerative one, for what he produces, how can he be liberal to his workpeople? If prosperity sets in it would be right that the labourer should participate in the better prospects of his master, and it may be admitted that in

190

prosperous times gone by he was not admitted to the due share of increased prosperity. The labourer could much benefit his position if he could purchase his articles of wear and consumption on more reasonable terms and of a better quality than the struggling shopkeeper usually offers, and if the girls were taught cookery and needlework, in both of which essential duties of a housewife the women of the labouring classes are almost as deplorably ignorant as the factory girls of our towns.

F.W.H. writes:- Mr Gladstone recommends planting fruit trees! Yes, on my own "freehold land" I would plant fruit trees, but not on another man's land, let to me on his own terms. No, sir, the only way to effectually restore prosperity to the land is to restore it as "property" to those from whom it has been taken - the peasantry, the cultivator, and the labourer. They will not want to be taught how to get the most out of it when it is theirs. To show how to do this a Stein and Handenberg are wanted in England.

"A Farmer's Daughter of South Beds" takes exception to the letter signed "South Beds" in Wednesday's paper (page 160), in which the writer says that farmers are always complaining whatever the times are, and adds "Look at him, cricket and lawn tennis all summer, shooting, hunting, concerts, and balls all winter, living even far better than his landlord did." Why, "Farmer's Daughter" asks, "why take isolated cases of this kind? It is with the ordinary farmer we have to do. There are some with means who farm merely for pleasure; they can afford to indulge in the pastimes complained of by 'South Beds,' and I regret to say there are some who can ill afford it who allow their families to waste time and money in amusements altogether unbecoming their position. But there are other farmers who work hard themselves; and their wives and daughters do all the domestic duties of the household, and then find that it is only by the strictest economy they are able to keep the wolf from the door. Are the farmers not to share in the general prosperity of the country? 'South Beds' complains of the low wages given. If the rents were reduced better wages would be given. Farmers are not so hardhearted as 'South Beds' would have you believe."

"A Bucks Radical" advocates parish councils, and says district councils will not meet the case. Labourers cannot go six miles to attend a district council; it must be the parish, which is already complete in itself. These councils must have the power to acquire and possess property, and let it out for the general interests. First they must have immediate possession of all public lands, charity lands, &c. If they could have this land in their own hands what might, yes, what might not, be the result? They could at once let it out in a hundred portions, not equal, but according to each man's ability to manage. They would at once have a large income, which they would spend in providing what is the second great requirement of the people, cottage homesteads on the land itself, with accommodation for poultry, pigs, &c ., and a building for each holder to store his produce, and thus make the best of it. In a few years the value of the property would be doubled and all the requirements of the people met. They would not migrate if they could have a cottage and land, which would provide all they would require for employment and comfort. Let the Liberal party advocate Home Rule for England - rural England - and it will not lack enthusiastic support.

East Sussex writes: The articles in your paper headed "Life in our Villages" are very instructing to us in East Sussex, as they show how much better off farm labourers are here than in the Eastern Counties. Our labourers are divided into two classes: the day labourer and the yearman. The average pay of an ordinary yearman about here is fifteen shillings per week with a good cottage and garden. The yearsmen always get the best cottages. Their gardens supply them with fruit and vegetables for the year, and in some cases they have some to sell. They never have a single hour of lost time in the year; wet or fine every week they take their full money. If they are possessed of a family, there is work for the wife and boys from early spring to late autumn - work of a light description, but which materially adds to the year's earnings. For instance, in the month of September, the wife and a couple or three children may earn from 5*l.* to 8*l.* at hop-picking. In spring the wife earns a nice little sum at hop-tying. This is followed by regular day work till the end of August, made up of thistle spudding, mangold and turnip slightening, hop-branching, hay-making, harvesting, &c. I think those men of Suffolk of whom your Commissioner wrote would think country life of the description far better than life in a town brewery at 30s. per week, a high rent to pay, and all fruit and vegetables to buy and pay for. Then comes the day labourer. His wages when at day work are 13s. 6d. per week. A great part of the time that he is only earning these wages he is practically not wanted by the farmer, and is simply kept on somehow or other in order that the farmer may have first call on his services when he really must have him. This time begins in the early spring, when the men go on hop digging, and work by the piece, earning 18s. to 20s. per week. Then comes hop dressing, followed by hop-poling, at which from 15s. to 18s. per week is made. After this comes hoeing, in some cases at 13s. 6d. per week, in others paid by the piece, when rather more work is done, and the labourer earns more money and the cost per acre to the farmer is rather less. Hop chopping and other hop work follows, the men earning about 18s. a week. At grass mowing they earn about 5s. per day. At oat mowing 6s. or 7s. per day (4s. per acre being often paid now for such pieces as were formerly done for 2s. 3d. to 2s. 6d. per acre.) In the wheat cutting, the men are assisted by their wives and children, and large sums are earned; and the hop-picking in a good hop year is a nice little harvest for them. Hop-dryers earn about 7s. per day. Thatchers can earn as much as 10s. per day, by working very long days. What the labourer wants is a "Pure Beer Bill" then hops would pay, and there would be plenty of work at high wages. Next he wants a better cottage to live in, and in some cases a rather larger garden. The next thing required is a cheerful Sunday, a cheerful service in the church, with good music - something to cheer us on our way, and something to look forward to during the week - instead of the usual melancholy, depressing apology for a service which is so common, and which is calculated to give one "the blues" for a week.

"H" writes from Ealing:- As the subject of allotments is now one of considerable interest. I took the opportunity of a fine Sunday evening to visit a portion of my neighbourhood where I had never been before, though I had often passed it by. Immediately south of St. Mary's Church, and within a few yards of the churchyard, I found a space which I was told was 26 acres, as full of vegetables, with some flowers and small fruit bushes, as it well could be. It was divided into strips running north and south, with a pathway of about 15 inches between each strip. At this time of the year much of the produce of the place had been eaten, and several of the allotments grew far more weeds than they ought. About six years since, Lady Lawrence left the land, about twenty acres, to be let in allotments for ever to the people of Ealing. Then two years since about six acres more, previously in pasture, were added to her useful legacy. At first the plots were 20 rods each - one-eighth of an acre - but soon the demand was so great that no larger quantity than 10 rods was given to any one person. As the larger fall in they are divided into two. For 10 rods the rent is 6s. a year, payable in advance. The payment can be made in one or more sums, or by 6d. on the last Friday in each month, which as a friend informed me "no one missed." This rent, which is at the handsome rate of 4*l.* 16s. per acre, covers rates and taxes of all kinds. The principal crop was potatoes, which unhappily, are much diseased, cabbages, cauliflowers, turnips, carrots, French beans, scarlet runners, parsnips, lettuce, endive, celery, red beet, tomatoes, rhubarb, onions, leeks, vegetable marrow, pot herbs of several kinds, and horseradish. As fast as one crop was removed the ground was re-dug and winter cabbage, broccoli, and other hardy vegetables are planted. On some of the plots many flowers were grown, on others strawberry plants, currant and gooseberry bushes, and raspberry canes were to be seen. As long as the rent was paid the people were not disturbed, and so looked upon their plots as their own. Being so much interested in what I saw, I walked on about half a mile to the allotment fields at Ealing Dean, which are much larger in extent. I was told by one that the allottees were principally working-men labourers, and men employed by the gardeners about, policemen, petty shopkeepers, &c., and that the gardeners soon taught the others all they required, to be able to turn their ten rods to good account. The vegetables were so dear in the shops that poor people would have little chance of having any except occasionally, were it not for these most welcome allotments, which only take up time that would otherwise be wasted or spent in a public-house. The Old Church Allotments are quite close to the South Ealing Station on the District Line, and the others to the Castle-hill Station of G.W.R., within half a dozen miles of South Kensington and Paddington Stations.

Mr. Herbert G. Moberly, hon. sec. Land Nationalisation Society, says if the land were held on direct tenure from the State - that is to say, if land were national property in fact as it is in theory - then land users and rent receivers would in the aggregate be identical, and each land user, while paying his just contribution in the shape of rent, in proportion to the value of the land he used, would share equally with all his fellow-citizens in the national benefits derived from the collective rent fund, the magnitude of which was due to that general pressure which each helped equally to cause. Rent would then be the great equaliser, for each would pay according to his privilege, and receive according to his due. The economic theory of rent, properly understood, declares emphatically that no half measures, such as abolition of entail, registration of title, or free trade in land, which leave the national inheritance in the hands of private individuals, can possibly remedy the injustice inherent in the existing system. The present system is the result of centuries of force and fraud, cemented into quasi-legality by ignorance and lapse of time, but the wrong is ever-recurring, and the only possible remedy is to nationalise the land, viz., to restore to the people collectively, as a national fund, the rent which they create, and to enable every man who wishes it to rent land direct from the State, or from local authorities as representing the State, on fair terms and with full security, for use and not for profit.

"J.D.," Loughboro, says:- In Mid-Leicestershire, where I live, the lot of the agricultural labourer is certainly better than that of his fellows in the south-eastern counties. But still that brightness which hope gives is lacking in his life. One of some twenty labourers on an estate near here has 14s. a week, which his wife supplements by a little mangling. By looking after poultry the handsome sum of 2s. 6d. per annum is added, and some trifle for collecting eggs and rearing chickens. For a month during harvest the labourers get an extra 1s. a day, but this addition is counterbalanced by the stoppage of wages in wet weather. Allotments of about 400 square yards each are allowed by the master landlord at the rate of 1s. per 100 yearly. And these, as is generally the case about here, are some distance from the houses. Little is left for luxuries when five mouths have to be fed out of 12s., 2s. being claimed for rent. On another estate in this district I lately came across a field company of harvesters, where a more rough and ready system of payment was made, but withal a more profitable one for the labourers. A couple of men were preparing a field of wheat for the reaping machine, and in reply to my inquiries they told me it was customary on that estate for the agent to pay 5s. an acre for cutting, and lead the machine and horse-power. The machine would cut ten acres a day, working from 6 a.m. to 7 p.m. Six men were required to tie and shock the corn and one to manage the machine. Well, some of your readers will perhaps think this a good wage for agricultural labourers, 42s. per week. But I was informed that the golden time quickly sped, lasting seldom more than two weeks. An extra sixpence a day is given while the corn is being gathered to the stacks, and then the men return to the routine of 15s. a week. Most of those in commercial life look forward to age and ripe experience as a time when the salary decreases not, and the work grows less irksome. But with these poor folks, as the labourers get old in the service, their wages become less, 10s. and 12s. a week being about the sum. To have a better class of workers on the land, an inducement must be held out to the labourers to put forth the energy which is born of hope. Is not this inducement conveyed by the division of the land into small holdings with fixity of tenure, at a fair rent? I have talked with both labourers and agents, and they give the area of such holdings at about 25 acres, though much depends upon the soil and the situation.

Monday, September 14, 1891

(FROM OUR SPECIAL COMMISSIONER.)

I am afraid the people of Woodstock have imbibed something of the discontented spirit that appears so very generally to be animating the agricultural world around them, and that they are not sufficiently thankful for the blessings they are privileged to enjoy. Not unto every small town is it given to have a great ducal landowner overshadowing it as the Duke of Marlborough overshadows Woodstock, and one would think that the inhabitants of this interesting old town could not be too grateful for the happy fortune which has given them one Providence above and another at Blenheim Palace. Possibly there may be some of them who have a due sense of their happy lot, but if there are I have not yet met with them. I have been moving, I fear, in rather a bad set, and they have been doing their best to prejudice me against great landowners and the sort of influence they exercise. Clearly there is a democratic ferment at work in this part of the world, as in so many others, and after what I have seen to-day, I cannot help feeling that it is quite time there was. Starting from Woodstock, I have had to-day a most interesting and instructive drive through Bladon, Handborough, Combe, Kidlington, Glympton, and Wootton. One or two of these villages are beautiful little places - in some respects all one could reasonably desire. Bladon, for one, just outside the wall of Blenheim Park, is quite a little show place. It is nearly all owned by the Duke of Marlborough, and though he and the vicar of Woodstock are at loggerheads over a matter which I am not concerned here to discuss, they have between them given the people good cottages and gardens, a fine church, and free schools, and many other things that must contribute largely to their comfort and welfare.

Kidlington and Glympton - owned by different wealthy landlords - are also quite model villages. But the democrats of Woodstock seem even fiercer in their condemnation of these pet villages than of such places as Handborough, where the conditions of life are in many respects the very reverse of all that is to be found in the others. Both Kidlington and Glympton have within living memory been largely reduced by the ruthless pulling down of cottages. At one time this was done for the simple purpose of clearing out poor people, who were not wanted for the profit and convenience of the landowner, and who were likely to be a burden on the rates. "Here are we, the great landowners, the only people on earth of the slightest importance. We don't want these cottagers; turn them out and pull down their houses, and let them drag their wretched carcasses to the workhouse in the next parish, where we shall not be responsible for their maintenance. What have we to do with them?" I don't know whether the present owners have done this; possibly not, for it is many years now since, by the union of parishes, this sort of thing was checked. But other motives have led to the demolition of cottages, and a resident in the district told me of many small houses he could remember to have been swept away. These places now apparently contain just about the number of dwellings required for the estates - not the least reference to the number of people the land could and would maintain, but just what the squires choose to have there. I am assured that it is literally true that if in one of these places a young man wants to get married and settle down, it is of no use merely to woo and to win the young woman. He must induce the squire to consent also. "Where's So-and-So?" "Oh, he's gone out of the neighbourhood. He wanted to get married, and the squire wouldn't put up a cottage and wouldn't hear of anybody taking in a lodger, so he has to go."

In these villages attempts to introduce Nonconformist ideas have been found to be quite hopeless. "In that village yonder," said my guide, "a man became a Nonconformist and had the audacity to hold a prayer meeting in his own room. He got notice to quit, and was turned out of house and home and employment - not of course for the prayer meeting; oh dear no." A Liberal politician here told me that in some election recently - County Council, I think he said - there were eighty voters in one such proprietary village, and he could only get one solitary individual so much as to speak to him. "No, sir, excuse me, I really can't. I don't want to lose my coals at Christmas." That is the sort of thing with which the forces of progress have to contend, and it is not surprising that there are many about here who regard "good landlords" with utter abhorrence. They are beneficent, but their beneficence implies the forfeiture of every particle of freedom, and the submission of the people to whatever may be imposed upon them. I heard to-day of a poor widow who shortly after her husband's death had a call by the estate agent. He came on Sunday evening, and told her she must get out of her cottage and shift into another. Certain changes had been decided on, and she must make room for somebody else. The poor woman didn't want to leave her home, and protested against it. Even if she went, surely she was entitled to some notice. Yes, no doubt - legally. For all that she must go, and at once; if not she must expect no more benefits. And, poor soul, she meekly submitted and went - swept out like so much dirt before a besom. "You have no idea what a condition of serfdom the people are reduced to on some of these big estates," said a resident here to me to-day. The squire owns the cottage, he can give or withhold allotments, he is practically the sole employer; his wife and daughters give coal and lend blankets, and look after the people when they are sick, and the parson finds schooling and religion, and there is no resisting any of them in anything. There is literally nothing for the people to do but plod quietly on as they are told, take what is given them, and be thankful. It is all well intended, all beneficent and beautiful, but it is the abnegation of all manhood, of everything like citizenship. The power of the clergy, when they happen to be men of independent means, is often a deadly blight upon the freedom of the poor. I don't know the Vicar of Woodstock. I hear that he is a high Churchman, and a man of many excellencies of character, but he is also a man of wealth, and the way in which he uses it to bribe down all independence of religious thought is little short of scandalous.

The superintendent of one of the Nonconformist schools in Woodstock tells me that his school has been almost ruined by the purse-power of the parson. "You know, Vicar, this isn't right," he said to him one day. "This isn't fair fighting to bribe away our children in this way. We never treat you like that." The Vicar's answer, I understand, was to the effect that the superintendent had no right to be teaching the children; he, the parson, was the only true spiritual guide in that parish, and that he was justified in resorting to every means in his power to get the children into the true Church, and would certainly do so. Just combine this power of the clergy with that of the squire to turn out a man, with wife and children, from his house and his village and his employment, and add to this combined power the blandishments of the Primrose dames, and you have a phalanx which - though thank God it is even now being broken, and shall one day utterly be put to rout - will yet give us many a long day's hard tussle.

Deeply conscious as one cannot but be of the tremendous weight under which the liberty and independence of spirit of the agricultural poor are being crushed, it is with grim and hearty satisfaction that one comes across here and there manifestations of a little good English pugnacity - aye, even though the pugnacity may be not altogether in the right. I could not help feeling this in the little village of Combe. Combe is on the far side of Blenheim Park from Woodstock, a benighted little place if its reputation counts for anything. In driving into it from Woodstock you pass a ruinous old structure which I had pointed out as a stable put up by a former Duke of Marlborough for the shelter of his horse, while he was paying his respects to Miss Glover in the village of Combe. His workpeople were always long in arrears with their wages, and they used to waylay his Grace near this stable and dun him for money. "Oh, you shall be paid; you shall all be paid," he would say. "Ah, but when and wheer, yer Grace?" demanded the men. "I remembers 'em doing it many a time." said a countryman to me yesterday. I suppose his Grace - let us be careful to give the most noble duke his proper title - I suppose his Grace found this unreasonable dunning of his starving labourers troublesome and inconvenient. They were thorns and brambles in his primrose path, and the lady was soon transferred to Blenheim, and the villagers will tell you now how Duchess Glover used to come dashing about Combe in her carriage.

A little further on in the village you have another interesting little object in the shape of a liliputian Wesleyan chapel. I don't know how the bit of land upon which it stands came to be available for the purpose, but I was informed that it was the only bit in the place that could be got, and in order to make it do one side of the building had to be planted in a pond, and the consequence is that it has always been damp and uncomfortable. A little higher upon is the church, and an intelligent native with whom I strolled round pointed to one of·the porches as having been at one time the Sunday-school room. There was no Dissent in the village at that time, and the parson's deputy in the school was one of the gardeners at Blenheim. The parson would look in and have a bit of chat about the gardens and flowers up at the palace, and as soon as he was gone old Jemmy Whatever-his-name-was would send one of the children over to the Cook for a pot of beer. "Many's a time I've seen children goin' into Sunday school with a pot of fourpenny," said my informant. Under this spiritually-minded and enlightened regime of the Church on the one hand and the great landed proprietor on the other, Combe seems to have been in the past a byeword and a scoffing to all the villagers around. Anything specially simple-minded and stupid it has been the habit to put down to "Silly Combe," and in the country around you may hear how that one native of the place sat on the branch of a tree while he sawed it off, forgetting that he would let himself down; how that another turned a horse out to graze with the nose-bag on, and so forth. Practically all the land and all the houses belong to the Duke, but it is far from Blenheim Palace and the management of it seems to be left to agents, and they do or they don't do just as it seems good to them.

As I moved up the village past the old stable and the Wesleyan Chapel and the parish church, I noticed the wall of a cottage bulging outwards to a degree which I thought looked quite dangerous. I examined the house further, and it struck me that a good strong wind would be sufficient to bring the whole place down in a mass of crumbled ruin. I was told that an old couple lived there, and I stepped into the garden and spoke to the woman. The poor miserable-looking old creature, I should say between seventy and eighty years of age, was full of complaints that they would do nothing to the place. She couldn't remember that they had ever done anything. "Come and look round 'ere, sir," she said; and I made my way through what had been once a thriving garden, full of raspberry canes and standard fruit-trees and strawberry beds. The rafters were all broken away, and were projecting over the eaves; the thatched roof had sunk in in the middle, and there was a hole through which you might have dropped a wheelbarrow stopped up by nothing but a few old rusty tea-trays, or something of the kind, loosely thrown into it. The walls were cracked and broken, and the window of the bedroom was lacking half its glass. "How do you manage with that bedroom window?" I asked. "Oh, I got a bit o' board as I stop that up wi'," said the woman. "I never remember as they put a bit o' glass in the window, and I never lived nowhere else," she added. There were two bedrooms; the one with the hole in the roof was totally uninhabitable. The water during all this wet, squally season had literally poured in there, flooding the place from top to bottom. The thatch over the smaller bedroom was not so bad as in the other room, but it let the rain in freely, and, as I have said, the window had only about half its glass in, and the wind must have blustered freely about every corner of that wretched hovel. Yet, up there, under the driest corner of that ruinous roof, lay all last winter a poor bed-ridden old man said to be eighty-six or eighty-seven years of age. If anybody wants to verify this he is there still, and the neighbours say that in the night-time they sometimes hear him crying and moaning piteously. The condition I have described must have been pretty much the state of the place for years past, yet the Duke of Marlborough's agent has, I am assured, been taking three pounds a year rent for it, and, if he cannot be said to have turned a deaf ear to all appeals to him, has again and again met them with promises that have never been fulfilled. As I have said, these people do or they leave undone just as they think proper, and there is no public opinion which dares express itself. But where's the parson? Where's the one Christian gentleman in the village who goes to the agent or, if need be, to the duke, and says, "I am the friend of these poor people. This is wrong, and it must be put right;" and when it isn't put right goes again and says "This is wrong, and if it isn't put right I'll raise the devil about your ears!" Where's the parson? Why not a hundred yards off. "What sort of a fellow is he?" I asked an intelligent old man in the village. "Oh," he said, with a smile, "he never interferes wi' nobody, 'e don't."

Nor is atrocious neglect of this kind the only thing of which this village has to complain. One would like, if one could, to discuss these rural matters in cold blood and with level judgment. But I confess that it has made my blood boil to drive round about Blenheim Park, and see how the labouring poor have been and are being defrauded of what belongs to them. There has been common land enough about some of these villages to make every family in them comfortable and prosperous. It would have given them room for cottages and gardens and allotments, or when by-and-by we get local councils it would have afforded the means of some form of public co-operative husbandry which would have made agricultural labourers only too eager to get

201

into the district instead of scuttling away from it as they are doing. Every man will tell you of somebody who has gone off to the railways or to the mines in Yorkshire, or to try his luck in London. Here, as elsewhere, farms have been consolidated into large holdings, expenses have been cut down, and machinery has supplanted labourers. "The corn at one time," said a man, "used to give the labourer about here nine and ten shillings an acre at harvest time; but machinery does the work now, and all the labourer has to do is to pick up the sheaves that the machine has cut and bound, and stand them up in shocks." He gets now about ninepence or tenpence an acre. The winter wages for many of the people, I hear, are nine shillings, with stoppages for wet days. But still if the common land could have been well tilled for the common benefit it would have made all the difference between starvation and comfort in the winter time. But what has become of the common land? Nearly all of it belongs to the Duke of Marlborough. There are these men whose park wall I have had variously estimated at from nine to fourteen miles in length, and with unnumbered thousands of acres, and whole villages of property outside have been generation after generation gobbling up piece after piece of the common lands of the poor, and they are doing it still. "Look there," said an influential Liberal of Woodstock, "the Duke of Marlborough has no business whatever with that land, but as Lord of the Manor he just simply takes it, and nobody dares oppose him." The thing looked plain as a pikestaff. There was the park wall bounding the duke's private property. Between that wall and the road was a space of waste land, common property. The transfer from public to private ownership is begun by sticking up a notice, "All persons depositing rubbish on this land will be prosecuted.- Marlborough." A little further on comes the next stage, and a low stone wall skirts the road and shuts in the open land. It is now the duke's, and if the people want it for allotments he has no objection to let it them at five-and-twenty shillings an acre. Again and again men said to me, "we are paying for our own land." For a mile or so before you get into Combe the road runs through some pasture land. There is not a doubt I think that that was all common land. Some of it is still unenclosed, but on both sides the road throughout the greater part of it a double railing and a quick-set hedge have been planted within the past year or two. All the people in Combe believe it belongs to them, and a pleasant walk that men have trodden from time out of mind has been taken away.

One old man told me he remembered his grandfather having a flock of sheep on that land, and it was all open and common property. Another said he couldn't recollect it being open, but the first he knew of it was that a farmer, whose tomb he pointed out in the graveyard, had rented it of the Duke at ten shillings an acre. One Sunday he remembers the agent getting the people together down in a field yonder and telling them he was going to drain it and otherwise improve it, and they could have it in plots at two pounds an acre. "It was their own land," said the man; "however, they took it at two pounds, and had it for years, and got it into good condition. Well, th'old dook died, and the next dook took it away from 'em. I remember it well." Up in the little old church there is a painted board stuck up in front of the gallery, registering a solemn compact that for one piece of this "common or waste land," the Duke of Marlborough is to pay six guineas a year. Whether that six guineas is still paid to the overseers for the benefit of the parish I cannot say; but it is unanswerable evidence as to the original common rights in the land, and everybody in Combe will tell you that in exchange for their rights of cutting furze and turf on another piece of the same common the Duke of the day solemnly pledged himself to send into the village loads of faggots on certain days. The Duke of Marlborough still of course holds that piece of land, but never a stick of their firing do the poor people get. How long will the common-sense and right feeling of the people of England endure this sort of thing? Not very long, I think, unless all signs of the times are utterly misleading. In just the same way that the Duke of Marlborough has acquired that piece of land at Combe by engaging to perform public services that are no longer rendered - to say nothing of a good deal more that they appear to have taken merely by cool impudence - so were their manorial rights acquired in exchange for duties that are no longer required of them.

These matters must be thoroughly overhauled, and the great reforming party of this country must administer to these great lawless landowners of insatiable maw emetics powerful enough to make them disgorge. On some system or other the people must get back to the land, and there could hardly be a better beginning than to begin with the lands that are justly their own. Even here in this little obscure corner of the rural world the people are beginning to put down their foot, and when a little time ago another piece of their common land was going to be appropriated to a purpose to which they had given no consent, they doggedly refused to permit it. "We ha' had enough of our land filched away from we," they said, "and we'll ha' no more on't." In this case to which I had intended to refer at length, but which I must leave for another letter, they were, I think, unfortunate and wrong; but, notwithstanding that, the mere fact of their resistance is a healthy sign of the times, and such signs are multiplying on all hands.

SIR,- I am not a Church of England man - anything but that; yet I cannot but endorse what "A Country Vicar's Wife" says (page 188) in your issue of last Saturday in reference to Nonconformist intolerance of innocent pleasures. The "Country Vicar's Wife" says she anticipated the advice of your correspondent the Rev. J. Denny Gedge (page 163), by starting dancing classes and other forms of recreation for her village children, but that her efforts were frustrated by certain leading Nonconformists of the locality. It would be ridiculous to say that this species of bigotry prevails to a really large extent even among rural Nonconformists - among urban Nonconformists it may be said to be non-existent. But judging from my own experience, I must say that in rural England the spirit which the "Country Vicar's Wife" most properly condemns is immeasurably more prevalent among Dissenting ministers and deacons and their flocks generally than among the corresponding persons and classes of the Church of England. Dancing and games such as dominoes and chess may on occasion be no less edifying than certain other "exercises" which the over serious would have in season and out of season. Mr. Gedge and the "Country Vicar's Wife" merely touch the fringe of a great question. Allotments or no allotments, the life of the rural labourer and his children is about the dullest and dreariest conceivable. Unless your labourer be a silent Wordsworth, it is useless to tell him that the colourless poverty of the country is preferable to the garish poverty of the gin-palace lighted slums.- Yours obediently,

"RUSTICUS".

SIR, - Your Commissioner's letters and the voluminous correspondence to which it has led point to the conclusion that no reform short of national ownership of the soil will settle the agrarian question. That, however, is the conclusion neither of your Commissioner nor of the majority of the letter-writers. None of them appear to be aware of the fact that State landlordism is not only the theory but the practice over vast portions of the British Empire. Those provinces of India are the most prosperous where the State is the direct landlord. In Bengal, for example, "permanent settlements" in favour of landowners have long since created a do-nothing, rent-receiving class of the type with which we are too familiar in Great Britain, and especially in Ireland; and these ridiculous, immoral, and predatory settlements have in the long run proved as fruitful a source of mischief to the landlords as to their tenants. The State alone should let land - a reservation which would ensure that none occupied land but those who worked it, and that the benefits of enhanced rents - natural increment, would accrue to the nation, and not to its individual idlers.- Your obedient servant,

"RAYAT".

SIR, - I see that one of your correspondents considers the rent of allotment land (4*l*. 16s. an acre) on the Lawrence estate, Ealing, to be a high one (page 190). But there are much higher prices than that paid in different parts of rural England. How is it that allotment land is so often twice, three, four times dearer than immediately adjoining land of the same quality occupied by the big farmers? Hodge insists upon paying an uncommonly high price for the satisfaction of "working himself to death," as the parson, the squire, and the big farmer say he must do if besides doing his duty by his employer he cultivates on his own account. "The labourer cannot, if he attends to a plot of his own, serve his master honestly," is the objection I have repeatedly heard in country districts, from clergymen especially. But I have never yet come across an authenticated case of lapse from duty on the part of allotment labourers. On the contrary, the fact that a labourer has the courage and the independence to work an allotment when (generally after infinite trouble and worry) he

succeeds in getting one is the best possible guarantee of his profitableness to his employer.- Yours,
"COUNTRYSIDE".

SIR, - With many thousands I have been deeply interested in your articles "Life in our Villages," and thank you for letting in a flood of light on its present state, which is a disgrace to us as a Christian nation. But to my own mind the most painful and saddening part is the fact that your Correspondent entirely or almost entirely ignores the work of the clergyman in the village, and I suppose it is because there is none to record. We have now and then the wife of the clergyman on the scene, with her blankets, &c., for all good churchgoers, but of the husband little or nothing is said. And, yet, is it not one great argument for an Established Church that it provides for every village a man of culture and light to whom the poor can look for guidance, instruction, and help? Such is the theory, but what are the stern facts? Are they not that the parson and the squire are hand and glove in all things, and no voice is lifted against the social evils and tyrannies under which the people groan, and to help which they are powerless? Is it any wonder such conduct makes hypocrites or infidels, in heart if not in word, when they see the man who should be their shield and defender siding with their oppressors, or at any rate is dumb and blind when he should stand forth boldly and rebuke rapacity and oppression which are being done under his very eyes? There are a few noble exceptions to this I gladly and thankfully admit. But would there be, or could there be any such cottages as some your Commissioner has portrayed if the clergyman had done his duty, braving the wrath of the squire or other landowners, compelling them from sheer shame to house their labourers at least as decently as they do their pigs and their horses. Again I say, to my mind the most saddening part of the story is the absence of the man who should be foremost in the village life for good.- Yours,
H.A.

SIR, - Will you kindly allow me to say a few words in answer to the Rev. Henry Brandreth, Dickleburgh Rectory (page 180)? He said that to rightly appreciate the condition of the agricultural labourer, we should contrast their present condition with other times with the French peasant. He did not tell your readers that in France about one man in four owns land; he asserted that there is no class in the country that has made more substantial progress. For a man to make such a statement as that, who lives amongst them shows at once how little he knows and how little he cares about their well-being. I admit the labourers in Kent are better off now than they were fifty years ago. The reverend gentleman said they do not do more than half so much work as they did fifty years ago. Here again he is talking of what he knows nothing about, and yet with half the labour they enjoy twice the comforts of life; if he had put it for the same amount of labour they enjoy more comforts of life, it might have been something like the truth. He said their work was of an interesting character. If the reverend gentleman had to toil as they do, and as I have done, and as others do now at the scythe, the dung-fork, the hop-garden spade, and many other sorts of work, from early morn to dewy eve, go home at dewy eve with wearied limbs, probably chafed under armpits, skin wrung off the palms of his hands. or his shoes wearing one of his feet raw, to a very inferior meal of food, lay his weary body down to rest in the greatest fear lest he should, through excessive weariness, sleep too long, and get behind in the morning, which would probably mean a blowing up or the sack, which again would mean bad character, out of work, more severe privations still, with the thought in his mind that the workhouse would be his finishing goal; the rev. gentleman might, under such circumstances, begin to think that there was nothing very interesting in his life to himself, but was very interesting to others who secured the greater part of the fruits of his toil. He would then understand that what belonged to him was the aches, the pains, the hunger, the thirst, the beats, and the colds. He might, under such circumstances, begin to think, as the labourers do now. that he was entitled to a larger share of the fruits of toil.- Yours truly,

WM. H. PAINE. 2. Grove-villas. Osborne-road, Willesborough.

SIR, - In the course of his graphic letters your Commissioner refers to the quantity of land that has gone out of cultivation in districts he has visited. His remarks are evidently the result of personal observation; he has wisely not consulted the agricultural returns or he would have told a different tale. In view of the importance to agricultural interests of reliable information as to the acreage of crops, and the number of live stock in the country, will you permit me to say that the agricultural statistics issued annually by the Board of Agriculture are valueless as a basis for the arguments, calculations, and conclusions regarding them which appear every year in the leading journals? Last year I directed the attention of the President to the fact that these returns, over which nearly half-a-million has been spent, were statistically worthless owing to the conditions under which they are obtained. Mr. Chaplin informed me, as the result of his inquiries, that the inaccuracies did not appear to be such as to affect the validity of the returns. I am not aware of the nature of the steps taken to ascertain the correctness or otherwise of the statement I submitted, but I should apprehend that it would be very difficult to get at the truth of the matter through the ordinary official channels. Since Mr. Chaplin's investigation there have been numerous letters published from the collecting officers themselves still impeaching the reliability of the returns. As an example of the doubtful accuracy of the returns, I may mention that in the returns published last November, after my correspondence with Mr. Chaplin, it is stated that last year there were 2,361,000 acres more land under cultivation than in 1870. Several explanations of this notable, and, to me, not credible extension of the area under cultivation during a period of agricultural depression are given by the Director of the Statistical Department of the Board of Agriculture; yet in the debate in the House of Commons last February on the taxation of land the Minister of Agriculture observed that such schemes would have the effect of adding largely to that amount of land which, unhappily, had gone out of cultivation. The President and the Director are at direct variance on this important point. Which statement is correct? Since my statement to Mr. Chaplin the 11,000*l.* hitherto paid to the collecting officials as remuneration for their services has been withdrawn, and in the instructions respecting the collection of the present year's returns particulars were required which were regarded as indicative of some future reform in the system of collection. I shall be glad if my efforts led to any improvement. At present the returns are not worth the paper on which they are printed.- I am, Sir, your obedient servant,

MALTUS Q. HOLYOAKE.

SIR,- Your Commissioner in to-day's issue blames the clergy for not interfering with the licences of public-houses in which drunkenness is allowed (page 170). What he pictures to himself apparently is something of this kind. A clergyman having seen a man come out drunk from a licensed house, appears before the J.P.'s on the next licensing day, and opposes the renewal of the licence on the ground of what he has seen. His evidence, being obviously disinterested, is accepted, and the licence endorsed or possibly cancelled. What would actually occur is this: The owner of the house (probably a brewer) would give the publican money to pay a clever lawyer to defend him, of which lawyer the J.P.'s would be "horrible afeard." The clergyman would be called upon to swear that the man alleged to have been drunk was actually drunk inside the house. More than that, he would be called upon to swear that the man was not ejected as soon as he began to show symptoms of drunkenness. Meanwhile some of the man's companions would appear as witnesses for the defence who would swear that he was not drunk inside the house or that he was ejected as soon as he began to get drunk. If the clergyman ventured to argue that the fact of the man being dead drunk a minute or two after he left the house was sufficient evidence that he must have been more or less drunk inside the house, he would be informed that he did not understand the laws of evidence. He would return home, having wasted his time, not only discomfited by the magisterial decision, but discredited in his parish as having maliciously attempted to injure the publican in his business. If besides being a clergyman he happened to be a reasonable human being (and, strange to say, some clergymen really are), he would know that in attacking the publican he was not acting quite fairly; for he would know that the people chiefly to blame for drunkenness in licensed houses in the country are not the publicans but the publicans' owners, and, whereas the loss of a licence would be a comparatively trifling matter to one of the latter, it might be ruin to one of the former.-
Yours faithfully,

"A COUNTRY VICAR".   Sept. 11.

Mr. J.W.D. Kingsley, Kilburn, says: Every labourer should have an allotment, and also a pigsty, so that he could keep a pig. He must not grown corn; he must grow vegetables, onions, carrots, runner beans, onion seed, turnip seed, &c. There is a large demand for onions, especially for the small ones for pickling, and they make lots of money. I have known them make 100*l*. per acre, and onion seed and cucumbers over 100*l*. per acre. With potatoes and runner beans, the potatoes are dug up early and sent to market and the beans are a second crop. Sometimes when potatoes are dug up the ground may be planted with cauliflowers, which makes lots of money. I have known lots of men who have grown the above-named crops. They begin with about one acre of land, and some of them are now owning house property and have ten or twelve acres; some have 100 acres, and would have more if it was to be obtained. One man that used to have one acre of land and used to grow things and take them round the town in a barrow had at his death one of the largest farms near London. Where there are allotments there should be some one in each village to get all the vegetables from the allotments holders and get them in one railway truck, and so the cost of carriage would be reduced. In a village where there are allotments if you trust the poor people you are sure of their money, and there is very little lost in bad debts. The county courts and magistrates have little work in such villages, but where there are no allotments there are always people in the county court or summoned in the police-court.

"An Oxfordshire Landlord" writes: If your corespondent will honour us with a visit, he may judge for himself whether my statement about wages is correct or not. I only spoke of Kingham. What the average throughout Oxfordshire may be I don't pretend to know. If he comes on Saturday he will see me pay my men 22s. and their wives 8s. for harvest work. If he will stay over Sunday and go with me to church, he will see the labourers, their wives, and children dressed, so far as I can judge, as well as those in a fashionable London church, barring, perhaps, "trimmings." Oddly enough, when I put down your Correspondent's statement of deploring the wretched state of agriculture in England now, I took up a similar complaint made nearly two thousand years ago:

> non ullus aratro
> Dignus bonos. squalent abductis arva colonis.
> (Georg. i., 506.)

The writer throughout is on all fours with me and your correspondent "Hodge" regarding the advantages and pleasure to be derived from a proper cultivation of the land.

Tuesday, September 15, 1891

SIR, - "A Vicar's Wife" has asked me a question (page 188) to which it is only polite to reply. We have tried dancing at our village fetes and choir entertainments, and our experience has been that the young people behave with a courtesy and simplicity, and an absence of all horse-play, that is very pleasant to witness. Nor do I find that the Wesleyans, who are largely in the majority in this village, offer any hindrance to what is somewhat no doubt of an innovation. Indeed, I think they must see with me how far more decent is such orderly and elegant movement than kiss-in-the-ring and hunt the slipper, and other such coarse sports as suited the rudeness of manners in the past. It is a pleasure to us to see at neighbouring fetes how, by this time, our young people, without any mauvaise honte, will lead the way where dance music is provided, in dancing cheerfully and with grace, and with becoming courtesy and respectful attention to their partners; and to notice how rapidly the onlookers become aware that what they are looking at is no rough and hoydenish sport for the young people, but one that necessitates good behaviour. Brought up myself to regard dancing very differently, I have become a convert to the seemliness of it through careful observation. My ideas on Sunday reading differ from "A Vicar's Wife"; but a relative of mine, who was a Suffolk rector, found it quite possible to attract large numbers to a Sunday evening in his schoolroom, where reading, illustrations, and music of a suitable character were provided. There is no doubt that country life has become more dull since the Sunday has ceased to be, as it was seventy years ago, a day of sports and general amusement; but I have no wish to see the day lose its distinctly religious character. My proposal would rather be that on every Wednesday there should be a half holiday for cricket, football, and every form of relaxation; in which case there would be no excuse, and less temptation, for

211

secularising our Sunday; and I am certain that the labourer could, and I believe he would, without effort, make up by sprightlier labour during the rest of the week for the time abstracted from his too often perfunctory performance of his daily task.

J. DENNY GEDGE, Methwold Vicarage.